Sleep Better!

Sleep Better!

A Guide to Improving Sleep for Children with Special Needs

Revised Edition

by

V. Mark Durand, Ph.D.
University of South Florida St. Petersburg

·P·A·U·L·H·
BROOKES
PUBLISHING CO.®

Baltimore • London • Sydney

Paul H. Brookes Publishing Co.
Post Office Box 10624
Baltimore, Maryland 21285-0624
USA

www.brookespublishing.com

Typeset by Scribe Inc., Philadelphia, Pennsylvania.
Manufactured in the United States of America by
Sheridan Books, Inc., Chelsea, Michigan.

Cover photo © iStockphoto.com/idal. Clip art © 2013 Jupiterimages Corporation.

Library of Congress Cataloging-in-Publication Data
Durand, Vincent Mark.
  Sleep better! a guide to improving sleep for children with special needs / by V. Mark Durand,
Ph.D.—Revised edition.
      pages   cm
  Includes bibliographical references and index.
  ISBN 978-1-59857-294-0 (pbk. : alk. paper)—ISBN 1-59857-294-6 (pbk. : alk. paper)—
ISBN 978-1-59857-466-1 (epub)—ISBN 1-59857-466-3 (epub)
  1. Sleep disorders in children—Popular works. 2. Children—Sleep—Popular works. I. Title.

  RJ506.S55D87 2013
  618.92'8498—dc23   2013031407

British Library Cataloguing in Publication data are available from the British Library.

2018   2017   2016   2015   2014

10   9   8   7   6   5   4   3   2   1

Contents

Contents

Prevention Strategies
    From Birth—Establishing Good Sleep Habits
    At 3 Months—Fading Nighttime Feedings
    Fading Nighttime Feedings
    Conclusion: The Beginning of Better Nights and Better Days

About the Reproducible Forms

Purchasers of this book may download, print, and/or photocopy the blank forms in Appendixes D–H for clinical use. These materials are included with the print book and are also available at **www.brookes publishing.com/durand/eforms** for both print and e-book buyers.

About the Author

V. Mark Durand, Ph.D., is known worldwide as an authority in the area of autism spectrum disorder. He is Professor of Psychology at the University of South Florida St. Petersburg (USFSP), where he was the founding Dean of Arts and Sciences and Vice Chancellor for Academic Affairs. Dr. Durand is a fellow of the American Psychological Association and has received more than $4 million in federal funding to study behavior problems in children with disabilities.

Dr. Durand was awarded the University Award for Excellence in Teaching at the State University of New York–Albany in 1991 and in 2007 was given the Chancellor's Award for Excellence in Research and Creative Scholarship at USFSP. Dr. Durand is currently a member of the Professional Advisory Board for the Autism Society of America. He is the coeditor of the *Journal of Positive Behavior Interventions* and has written 12 books, including abnormal psychology textbooks that are used at more than 1,000 universities worldwide (translated into Arabic, Greek, Spanish, Portuguese, French, Hindi, and Chinese). In addition, he has more than 100 research publications.

Major themes in Dr. Durand's research include the assessment and treatment of severe behavior problems for children and adults with autism, parent training, and the development of treatments for child sleep problems. He developed one of the most popular functional behavioral assessment instruments used today—the Motivation Assessment Scale (MAS; Monaco & Associates, 1992)—that is now translated into 15 languages.

Dr. Durand developed a unique treatment for severe behavior problems—called *functional communication training*—that is used worldwide. More recently, he developed an innovative approach to help families work with their challenging children and published a guide for parents and caregivers parents and caregivers of children with challenging behavior (*Optimistic Parenting: Hope and Help for You and Your Challenging Child;* Paul H. Brookes Publishing Co., 2011). The book has won several national awards.

Preface to the Revised Edition

It has been approximately 15 years since the initial publication of *Sleep Better! A Guide to Improving Sleep for Children with Special Needs.* During the decade and a half since its release, a significant number of studies advanced our understanding about the nature of sleep problems in children with a range of disorders (e.g., attention-deficit/hyperactivity disorder, Asperger syndrome, autism spectrum disorder, Williams syndrome). In addition, an increasing number of studies now document a growing evidence base for the interventions initially described in the *Sleep Better!* book. Unfortunately, what has not advanced significantly in the intervention literature is the theme of "contextual fit" that ran throughout the book. Studies that look at the effectiveness of particular techniques (e.g., bedtime fading, sleep restriction) continue to examine the effectiveness of each approach or compare approaches as if all families are willing and able to use these interventions successfully and interchangeably. Little attention is paid to individual differences in families and their circumstances that can serve as obstacles to the effectiveness of certain treatments.

A major theme of the first edition of *Sleep Better!* was making clear that many families struggle with some of the more frequently recommended intervention approaches. For example, families often told us that using one of the more popular treatments of the day—graduated extinction, which required parents to listen to the cries of their child—was too upsetting to them. Their feelings of guilt ("Why am I doing this to my child, who already has so many other challenges?") made them stop this approach prematurely. On the other hand, some parents prefer this type of intervention over ones that involve their staying up late at night or waking early in the morning (e.g., sleep restriction). The book highlighted the pros and cons of each approach and offered families choices based on their own needs and preferences. In fact, the feedback from families indicated that this was one of the book's greatest strengths. They liked that no one particular approach was being "sold" to them but rather, that they could pick and choose and sometimes modify techniques to fit their own schedules and needs.

We have taken this approach one step further and looked directly at these obstacles. In our work with families who are dealing with sleep problems as well as many other behavioral challenges presented by their child, we find that emotional reactions and self-talk (e.g., "I must be a bad parent if I can't control my child's behavior," "Other people are judging me because my child misbehaves," "My child's disorder is the reason behind this disruption and therefore can't really be changed") get in the way of following behavioral plans. In other words, when families do not follow through on suggested programs, this can sometimes be attributed to these attitudinal barriers rather than their being unmotivated or not receiving enough training. In a large randomized clinical trial, we documented that helping families with these interfering thoughts and feelings could help them assist their child more effectively and led to reports of improved quality of life (called *optimistic parenting*; Durand, 2011; Durand, Hieneman, Clarke, Wang, & Rinaldi, 2013).

A major goal of creating a revised version of *Sleep Better!* is to better incorporate this *optimistic parenting* approach for families who struggle with trying to help their child sleep better. Our experience suggests that almost half of the families with whom we work face these attitudinal obstacles to the point that it prevents them from being more successful parents. As a result, including help for these families in a revision of *Sleep Better!* may broaden the range of individuals whom we can assist.

Preface to the First Edition

This book was born out of my personal experiences with sleeping difficulties. To be more exact, it is the direct result of my own son's multiple troubles with sleep, which included problems falling asleep at night, difficulty sleeping through the night, his occasional episodes of sleep terrors (a disturbing sleep disorder that looks like a frightening nightmare but is not), as well as nightmares, sleep talking, sleep walking, and even bruxism—or teeth grinding—during sleep. It was his disturbed sleep, and mine and my wife's efforts to help him and us sleep better, that was the early force that sparked my subsequent research on sleep difficulties and ultimately this book.

Over two decades have passed since the worst of my son's sleep problems have been resolved, yet I can still recall many episodes quite vividly. Unless you have experienced it yourself, it is almost impossible to describe the pit-in-the-stomach feeling you experience when hearing your child begin to cry at 12:30 a.m.—one more night of hundreds of such nights. Just as your body and your mind have begun to give up the tensions of the day, the stirring followed by the inevitable crying jolt you into the dreaded realization that it is happening one more time. One more night your child will have disrupted sleep and, despite your feeling guilty about thinking this way, you are aware that you too will not get a full and complete night's rest—by now a luxury for which you would be willing to trade much.

But because you are reading this book, you know this feeling all too well. If your child or someone you care for is experiencing sleep problems, then let me reassure you right away—there is reason to feel optimistic. *It is likely that the procedures described in this book will help you and your child sleep better, perhaps within the next few weeks.* This is not a careless statement. These procedures have been tested in scores of studies on people who do not have special needs and in a growing body of exciting new research studies that focus specifically on people who do have special needs. The news from these studies is worthy of our optimism, suggesting that most people who have problems with their sleep can be helped in a meaningful way.

After my experiences with my son's sleep problems, I had a new understanding of what it must be like for other parents. I could now empathize with the feelings of anxiety that result from not knowing what to do with your child who appears so distressed. At the same time, these helpless feelings can turn into depression—a common occurrence for people who feel that they have no control over important aspects of their lives. There is often embarrassment as well. I must be an inadequate parent (especially one who has a Ph.D. in psychology!) if I cannot even get my child to go to bed at night.

Couple these feelings, and the stresses that go with them, with the thousands of parents who have children with special needs, and you have an almost intolerable situation. I have worked with children with special needs for more than 30 years and have been privileged to work also with many of their parents. I was alarmed to learn that children with special needs are *more likely* to have sleep difficulties. It is hard to imagine how stressful life must be for these families to deal with the multitude of problems these children can present—all without having a good night's sleep! This concern led us to examine more closely the unique difficulties posed by the sleep problems of these children. For example, none of the books on sleep talk about how to deal with the little girl who not only wakes up several times each night but who also severely bangs her head into the headboard of her bed at the same time. Nowhere could I find advice for the boy with attention-deficit/hyperactivity disorder (ADHD) who never seems tired and whose medication for attention difficulties might contribute to his sleep problems. Little advice was available for the parents of the boy with autism spectrum disorder (ASD) who roamed the house each night and who sometimes would climb out his window at 3:30 a.m. It was for these children and the multitudes of others with similar idiosyncratic needs that I decided to embark on a series of studies to evaluate sleep interventions and to write this book describing our successes.

It is important to point out that not all of our efforts were initially successful. Some of the people we work with need additional medical attention. I try to point out some of these situations as I discuss the sleep problems and their treatments. Readers should be warned that for severe and/or persistent sleep problems that do not respond to the suggestions in this book, more extensive evaluation may be needed. There are sleep disorders centers that provide these services throughout the United States and internationally, and we provide information for locating a center near you in Appendix C of this book.

The language adopted in this book bears mentioning. First, I primarily use the phrase *people with special needs* to indicate a range of individuals with varying abilities. In our work, we have helped and consulted with families who have children with labels such as ASD, intellectual disability, and ADHD. At the same time, other children have not received official labels but have had difficulties learning or may have experienced some traumatic events (e.g., abuse, accidents) that have interfered with their sleep. I hope readers do not find using the phrase *people with special needs* in any way offensive. It is simply a literary convenience. I also go back and forth describing mostly children and adolescents, but I sometimes discuss the problems of adults as well. Children grow up, and frequently parents struggle with the sleep problems of their adult child, so I include a range of issues that are relevant to children, adolescents, and adults. I begin the book with a discussion of sleep (Chapter 1), followed by a description of a range of sleep problems (Chapter 2), and then a step-by-step interview (Chapter 3) that will help you identify the type of sleep problem your child is experiencing. There are many reasons why people do not sleep well, and it may be helpful for you to understand the nature of the sleep problem before attempting any treatment. Having said that, readers can still go directly to Chapter 3 for the Sleep Interview and to identify specific sleep problems. The good news is that most of the sleep problems we experience can be identified easily. Once you have found the type of sleep problem, you can move on to the chapters on treatment. The last chapters of the book describe the multitude of treatment options available for these sleep difficulties, most of which involve drug-free approaches. I tried to include a number of actual cases to show you how we proceeded with the complexities of these treatment plans. If you carefully follow the steps described here, sleep should be greatly improved soon. I wish you luck.

Acknowledgments

There are many people to thank for their help in creating this book. Clearly, I owe a great deal to the many families who opened up their lives and their homes to my colleagues and me. Often, it was embarrassing for families to tell strangers how their lives had been turned upside-down as a result of their child's sleep problems. I thank them for their honesty, for their patience, and for their determination to once again help their children in difficult times. Several of my graduate students, both past and present, served as primary therapists for many of the cases described in this book, and their help is greatly appreciated. Among the students who have had the greatest impact on this work are Dr. Kristin Chistodulu, Dr. Peter Gemert-Dott, Dr. Eileen Merges, and Dr. Jodi Mindell. Their efforts and wisdom are woven throughout this book. For the first edition, I thank the staff at Paul H. Brookes Publishing Co., especially Christa Horan and Jennifer Lazaro Kinard, for their work in getting my words into print. For the revised edition, I want to thank Rebecca Lazo for her many words of encouragement. Finally, my thanks and my love to my wife and son—Wendy and Jonathan—for helping me learn about sleep and for being my support whenever I needed it.

To Wendy, for being the perfect partner,

and

to Jonathan, for being the perfect teacher

The Nature of Sleep and Its Problems

An Overview of Sleep

Sleep has intrigued us for centuries. Authors throughout the ages have written about sleep. They write quite positively when sleep is good:

"Oh sleep! it is a gentle thing,
Beloved from pole to pole."
—Samuel Taylor Coleridge, *The Rime of the Ancient Mariner, Part V*

But often they write quite negatively about sleep as well:

"Sleep is a death; oh, make me try,
By sleeping what it is to die"
—Sir Thomas Browne, *Religio Medici*

Before I begin our exploration into the problems people experience with sleep, I first take a look at what sleep is. Some basic understanding of how and why we sleep is necessary to help explain what can go wrong with this important part of our lives. At this point, some of you may be understandably anxious for some answers. If you have suffered through many nights with a child who is having sleeping difficulties, you may simply want to "get on with it" and move ahead to Chapter 3, which helps you identify specific problems and why they may be occurring. However, you might find that knowing what sleep is will be interesting and that this knowledge will help you understand when sleep goes wrong.

Sleep refreshes and restores us. Although many people today seem to try to cheat sleep, to "burn the candle at both ends" and avoid wasting precious hours unproductively, we actually need sleep as much as we need food to eat and air to breathe. We are just at the beginning of our search for knowledge about sleep and how it affects us, but it is becoming clear that sleep serves several essential purposes in our lives. For example, sleep seems to be important for learning and for memory. Somehow during sleep, the brain processes information and makes it accessible to us later. Research has suggested that sleep may also be involved in the body's ability to ward off illness, helping to restore the immune system.[1] A lack of sleep can also set off internal processes that make us feel hungry even after eating.[2] And without sleep, we die: Although many believe that there are people who do not sleep at all, in fact, if you go too long without sleep, it is fatal. Clearly, sleep is important to physical well-being. It is also essential for mental well-being. Without sleep, we become irritable, our motivation declines, and our ability to concentrate on everyday tasks diminishes. The seriousness of not sleeping is illustrated by the number of traffic-related accidents due to a lack of sleep, estimated by the U.S. National Highway Traffic Safety Administration to cause as many as 30,000 accidents per year.[3] Lack of sleep was mainly responsible for the crash of the Exxon *Valdez* oil tanker and is thought to have a role in most nuclear reactor accidents, which usually occur in the very early morning. Sleep is an essential part of our lives, and sleeping well is necessary for the soundness of the body as well as the mind.

Before I begin to describe what *problem sleep* is and how to sleep better, it is important that I first describe what "normal" sleep is. You should already be a little uneasy with this term. We know that *normal* has been misused when it comes to people with special needs, and the same is true for sleep. We have a number of myths about what good or normal sleep is, and it is best to take a look at these myths before I try to discuss the problems people experience when it comes to sleeping. What follows is an overview of important information about why and how we sleep. I will then begin to discuss how sleep can be disrupted.

HOW MUCH SLEEP DO WE NEED?

Most people believe that everyone needs about 8 hours of uninterrupted sleep each night to be rested and alert the next day—and for many people this is true. However, the 8 hours of sleep that we all think is ideal is really only an average—which means some people need less sleep and some people need more. There are people who sleep as few as 4–5 hours each night and feel rested. On the other hand, others report sleeping 9 or more hours but continue to complain that they do not feel refreshed. We still do not understand why sleep needs differ so much among people, but our individual needs seem to be pretty constant. The number of hours each of us sleeps might differ from night to night depending on changing schedules or stress during the day, but if you look week to week or month to month, we tend to sleep, on average, about the same amount of time each day.

Age is one factor that tells us about how long people will sleep. Figure 1.1 shows how total sleep time gradually decreases as we age. In the first few days of life, infants sleep as many as 16 hours in a day. As they grow older, children begin to sleep less, needing only about 12 hours by age 2 and about 8 hours by age 13. Remember, these numbers represent an average, so your 2-year-old may sleep more or fewer than 12 hours but still be rested. Sleep needs continue to decline through adulthood so that by age 50, people sleep only about 6 hours on average per day. In addition, older adults frequently experience sleeping problems in the form of frequent night waking and often feel that they are not getting enough sleep.

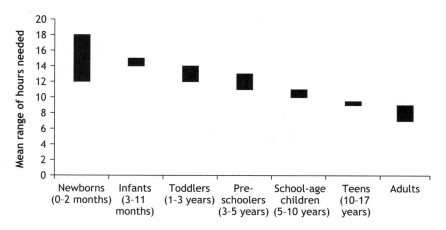

Figure 1.1. Range of sleep needs by age. ((*Source*: National Sleep Foundation, 2011.) (From Durand, V.M. [in press]. Sleep problems. In J.K. Luiselli [Ed.], *Children and youth with autism spectrum disorder [ASD]: Recent advances and innovations in assessment, education, and intervention.* New York, NY: Oxford University Press; reprinted by permission of Oxford University Press, USA. www.oup.com))

WHEN ARE OWLS AND LARKS NOT BIRDS?

There is one rule in our house that is rarely discussed but is understood by all—do not talk to me in the morning. Actually, this is not a rule so much as a reminder that if my wife, a relative, or a friend does try to engage me in conversation early in the morning, she or he will come away quite dissatisfied. Because work forces me to awaken earlier than my body likes, I am often uncommunicative—using mostly grunts to respond to questions—until about an hour after I have awakened. I am one of about 10% of adults who is an *owl* (or "night owl"): a person whose preferred time to be awake is from late morning until early the next morning. Another 10% of adults are *larks*: people who relish the early morning.[4] As we will see later, all humans are programmed to sleep in the evening and to be awake during the daylight hours. But there are those of us who push the edges of our nighttime preference for sleep.

Owls' preference for the latter part of the day and evening and larks' preference for early rising have been documented in research studies. In one study, owls were found to be at their peak performance of logical reasoning skills at 11 a.m., whereas larks were at their best at 8 a.m. (by the way, it is 10:30 a.m. as I write this, so I am almost there!). These sleep differences hold up even if these people are kept in the dark and away from typical sleep cues, which means that their different preferences for sleep are more than simply a result of their learning different sleep habits. Larks usually exercise in the morning before work, owls in the evening after work. The behaviorist B.F. Skinner was a lark, typically rising at 1 a.m. to work for an hour, sleeping for several hours, and ultimately beginning his day at 5 a.m. Famous owls include Socrates, French philosopher René Descartes, and inventor Thomas Edison.

We will see later that knowing if a person is one of the minority of us who is either an owl or a lark sometimes helps to explain presumed problems with sleep. A child's disruptive behavior and refusal to go to bed at a particular time may simply be the result of a clash between a child's owl preference for a later bedtime and a parent's lark preference for an earlier one. I next turn our attention to sleep itself: what it is and why we do it.

WHAT IS SLEEP?

We take sleep for granted because we experience it each day, and most assume that science long ago unlocked its mysteries. However, the complete answer to the question "What is sleep?" continues to elude us. We certainly know a great deal about what happens to the brain and the body during sleep, and next, I briefly review some of the more important changes. But the answer to what sleep is and why we all do it continues to be one of the more fascinating mysteries left to solve about human beings.

The first thing to understand about sleep is that it is *not* a time when the brain shuts down for a rest. Despite the fact that we are unaware of what is going on around us, the brain is quite active during sleep, as is the body. We go through several stages of sleep that seem to serve different purposes, and these stages look very different from each other. One reason we are interested in the different stages of sleep is that each also has its own characteristic sleep problems. As you will see, understanding the way sleep progresses typically can also help us understand what is going wrong with sleep.

There are two main types of sleep phases: *rapid eye movement (REM)* sleep and *nonrapid eye movement (NREM)* sleep. Most will recognize that the REM phase of sleep is when we dream. The eye movement under our closed eyelids during sleep signals the time when we report the universal phenomena we call *dreams*. REM sleep was discovered in 1953 at the University of Chicago by Dr. Nathaniel Kleitman and his graduate student Eugene Aserinsky. These sleep researchers were amazed that every sleeping person they studied had these periods of rapid eye movement, and these episodes began in each person around 90 minutes after he or she first fell asleep. Not knowing what these eye movements might mean, they later performed a very simple experiment: They woke up people during these times and asked the subjects what they were experiencing. About 80 percent of the time, people reported dreaming. The discovery of REM sleep revolutionized the field of sleep research because it indicated that there was some order to sleep: regular phases that were common to all people.

Kleitman and Aserinsky observed a period of about 90 minutes prior to the onset of REM sleep where the person was clearly asleep but where there was no apparent eye activity. This phase was called NREM and continues to be somewhat of an enigma to us today. We begin our sleep in NREM sleep and go through several stages (see Figure 1.2). The three stages of NREM sleep roughly correspond to how deeply we sleep, with the first stage being "light" sleep, the second stage being a "deeper" sleep, and the third stage being the "deepest" sleep. During the first stage (creatively referred to as Stage 1), we are

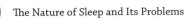
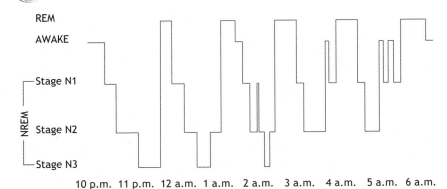

Figure 1.2. Sleep stages. (From Durand, V.M. [in press]. Sleep problems. In J.K. Luiselli [Ed.], *Children and youth with autism spectrum disorder [ASD]: Recent advances and innovations in assessment, education, and intervention.* New York, NY: Oxford University Press; reprinted by permission of Oxford University Press, USA. www.oup.com)

in transition between being awake and being asleep. (If you recall the movie *Hook,* this is the place where Tinker Bell told Peter Pan she would wait for him!) During this stage, people tend to feel that they are awake, although their thoughts begin to drift. Early researchers attempting to study Stage 1 sleep taped open the eyelids of volunteers and found that these people could not later remember pictures shown to them during this time.

Following this beginning stage of sleep, the pattern of brain waves begins to change, and we drift into the deeper stages of sleep (Stages 2 and 3). In the deepest stage of sleep (Stage 3), it becomes very difficult to awaken someone.[5] I remember the day my son was born, and I had been up for almost 48 hours (along with my wife, of course). After the birth, I came home to sleep. About 60 minutes after I first fell asleep—which is about the time we enter the deep stages of sleep—the phone rang numerous times. I was finally awakened and found myself speaking with a friend who was curious about the birth's outcome. My friend was astonished that I could not recall any of the details of the birth, including whether it was a boy or a girl! This was not unusual, for although someone can be awakened from these deep stages of sleep with some prodding, it takes a few minutes for the person to become fully alert.

After we cycle through approximately 90 minutes of NREM sleep, we then move into REM sleep. As I said, this is the time when our eyes move rapidly under our eyelids and people report dreams. What may surprise you about this sleep phase is that, although the brain is very active during this time, our muscles are almost paralyzed (or atonic). Did you ever have a dream where you were trying to run away from someone but felt as if your legs were dragging? Or you dreamed something terrible was happening to you but you could not scream? These are common dream experiences because they correspond to the body's inability to move during this time. Our muscles being almost completely paralyzed accounts for dreams of leg dragging as well as the inability to use vocal muscles to scream. If you have witnessed someone crying out during a dream, it was probably just as he or she awoke, which signaled the end of REM sleep. This information helps us understand that several types of sleep problems, such as sleep talking and sleep walking (also called *somnambulism*), occur during NREM sleep and probably do *not* represent the acting out of a dream.

We progress through these sleep stages several times through-out the night, going through the three stages of NREM sleep, into REM sleep, then back again to NREM. During the transition to NREM sleep after a period of dreaming, we experience a phenome-non known as *partial waking*. This is a brief period (sometimes only a few seconds) where we actually wake up from sleep. You might have had the experience of being in bed next to someone who awakens, sits up and says something, and then immediately falls back to sleep. When asked about it the next morning, the person has no memory of the event. This was probably an episode of partial waking, which we all experience as a typical part of sleep. This partial waking becomes important to us when we try to understand the night waking of chil-dren. As we will see later, all children experience these partial wak-ings; however, some children awaken fully from these episodes and then cry out or leave their beds for the comfort of their parents. I will explore why this might happen and how to respond to these episodes in later chapters.

Dream sleep appears to be extremely important to us. Although many authors have written quite eloquently about the content of dreams and how to interpret them, the mere act of going through this phase of sleep also seems necessary for our well-being. You may have noticed that if you miss a great deal of sleep, you may sleep a bit lon-ger on subsequent nights, but you do not usually need to make up each hour missed. However, when you study the sleep of people who are sleep deprived, you find that they do make up their missed REM sleep. In other words, the brain seems to compensate for this type of sleep by more quickly moving into REM sleep, even at the expense of NREM sleep. It is important to note that REM sleep is involved in memory and in consolidating newly learned information. Newborns spend approximately 50% of their sleep in REM sleep, possibly because of their need to make sense of all the new information they are exposed to throughout the day. The importance of REM sleep in learning and memory—coupled with the relative lack of REM sleep experienced by people with sleep problems—suggests that people with sleep problems may not only become irritable if they continue to go without enough sleep, but they may also experience cognitive impairments as a result. Obviously, for people with special needs who may already have learning difficulties, the added interference with learning and memory caused by their sleeping difficulties is of great concern. For example, we know through a number of research studies that amounts of REM sleep tend to be lower among individuals with more severe forms of intellectual disability.[6] What is unknown is whether the relative lack of REM sleep further adds to their learning difficulties. This is simply one more reason the sleep of people with special needs is an important area of concern.

WHAT IS OUR BIOLOGICAL CLOCK?

"I know who I was when I got up this morning, but I think I must have changed several times since then."

—Alice, *Alice's Adventures in Wonderland,* by Lewis Carroll

Probably some of the most fascinating information about the body and sleep comes from researchers who sometimes call themselves *chronobiologists*. Chronobiology is the study of "body time," or how the body's temperature, hormones, and other biological functions fluctuate day to day and hour to hour. Like Alice, we all change quite dramatically over the course of the day, and these changes seem to have a profound effect on us. The sleep–wake cycle is considered one of the *circadian* rhythms—with the word *circadian* meaning "about a day." You can expect significant information about the effect of these changes on our lives to make its way into the public consciousness over the next few years.

Deep inside the brain is a little bundle of cells—about the shape and size of this letter *v*—called the *superchiasmatic nucleus (SCN)*. The SCN is our "biological clock"—the part of our brain that keeps many of our bodily rhythms in sync. The SCN is located on top of the main junction of nerve fibers that connects to the eyes—a connection that becomes important, especially for sleep. The SCN seems to signal the brain when it is time to sleep and when it is time to be awake, and this sleep–wake cycle runs through its course over a period of about 24 hours. An unusual thing happens, though, if people are literally kept in the dark and not given information about whether it is day or night. If people are kept away from light cues, they will fall asleep and awaken on a cycle that runs about 25–27 hours. It appears that the increasing light in the morning and the decreasing light at night trigger the SCN to reset itself each day to run through a 24-hour rather than a non-24-hour day.

One group of people for whom this phenomenon is especially important is individuals with severe visual impairments (blindness). Because people with blindness cannot receive light cues from the sun, their sleep–wake cycles sometimes run through a 25- to 27-hour cycle. At first glance, this may not appear to be a serious problem; however, consider how their sleep patterns will change over the course of several weeks. If, for example, a person without the benefit of light cues falls asleep at 10 p.m. on Sunday evening, he or she will not be tired and fall asleep until about 11 p.m. on Monday (25 hours later). This advances to about midnight on Tuesday, 1 a.m. on Wednesday, and 5 a.m. by the next Sunday—he will be awake all night and not feel tired! This pattern will continue, with the person sleeping during the day and being awake at night the following week until the pattern gradually comes around again. When we have worked with such children, often parents are unaware that their children's sleep is affected in this way. The parents instead report that their children cycle through good and bad times, sometimes seeming to be "in tune" during the day and other times seeming to be "out of it" or irritable and cranky. In fact, these children are often referred to us for help because they are being aggressive during the day, although not every day. Their parents and teachers frequently do not suspect that these mood swings correspond to the synchronicity or lack of synchronicity between their children's sleep–wake cycles and everyone else's.

Lest you think that the prognosis for people with severe visual impairments and their sleep is all bad, a breakthrough in this area is beginning to provide relief for these individuals and their families. We now know that a certain hormone—melatonin—is partially responsible for transmitting the message to the SCN that it is dark outside. Melatonin is primarily produced in the pineal gland and is secreted in large amounts when the decreasing amount of light at nighttime is detected by the eyes. Many of you will be familiar with melatonin because of the media attention it has received as not only a natural cure for all sleep problems but also the answer to longer life and any number of other ailments. I think we have become savvy enough to recognize that such dramatic claims are often nothing more than calculated attempts to sell books; however, melatonin does provide some real benefit to the sleep of some groups of individuals, with people with blindness being one such group. Initial research suggests that small amounts of melatonin, when given prior to the desired bedtime, can stimulate the brain's biological clock to signal the time to sleep. This seems to be very helpful for regulating the sleep and wake times, especially for people with blindness. I will return to the use of melatonin later when I discuss the group of sleep problems known as *circadian rhythm disorders*.

The discovery of how the sleep–wake cycle naturally leans toward a non-24-hour day helped answer several questions about sleep. For example, we know that, for most of us, it is easier to stay awake an hour or so later at night than it is to fall asleep earlier. This is because of the body's natural tendency to move time ahead toward the 25- to 27-hour pattern. This also explains why it is more difficult to adjust to flying eastward across time zones than westward. For example, if you fly from New York to Los Angeles, you "gain" 3 hours because when your body (which is still on New York time) says it is 11 p.m. (your typical bedtime), it is only 8 p.m. in Los Angeles. Your body naturally wants to stay awake a bit longer anyway, so it is not difficult to adjust. On the other hand, flying from Los Angeles to New York, you "lose" 3 hours. Therefore, when you arrive in New York and it is your usual bedtime of 11 p.m., your body—which is still on L.A. time—says it is only 8 p.m., too early to fall asleep. It takes a few days for your body's circadian rhythms to adjust to this new time. Similarly, shift workers find it easier to change schedules ahead from an afternoon to an evening schedule rather than back from an evening to an afternoon shift. Sometimes changes in schedules due to events such as changing time zones or shift changes will have more than a temporary effect, and I will examine these sleep problems later in the book.

HOW DOES TEMPERATURE AFFECT SLEEP?

In addition to changes in the hormone melatonin, the body's internal temperature also seems to be involved in how and when we sleep.[7] The body does not maintain a constant temperature of 98.6° F, but rather, its internal temperature increases and decreases over the course of the day, making temperature another of our circadian rhythms. More recent and accurate measurements of body temperature indicate that the "normal" average temperature is 98.2° F, a little lower than we once thought, and that this ranges from about 97° F at its lowest point to about 99° F at its highest. These changes in temperature during the course of the day seem to closely follow periods of sleep and wakefulness.

Body temperature is at its lowest in the early hours of the morning (between about 4 a.m. and 6 a.m.) and begins to rise just before we awaken. This rise in temperature is involved in our alertness, signaling the time to wake up in the morning. Throughout the rest of the day, our body temperature rises gently, with the exception of a slight dip in temperature at midday. Our high temperature of about 99° F occurs in the early evening (between 7 p.m. and 8 p.m.) and then begins its decline. The drop in temperature signals a time of decreased alertness and corresponds to when most people feel the need to go to sleep. The general rule of thumb is that we are most alert when our natural body temperature is high and least alert when it is low.

In addition to giving us more information about how and why we sleep, understanding the relationship between body temperature and sleep also provides us with very helpful information about how our lifestyles will affect sleep. Exercise, for example, raises our internal body temperature. In terms of helping us sleep, the best time to exercise is in the late afternoon, somewhere around 4 or 5 p.m. The rise in body temperature after we exercise at this point in the day lasts for about 6 hours, and then declines, making it optimal for helping us fall asleep in the late evening. You can see that exercising later in the evening just before bedtime may interfere with sleep. Because of the importance of body temperature to sleep, people often wonder if taking a warm bath or shower at bedtime will actually cause difficulties falling asleep. This does not seem to be a problem, perhaps because a bath or shower does little to affect our internal body temperature.

CONCLUSION

This introduction to sleep should help us as I next turn our attention to the problems people can experience with their sleep. What follows is not an exhaustive list of sleep problems (which itself could fill the pages of this book) but rather is a description of some of the more common sleep problems experienced by people with special needs.

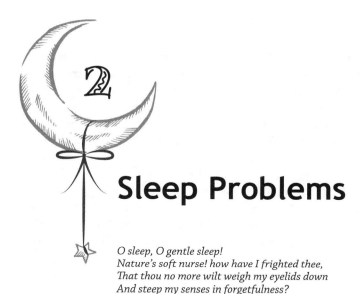

Sleep Problems

O sleep, O gentle sleep!
Nature's soft nurse! how have I frighted thee,
That thou no more wilt weigh my eyelids down
And steep my senses in forgetfulness?

—William Shakespeare, *King Henry IV*, Part III, Act I, Scene 5

King Henry IV's longing for sleep seems at odds with modern-day society's desire to wring the most out of a day. Many of us are trying to do more with less sleep. Yet many more people yearn to sleep better but, for a variety of reasons, cannot. Some have difficulty falling asleep or have their sleep disturbed frequently throughout the night. Others feel tired even after what seems to be a full night's sleep. Still others may encounter a number of abnormal sleep experiences such as frequent and disturbing nightmares, sleep terrors (which at first resemble nightmares but represent a very different sleep disturbance), sleepwalking, or sleep talking. This chapter addresses the many ways that sleep can be disrupted along with what we know about the causes of these problems.

HOW COMMON ARE SLEEP PROBLEMS?

You may be surprised to learn that as many as one out of every three otherwise healthy adults experiences significant problems with sleep.[1] At the same time, a similar ratio of children experience sleep problems. What is most alarming to many of us is that sleep problems seem to occur *more* often in people with special needs. As if life was not complicated enough, adding a sleep problem on top of all of our other difficulties can make getting through each day a greater challenge for people with a sleep problem as well as for their families and friends.

People with autism spectrum disorder (ASD) may be among the most seriously affected when it comes to sleep problems, with some research suggesting that almost all of these individuals experience difficulty with sleep at some point in their lives.[2] A survey of children with a range of developmental disabilities found that about 80% of parents reported some problem with their child's sleep and that one in four described the problem as severe.[3] To make matters worse, the parents also indicated that, unlike children without disabilities, their children did not seem to grow out of these sleep problems and that their sleeping difficulties persisted into adulthood. Sleep problems commonly occur among children with a variety of disorders, including Tourette's disorder, Rett syndrome, Williams syndrome, Angelman syndrome, and cerebral palsy. Because a problem with sleep may be a sign of other related problems, a number of different groups of people experience difficulty sleeping. Nightmares, sleep terrors, and other problems with sleep are commonly reported among children and adults who have been victims of abuse or other traumatic events.[4] Obviously, this does not necessarily mean that a sleep problem is a sign of past or current abuse but simply that these upsetting episodes can increase the likelihood of sleep problems in the affected person. Even something as apparently unrelated as marital discord can disrupt the sleep of the couple's children.

One group of children for whom sleep is often reported as a problem is those with attention-deficit/hyperactivity disorder (ADHD). ADHD is a disorder that affects an estimated 7% of all children and results in difficulties with attention and, for many children, also involves impulsivity and hyperactivity.[5] The most common treatment for these children is a medical one—typically a stimulant medication such as Ritalin or Adderall. Parents of these children often describe how their children develop sleep problems after being placed on this type of medication. I describe how to balance the medication and sleep needs of these children later in the book. It is clear, however, that many children with ADHD also require assistance with their sleep.

HOW SERIOUS ARE THESE PROBLEMS?

As you can see, many groups of people with special needs also experience disturbed sleep. In addition to the sheer number of people who have difficulty with their sleep, the effects of sleep on their behavior also contribute to the concern of families and professionals. We know, for example, that disturbed sleep has a negative impact on performance during certain tasks—motivation to work decreases and the ability to concentrate becomes impaired. Similarly, people who have not had enough sleep often report feeling irritable or depressed. What can we say, then, about the effects on people with special needs—especially those who have difficulty learning and carrying out daily tasks?

Unfortunately, research looking at the effects of sleep problems on people with special needs is rare, so we have very little direct knowledge about how those people may be affected. But some general conclusions can be made based on research usually conducted on adults without disabilities. It is important to note that one night of disrupted sleep will probably have a minimal effect on a person's ability to carry out daily tasks. That is good news because, occasionally, all of us have experienced a night that—because of anxiety over a presentation you have to give, the cup of coffee enjoyed too late at night, the excitement over a trip the next day, or even just being anxious about not falling asleep—we have slept very little. Yet, despite being tired, we are able to get through the day relatively well. However, should this disturbed sleep persist for more than a day or two, there are likely to be noticeable effects. Persistent and chronic sleep disturbances will cause a decline in motivation or concentration as opposed to a loss of ability.[6]

As motivation decreases, concentration is impaired, and performance errors increase. Significantly, people involved in boring, repetitive tasks will show the effects of a poor night's sleep more readily than those involved in interesting and challenging tasks. Consider this in light of how we tend to treat children and adults with special needs. A person who has difficulty learning new skills (such as a person with an intellectual disability or learning disability) is usually given an easier—and therefore sometimes boring and repetitive—task until he or she is considered "ready" to move on to more challenging work. If the person also experiences sleep problems, his or her difficulty at work will be made worse by presenting the same unchallenging work over and over. You can see that we may be mistakenly attributing errors on school work or at a job to the person's cognitive difficulties, when this problem may be, in part, a result of sleep problems and our lack of understanding of their effects on a person's performance.

Sleep also affects our emotional well-being. Sleeping longer is associated with adaptability (being able to tolerate changes in routines) and positive mood, whereas sleeping less is associated with children described as "difficult"—those who get upset if you try to change routines and who always seem irritable. One young boy I worked with was referred because he lacked motivation in class and was generally noncompliant to his teacher's requests. The boy had a severe intellectual disability, and the teacher seemed to assume his difficulties were related to his diagnosis. After watching him at his desk in class for a few minutes, I turned to his mother, who was also watching, and said to her, "He doesn't sleep very well, does he?" His mother was astounded I knew that without her telling me, and his teacher was even more astounded because she did not know herself that the boy slept only 3–4 hours each night. They both looked at me in awe at my remarkable clinical skills and asked how I knew this by only seeing him for a few minutes. I ruined the adulation when I said, "Well, he looks tired!" This story not only highlights how a lack of sleep can affect your mood and behavior (which fortunately improved in this boy when we helped him sleep better, the full details of which I describe later in the book), but also how we tend to overlook sleep as an important influence on how we think, feel, and behave.

In some cases, the negative impact of poor sleep can be even more serious. In our own research on people who display self-injurious and aggressive behavior—too often observed among people with ASD and other developmental disorders—we have found that disrupted sleep can make these behavior problems worse. Not sleeping well can make some people hit themselves or others more often. On a positive note, we have been able to help reduce the occurrences of these very disturbing behaviors by improving the affected person's sleep.[7]

A final measure of how serious these sleep problems can be is easily seen in the families of people with disrupted sleep. In some cases, I have observed couples whose marriages have been threatened because of their child's sleep problems. Depression among parents—especially mothers—is also common in these families. The cause of these problems at home can be traced back to several factors. First, a child's disturbed sleep invariably means that the parents' sleep will also be disrupted. Getting up with your child each and every night for months and years means that both you and your child will be sleep deprived. We have just seen that your ability to concentrate and your mood will be affected in a negative way if you are not sleeping well yourself. In addition, we know from psychological research litera-ture that depression can occur when people feel they have no control over important parts of their lives. People begin to feel helpless and give up trying to improve this nighttime problem. I worked with one mother whose child woke up and cried every night for 7 years. She had long before given up hope that anything could be done to help them get a good night's sleep and felt guilty that she could not help her child. Obviously, sleep disturbances can have negative consequences for everyone who is in some way touched by this vexing problem.

WHEN DOES SLEEP BECOME A PROBLEM?

I mentioned in the last chapter how people have different sleep needs. Some people can sleep only 5–6 hours per night and yet they report feeling rested and refreshed. Others can sleep for 9–10 hours and still feel tired the next day. This issue of sleep differences raises an important question: If people have different sleep needs, how do you know if a child's inability to sleep more than a few hours per night is a sleep problem or just a normal difference? You might be surprised to learn that sleep experts rely heavily on the subjective impression of the person with the sleep complaint. In other words, if a person sleeps only 5 hours per night but is not bothered by this and can carry on daily activities, then it is not considered a sleep problem. On the other hand, if a person sleeps an average of 9 hours per night but is still tired during the day and is concerned about sleep, then it is consid-ered a sleep problem. For children, this often translates into how well they function during the day and how disturbing the sleep difficulty is at night. If a child appears tired and irritable even after 8 hours of sleep, he or she may have a sleep problem. Similarly, if bedtime is disrupted (e.g., the child cries for 20 minutes or more each night) or night waking is a problem (e.g., screaming out each night), then this too may signal a problem with sleep.

As I turn next to the common sleep problems experienced by peo-ple with special needs, bear in mind this subjective quality to sleep. If your child's sleep pattern adversely affects him or her or your family in any important way, then assume it is significant enough to look at more closely. Keep in mind, too, that there are more than 80 differ-ent and distinct sleep problems recognized by sleep professionals—far too many to cover adequately here. Fortunately, only a handful of these problems are commonly experienced by people with special needs. I will describe the most frequently occurring of the sleep disturbances and some information on their causes.

Insomnia

What image is conjured up in your mind when you think of a person with insomnia? Most people picture a person who never sleeps yet who functions well during the day. This is, however, just one more myth about sleep. It is not possible to go completely without sleep for very long. If you stay awake for more than a day or two, you will begin having brief periods of sleep that last for several seconds—called *microsleeps*. People with severe insomnia are often unaware that they have these brief sleep episodes, thus believing that they never sleep. In addition to experiencing microsleeps, being this sleep deprived will have a significant negative impact on a person's life. These individuals often have substantial impairments in the quality of their lives and have difficulty getting through even the simplest of life's daily tasks. I mentioned earlier in the book that a complete lack of sleep is catastrophic, suggesting how important sleep is to us. One sleep disorder that does involve not sleeping at all is called *fatal familial insomnia*. As the name implies, this progressive sleep disorder ultimately leads to death for those afflicted, but fortunately it is an extremely rare problem.

Insomnia is not one problem but describes instead a number of different problems with sleep. Sleep professionals break down insomnia into three different and distinct problems:

1. Difficulty falling asleep at night (called a difficulty *initiating* sleep)

2. Waking frequently during the night or waking too early and being unable to go back to sleep (called a difficulty *maintaining* sleep)

3. Not feeling rested even after a reasonable number of hours of sleep (called *nonrestorative* sleep)

As with all of the sleep problems I describe, a person is considered as having insomnia only if the cause of these sleep disturbances cannot be traced back to some other medical or psychological problem. If we find, for example, that a person is not sleeping well because he or she is experiencing pain, then this is not technically thought to be primarily a sleep problem. At the same time, a person who is anxious or depressed will often have difficulty sleeping. If the anxiety or depression is the primary cause of the sleep difficulties, then this is where clinical attention is first paid.

Being sleep deprived, whether it is a result of not being able to fall asleep, waking up too frequently, or not receiving refreshing sleep, affects about one third of people with special needs and is the most common sleep complaint. It also appears that these sleep problems will often not go away on their own. Although many children do seem to grow out of their early sleep difficulties, many do not, and as we have seen, these sleep problems can upset the lives of everyone in the family. Looking at the different types of insomnia is important, because it will lead us directly to the causes of these problems and ultimately to their treatment.

Trouble at Bedtime

One of the symptoms of insomnia involves difficulties going to sleep at an acceptable time. As many parents know all too well, this can involve emotional outbursts from the child. Some children will scream and cry for hours on end. Others are more subtle in their efforts to avoid bedtime and concoct elaborate routines that involve the whole family. At one point in our home, for example, we had a more-than-hour-long parade of events that would begin by reading my son a story, followed by "just one more" story. Then hugs and kisses were next, followed by back scratching. This was then followed by more hugs and kisses. After a few minutes in bed, there was a need for a glass of water, then a trip to the bathroom, then another trip to the bathroom. Then the sheets weren't just right, there was a noise outside, or it was too hot or cold—sound familiar? Still, other children will just lie awake in bed, not able to fall asleep. These difficulties can stem from a number of different problems.

For some children, bedtime difficulties stem from the inability or unwillingness of parents to set limits on their children's bedtime. Many parents report that they become extremely upset when their child cries or screams and that anything is preferable to listening to that kind of gut-wrenching emotional outburst. They find that going into the child's room to comfort him or her or bringing the child into their own bed will end that evening's battle, but as we all know, this will just postpone the problem until the next night. Worse yet, repeatedly "giving in" to a child's tantrums runs the risk of teaching him or her to tantrum every night, usually in an ever-increasing escalation of intensity.

It is important to remember that parents are not completely to blame in this case or in any other case of a childhood sleep problem. Although some parents are quite aware of the pattern that develops at bedtime and recognize their role in the situation, they oftentimes forget that their child has a role as well. We often have to remind parents that many children fall asleep on their own. In other words, some children's sleep patterns are such that they have no difficulty falling asleep at night and, in fact, seek out bedtime. The child who resists bedtime may be one who is simply not tired at the time most of us sleep. An additional difference we observe in children is known as *temperament*. Different children have different personalities or temperaments and will deal with problem situations in their own ways. Some children who may not be tired at bedtime may be more easygoing and will therefore do their best to fall asleep after being asked. Other children, however, are more strong-willed and feisty, and they put up a fight in most situations. The child who resists being told when to wash up or what clothes to wear may similarly resist your decision about bedtime. If you find that this describes your child, I can help you deal with this problem later in the book. Take some solace in knowing that it takes two or more people to create this problem, and there are relatively easy "fixes" that can resolve even the most disturbing bedtime disasters.

Why is it that some people are simply not tired at bedtime? One reason may be that what you do, eat, and drink before bedtime can sometimes be the cause of these problems. Referred to by sleep experts as *sleep hygiene,* these are daily living practices that influence your ability to fall asleep and stay asleep. Caffeine in coffee and soft drinks is among the biggest offenders because it can increase your arousal, and therefore you do not feel tired enough to go to sleep. What most people do not know is that caffeine stays in our systems for up to 6 hours. This means that drinking a cup of coffee or a soft drink at dinnertime may very well be interfering with a person's ability to fall asleep later in the evening. The nicotine found in cigarettes is, like caffeine, a stimulant, and it too can interfere with sleep. Other stimulants, including the medications Ritalin and Adderall, which are often prescribed for people with ADHD, can interfere with sleep as well. As I mentioned in Chapter 1, exercise too close to bedtime (3–4 hours) can also increase arousal and will hinder attempts to fall asleep.

Even where a person sleeps can keep some from falling asleep easily. For one of our cases, we videotaped the bedtime routine of a

young girl to see how the family was carrying out our recommendations. This little girl did not cry or scream when she was told it was
time to sleep, but she would constantly come out of her room. The
video was quite revealing because it picked up the family's television
programs and all of their conversations even though the video cam-
era was placed in the little girl's room. It was clear that the girl could
hear everything going on with the rest of her family because her bedroom was right next to the family room. The girl's room was much too
noisy for her to fall asleep in at night, especially for someone who was
already a light sleeper. Relatively minor changes helped her bedtime
problems dramatically. In addition to noise, too much light or even
an uncomfortable temperature in a bedroom can prevent a smooth
bedtime.

Daytime sleeping is a common cause of bedtime disturbances.
Many of the children with whom we work take naps during the day,
in part because they have not slept well the previous night. Some children sleep on the bus to or from school, others during school, and still
others take a nap at home after school. Naps by themselves are not
inherently bad. Leonardo da Vinci is reported to have *only* napped,
sleeping for 15 minutes every 4 hours throughout the day. In fact,
many sleep experts recommend that adults try taking short naps
during the day to make up for the lost sleep they experience each
night. Our "sleep debt" needs to be paid back, and napping may be
exactly the remedy many of us need. Unfortunately, for some people, sleeping during the day may also affect attempts to fall asleep
in the evening. A nap of more than a few minutes can decrease the
likelihood that the person will be tired at his or her usual bedtime.
This sets up the beginning of what can become a very vicious cycle.
Not being able to fall asleep easily at night will make the person tired
again the next day, which in turn will create the desire to nap, and the
nap will interfere with bedtime once more. Some children's daytime
sleeping habits are the root of their bedtime problems.

A related problem that can sometimes be the cause of a lack
of sleepiness at bedtime involves the different patterns or *phases* of
sleep that we all prefer. In Chapter 1, I discussed how some people
are larks (those who prefer waking early and going to bed early) and
others are owls (those who prefer sleeping late and staying up late).
The approximately 10% of people who are owls will not be tired at the
usual bedtime because of the differences in their circadian rhythms.
For children who are owls, this may result in a resistance to go to

bed. Later in the book, I discuss some very intriguing new techniques for helping people shift their sleep phases to more closely match the desired sleep times.

Anxiety surrounding bedtime can be a vexing problem. Children will often refuse to go to sleep at night because they are afraid of the dark, because some monster is waiting for them under the bed, or even because they are afraid of having bad dreams. For children who cannot talk, parents often wonder if their resistance to bedtime is a result of fears and anxieties. One of the first challenges of helping a child who reports being afraid about going to sleep is determining how real the anxiety truly is. Children are often quite creative in finding out exactly what to say at bedtime to get a parent into the room. A friend of mine had a great deal of difficulty getting his daughter to go to sleep at night. She complained that monsters might hurt her after the family fell asleep. Using a bit of ingenuity, my friend went to the store and bought a quite elaborate "magic wand" for his daughter. He explained to her that the wand had special powers and that, if any monster tried to get her, she could make it disappear with one wave of the wand. This worked well for less than a week, when his daughter began a nightly ritual of asking for water, a back rub, to be tucked in, and other activities. In other words, it appeared that the reports of monsters may have been a conscious or unconscious attempt on the part of the little girl to get her father into the room, and when the wand took away that method, she found a different way. The problem is that, because we cannot get inside the head of this little girl, we will never know if her fears were real, if she just began the new ritual to allay those fears in a new way, or if her distress was simply an attempt to obtain more of her parents' attention at night.

Children with a history of abuse or who have experienced other trauma often have very frightening dreams, and bedtime can become associated with a great deal of apprehension. Just as many of us associate a physician's office or a hospital with unpleasant events, these children learn that bed and sleep are linked to their bad dreams and are things to be avoided. Children who have problems with bedwetting may also avoid bedtime for the same reason.

Finally, medications given to some children to get them to sleep at night may quickly become the source of a sleep problem. Many of the parents of children with special needs who we see have at some point been told to give their child some type of sleep-inducing medicine—often the antihistamine Benadryl, which produces sleepiness as a side effect. Pediatricians will often suggest this medication because it can help a child go to sleep quickly at bedtime and can prevent many of the bedtime disturbances I just described. The problem with Benadryl and many other medications used to induce sleep is that, when parents try to stop using it, it can actually make sleep worse than before. The phenomenon of worsening sleep after medication withdrawal is called *rebound insomnia* and is sometimes the cause of nighttime disturbances in children. Medication for sleep, especially among children, is not typically recommended for long-term use, in part because it can make a bad sleep problem worse.

Night Waking

I once heard someone say that bedtimes are for parents. Whether a child goes to bed at 8, 8:30, or 9 p.m. may be less important for the sleep needs of the child than it is for the mental health of the parent. Parents work hard and, as much as we love our children, we do need a little break away from them at the end of the day. It is then a cruel twist of the natural order of things that just as parents begin to unwind and relax, their child awakens prematurely from sleep. Or worse, just as parents find themselves deep in sleep, the cries of their child snatch them back to reality. This is especially difficult for parents who may have just battled with their child for more than an hour to go to sleep in the first place.

Along with bedtime problems, night waking is among the most common sleep problems experienced by children. Like bedtime disturbances, night waking can be caused by a number of different factors. In many cases, night waking can be traced back to a child's earliest years. In Chapter 1, I described how all of us go through "partial wakings" throughout the night. These are brief periods in our sleep cycle where we awaken but then immediately go back to sleep and have no memory of them the next day. It is thought that, particularly for children who do not fall asleep on their own at night, their disruptive night wakings originate from these partial wakings. Imagine an infant who is being held in her mother's arms and who falls asleep. The mother places the child in a crib, turns off the light, and leaves the room. Some 60 minutes later, the infant experiences a partial waking, but instead of being in her mother's arms, she is now in a dark room, alone in a crib. This unfamiliar situation may be disturbing enough to cause the child to cry out. Further imagine that you are the child's parent and that you are a first-time parent or that this child has been ill or has some other problem. Your child's crying will cause you some concern, and you are likely to go into her room to see if she is all right. Your child, who may have only been partially awake, is now more fully awake at seeing you in the room. You comfort your child, maybe even hold her in your arms until she falls asleep again, and then you go back to sleep.

What seems to happen in this very common scene is that the child does not learn to fall asleep on his or her own. The child may only fall asleep with a parent in the room or with music on in the background. When he or she wakes up during the night, and the scene has changed dramatically, it can be frightening, and it is more diffi-cult to fall back to sleep. Crying out as a strategy is further reinforced because it brings the parents back into the room. So, instead of learn-ing how to fall back asleep alone after one of these awakenings, the child instead learns to get the parent back in the room to recreate the comforting scene he or she had grown used to. Sadly, many children learn one more stage to this episode. After many nights of this, some parents recognize that they should not be going into their child's room and try to ignore the cries. This is obviously upsetting to the child, so she cries longer and more loudly. At some point, most par-ents give up because they cannot stand to hear their child so upset. Unfortunately, what the child has now learned is the next time her parents do not come into her room right away, cry longer and louder, because if at first you do not succeed . . . As you can see, disruptive night wakings can originate from these first experiences with par-tial wakings.

Early feeding practices can also lead to night wakings in a number of different ways. One reason this occurs is because, as I just described with a parent's presence when the child falls asleep, the child may learn to associate going to sleep with feeding. This often begins in infancy, when the child is fed just before sleep. By the age of about 3 months, children no longer need to be fed at bedtime or at times throughout the night. However, parents often enjoy this closeness as the child goes off to sleep, or their child's occasional awakenings make them feel that the child is hungry. Because of these reasons, bedtime and night-time feedings will frequently continue well beyond 3 months of age. What can take over is the cycle of awakenings followed by the parent coming into the room and feeding the child. Nighttime feedings can also disrupt sleep by activating the digestive system at a time when it should be dormant. In addition, consuming liquids can cause the desire to urinate, which can contribute to awakenings. Night waking often results from a combination of a child who may be a light sleeper, along with learned patterns of falling asleep.

In addition to the learning that can go on surrounding these night wakings, certain medical problems can also contribute to nighttime disturbances. Conditions such as colic, urinary tract or middle ear infections, congestion, or any other condition that is uncomfortable or painful for the child may disrupt sleep. The side effects of certain medications such as antihistamines or antibiotics can also contribute to night waking. These conditions, combined with how parents respond to night awakenings, can also result in a pattern of chronic nighttime disruption.

Feeling Tired Throughout the Day

Some people sleep for what appears to be an acceptable amount of time yet feel unrested the next day. They may have a very difficult time getting going in the morning and feel tired during the day. Here we see children who sleep 8–10 hours per night and yet will still take naps during the day. Usually this is a sign that the person's sleep is being disrupted during the night, even if he or she is unaware of it. A number of medically related conditions can lead to this problem. One of the more common causes involves problems people experience with breathing as they sleep. In its extreme form, people will stop breathing for several seconds at times throughout the night in a condition called *sleep apnea*.[8] Less dramatically, many people have obstructed breathing, which can disrupt the normal progression of sleep stages. Like the partial awakenings, this sleep disruption brought on by breathing problems often goes unnoticed by the person affected, yet it can interrupt sleep enough to leave the person feeling unrested the next day. For children, they may not display excessive sleepiness during the day but may instead be more irritable, hyperactive, or have trouble concentrating. I describe sleep apnea and other related breathing problems later in this chapter and also recommend that, if this problem is suspected, a formal medical evaluation should be conducted of the person's sleep.

Sleep and seizures (sudden and unpredictable discharges of electrical activity in the brain) are related. Given that both involve electrical activity in the brain, it should not be surprising that sleep can activate certain types of seizures. Seizures during sleep often do not cause the person to awake fully but, like breathing problems, can disrupt sleep enough to cause daytime drowsiness. This condition is further complicated if the person is taking antiseizure medication because this medication can contribute to daytime drowsiness as well. Medication for asthma symptoms, especially if taken close to bedtime, can also disrupt sleep and be a cause of sleepiness during the day.

Hypersomnia and Narcolepsy

The word *insomnia* means not enough or insufficient sleep. We have seen that insomnia covers a variety of problems that all involve not getting enough sleep. *Hypersomnia,* on the other hand, refers to getting too much sleep. Hypersomnia and a related sleep disorder called *narcolepsy* involve sleeping excessively during the day despite getting sufficient sleep at night.[9] With these disorders, people find themselves falling asleep, sometimes at very inconvenient times, even after a night of 8–10 hours of sleep. Both hypersomnia and narcolepsy are relatively rare—occurring in less than 1% of the general population—but they can be very debilitating to the person affected.

We know very little about what causes hypersomnia. Family history of this sleep problem seems to be common, with about 40% of the people with this problem having a family member who also has hypersomnia. This suggests that one's genetics may be involved in its cause for at least among some of the people who suffer from this problem. One additional finding about hypersomnia is that a larger proportion of people with this sleep problem than you would expect seem to have a history of having the infectious disease mononucleosis. Unfortunately, we still do not fully understand how genetics or mononucleosis is involved in the development of hypersomnia.

We have more information about narcolepsy, a sleep problem that also involves excessive sleeping during the day. The symptoms of narcolepsy take on a more dramatic quality than those involved with hypersomnia. With narcolepsy, people will be awake and alert one minute and slump down to the floor and be fast asleep the next. In addition to falling asleep, people with narcolepsy experience a sudden loss of muscle tone (called *cataplexy*). This muscle tone loss seems to be caused by the sudden onset of REM sleep. If you remember, REM, or dream, sleep typically begins about 60–90 minutes after we fall asleep. This is also a time when we are relatively paralyzed, not able to move any of our major muscles. What appears to happen for people with narcolepsy is that their daytime sleep attacks involve an immediate transition into REM sleep along with the accompanying paralysis. Thus their heads might fall to one side, they may slide down in their chairs, or they may even fall to the floor as a result of this immediate movement to REM sleep. Another aspect of this sleep attack is that people often report that the attacks occur in the middle of some emotional event. People have been known to be watching their favorite sports team on television and, right at a crucial moment of the game, fall fast asleep.

Two other unusual events surrounding sleep affect people with narcolepsy. These individuals will often report experiencing *sleep paralysis,* which is a brief period of time upon awakening where they cannot move or speak. As you can imagine, this feeling of not being able to move or speak can be quite frightening to these individuals. It is important to note that sleep paralysis occurs occasionally for people who do not have narcolepsy, although it is more common among people with this sleep problem. The last major symptom in narcolepsy is an experience called *hypnagogic hallucinations.* These hallucinations are particularly vivid experiences that occur during sleep and are said to be unbelievably realistic because they include perceiving not only visual aspects but the full range of the senses, including touch, hearing, and even the sensation of body movement. People have retold stories, for example, such as hallucinating being in a house on fire and that they could smell the smoke and feel the heat.

Before I discuss the causes of narcolepsy, it is intriguing to note that sleep paralysis and hypnagogic hallucinations have been used to explain a most unusual phenomenon—UFO experiences. As you know, people routinely report seeing unidentified flying objects and also more active incidents, including being abducted by aliens. In an interesting study, researchers questioned people who had these experiences and separated them into two groups: those with more passive reports, such as just seeing lights in the sky, and those with more active experiences, such as seeing and communicating with aliens. The researchers found that a majority of these experiences occurred at night, and 60% of the more active events were said to have happened during sleep. If you look at their reports, the people with these active experiences describe events that resemble the frightening episodes of sleep paralysis and hypnagogic hallucinations.

> I was lying in bed facing the wall, and suddenly my heart started to race. I could feel the presence of three entities standing beside me. I was unable to move my body but could move my eyes. One of the entities, a male, was laughing at me, not verbally but with his mind. He made me feel stupid. He told me telepathically, "Don't you know by now that you can't do anything unless we let you?" (Spanos, Cross, Dickson, & DuBreuil, 1993, pg. 627)

The realistic and frightening stories of people who have UFO sightings may not be the products of an active imagination or the result of a hoax but, at least in some cases, may be a disturbance of sleep. Sleep paralysis and hypnagogic hallucinations do occur in a portion of people without narcolepsy, which may help explain why not everyone with these "otherworldly" experiences has narcolepsy.

Knowledge about the causes of narcolepsy is growing, and it appears that this sleep problem has biological origins. Specifically, it seems clear that narcolepsy is influenced by one's genetics. The first clues about the genetics of narcolepsy came from a most unlikely source—man's best friend. Some years ago, the highly regarded sleep researcher Dr. William Dement was lecturing to a group at the American Academy of Neurology in Boston. In the audience was a veterinarian who commented that he had observed a miniature poodle named Monique who seemed to display the same symptoms as narcolepsy in his human patients being described by Dr. Dement. Intrigued, Dr. Dement requested that Monique be flown to his sleep laboratory at Stanford University for further study. It was there that he discovered that the dog had a disorder identical to narcolepsy in humans. As a result of this chance encounter, researchers have been able to identify that Doberman pinschers and Labrador retrievers also inherit this disorder and that it may be associated with a cluster of genes on chromosome number 6. It appears that this genetic mutation causes the loss of certain brain cells (those containing a brain chemical called *hypocretin*) in an area in the hypothalamus. It is hoped that this advancing knowledge will lead to better treatments for humans.

Breathing-Related Sleep Problems

Sleepiness during the day that is the result of disrupted sleep at night sometimes is caused by physical problems. A common physical problem that disrupts the sleep of approximately 1%–2% of the population involves difficulty breathing during sleep. For all of us, the muscles in our upper airways relax somewhat as we sleep, and this makes breathing a little bit more difficult. Unfortunately, this constriction of breathing is more pronounced in some people, and it can cause very labored breathing during sleep (called *hypoventilation*). As a result of breathing difficulties, people will experience numerous brief episodes of being awakened during the night, although a person will not be fully awake and will probably not remember the awakenings. However, because they are not sleeping deeply, they do not feel rested the next day even after 8 or 9 hours in bed. At its most extreme, some people will have short periods of time during sleep where they stop breathing altogether—sometimes up to 10–30 seconds—which is referred to as *sleep apnea*.

Although immediate signs of breathing difficulty may not be obvious to anyone other than a bed partner, there are other important indications. Loud snoring is sometimes a sign of a breathing difficulty. Also, heavy sweating during the night, morning headaches, and episodes of falling asleep during the day may be evidence of breathing problems during sleep. Finally, these breathing difficulties occur more often in people who are overweight, perhaps because of increased pressure on the airways. As I have mentioned before, if breathing difficulties are suspected of being the cause of a sleep problem, a medical evaluation is essential.

Sleep Schedule Problems

The artist Edward Hopper often painted people at the extremes of our sleep–wake cycle. In "Morning Sun," a woman is pictured fully dressed looking anxiously out of her window at the predawn light. In sharp contrast is the painting "Nighthawks," which depicts a couple lingering over their coffee at an all-night diner. What makes our sleep schedules so different? In Chapter 1, I described how our biological clock informs the brain to help us sleep at night and to help us wake up in the morning. We also found that light from the sun resets this clock each day so that we go through about a 24-hour cycle—known as a *circadian rhythm*. Unfortunately, sometimes this process is disrupted, and people sleep at times when they want to be awake and are awake at times that they want to be asleep. Unlike with insomnia where people may have trouble sleeping, people with sleep schedule problems may sleep fine but at the wrong times. They may awaken fully alert at 4 a.m. and have nothing to do then fall asleep later that day at 8 p.m., despite wanting to be awake. Others cannot fall asleep at night and then cannot get up the next morning. More than simply an inconvenience, being "out of sync" can cause individuals to be tired and have difficulty concentrating during the day if they try to fight their body's desired schedule. These sleep schedules usually do not fit with our typical school or work schedules, and activities can be seriously disrupted.

You have already experienced what out-of-sync sleep schedules can be like if you have flown across several time zones in a day and have felt jet-lagged. People who are jet-lagged usually report difficulty going to sleep at the proper time as well as feeling fatigued during the day. Certain people seem to be more negatively affected by time zone changes, including older adults, introverts (loners), and early risers (morning people). Repeated travel such as this disrupts the sleep of people so much that they can experience serious and chronic sleeping difficulties.

Another group of people who suffer from these types of sleep problems are people whose work schedules do not allow them to sleep at night. Many people such as hospital employees, police, or emergency personnel must work at night or work irregular hours; as a result, they may have difficulty sleeping or may be excessively sleepy during waking hours. These problems can actually become more serious, with reports of gastrointestinal symptoms, increased potential for alcohol abuse, low worker morale, and disruption of family life being more common among these shift workers.

In addition to these self-imposed causes of circadian rhythm sleep problems, there are people who suffer from the same symptoms because of more internal, although as yet not completely understood, causes.[10] Extreme night owls, or people who stay up late and sleep late, may have a problem called *delayed sleep phase syndrome,* a type of circadian rhythm disorder. Falling asleep is "delayed" or later compared to a typical bedtime. At the other end of the extreme, people with *advanced sleep phase syndrome* are very early to bed and very early to rise. With this syndrome, sleep is "advanced" in relation to our typical bedtime. Not going through the 24-hour phase of sleep and wakefulness—called *non-24-hour sleep–wake syndrome*—disrupts the lives of a significant number of people. For a variety of reasons, individuals with this sleep problem follow a 25-hour (or longer) phase and are constantly changing the time when they sleep. You may recall that I discussed how people with severe visual impairments (blindness) often experience this problem and how they go through very difficult phases where they want to sleep during the day and stay awake at night.

People with delayed sleep phase syndrome (night owls) often seem to develop the difficulty as a child or adolescent, staying up later and later at night and then sleeping late the next morning. On the other hand, those with advanced sleep phase syndrome seem to develop the problem later in life, perhaps as part of an acceleration of their biological clocks. Two related causes of these sleep schedule problems are currently being explored. I described in Chapter 1 how the brain chemical melatonin seems to be involved in resetting our biological clock. It is believed that, for some people who have sleep schedule problems, their production of this hormone may not be sufficient enough to trigger the brain to begin sleep.

The second area of study for people with sleep schedule problems involves sunlight. I described before how the hormone melatonin, which seems responsible for signaling sleep, is produced deep in our brain by the pineal gland. In some animals, particularly some birds and reptiles, the pineal gland is so close to the top of the skull that it can detect light from the sun directly and transmit this information to other parts of the brain. This ability has earned the pineal gland the label of *the third eye* in these animals. Our pineal gland, because it cannot detect light directly, is connected to the nerve fibers in our eyes. What happens, then, is that as our eyes take in less and less light in the evening; this tells the pineal gland to begin producing melatonin, which in turn triggers our sleep. However, if we do not receive sufficient light cues, this elaborate system does not work as it was designed, and our sleep is disrupted. There is one group where you see this problem quite clearly—people who live in extreme northern latitudes. The low levels of light that people are exposed to in the winter months seem to interfere with melatonin production and can wreak havoc on sleep schedules. I discuss in a later chapter how you can use bright lights to help "jump start" this light–melatonin mechanism to help someone sleep better.

Nightmares

The British author Robert Louis Stevenson is said to have suffered greatly from nightmares as a child. Fortunately, he turned this malady into creative success by using one of his nightmares as the basis of his famous book, *The Strange Case of Dr. Jekyll and Mr. Hyde*. We have all, from time to time, had a dream that was frightening or distressful. You dream that someone is about to kill you or that you are running away from some threat but cannot run fast enough, or that you are back in school and cannot find the room where the big final exam is being held. These dreams are so frightening that a person may awaken feeling very upset and can usually remember at least part of the dream. For some people, these nightmares can impair their ability to carry on daily activities. Recurring nightmares can lead to disrupted sleep, primarily because the person begins to fear bedtime.

"Bad dreams" are an almost universal phenomenon. Severe and recurrent nightmares are also common, occurring for as many as 20% of children and 5%–10% of adults. As with most of the other sleep problems I have discussed, there is little information about the frequency of nightmares among people with special needs. One exception is among children with histories of abuse, who do report much higher rates of nightmares than others.

You would expect that, because nightmares are so common, a great deal of research would focus on their causes. Unfortunately, we still know very little about why people have nightmares. One study, however, suggests that any form of trauma, even emotional trauma, may contribute to an increase in nightmares. This study looked at how the September 11th attack on the United States affected young children who lived near Ground Zero in New York.[11] The researchers found that there was a significant increase in reported nightmares following the event. In this case, one of "nature's experiments" allowed researchers to examine how emotional trauma can directly influence nightmares.

Sleep Terrors

One evening some years ago, my peaceful and as yet uneventful night's sleep was shattered by the blood-curdling screams of my then 3-year-old son. The screaming and crying continued as my wife and I raced to his room. Although it took only a few seconds to reach him, a thousand thoughts of the most horrendous nature went through our minds. Was he being attacked? Was he stricken by some hideous disease that would soon strike him down? What could possibly make him scream like that, a scream we had never heard from him before? We stumbled into his room to see him sitting up in his bed, still in a panic. My wife and I competed to be the one to hold and comfort him, finally able to rescue him from what then looked like a bad dream. However, this was different. We were not able to comfort him as we had in the past when he had a nightmare. In fact, we seemed to become the enemy. The unspeakable horror was projected on us as he fought our efforts to soothe him. Minutes seemed like hours until he finally stopped screaming and went back to sleep in his bed. Although my wife and I worried that this was the harbinger of some dreaded affliction, the next morning my son was his same cheery self, seemingly unaware and unscathed from the evening's trauma.

This scenario, which was repeated several more times in my son's early years, describes an experience of *sleep terrors* (sometimes referred to as "night terrors," although they can occur during daytime naps as well), a sleep problem that is often mistaken for a nightmare.[12] Called *incubus* in adults and *pavor nocturnus* in children, these sleep attacks usually begin with a piercing scream. The person appears extremely upset, is often sweating, and frequently has a rapid heartbeat. Sleep terrors look like nightmares because the child (it most often occurs among young children) cries and appears quite frightened. However, sleep terrors occur during NREM, or nondream, sleep and are therefore *not* instances of frightening dreams. In addition, during sleep terrors, children cannot be easily awakened or comforted as is possible during a nightmare. In the case of sleep terrors, children do not remember the incident, despite its often dramatic effect on the onlooking parents.

About 5% of otherwise healthy young children experience sleep terrors at some point in their lives, and a small percentage of adults also have these attacks. We do not yet know how often people with special needs endure these types of sleep problems, although our experience has been that they are at least as likely to occur in this population as well.

We know very little about the cause of sleep terrors. Early thinking was that psychological stress during the day brought on these attacks in some people, although research now suggests that this is not a major influence on this sleep problem. Some more medically oriented theories have pointed to things such as enlarged adenoids or an "immature" central nervous system as causing sleep terrors, although today there is very little evidence for any specific cause. Sleep terrors do seem to run in families, although again, it is too early to speculate about any specific genetic cause. The good news is that, for most children—including my son—these sleep problems tend to become less frequent as the child grows older and are usually gone by the teenage years.

Sleepwalking and Sleep Talking

It might surprise you to learn that *sleepwalking* (also called *somnambulism*), like sleep terrors, occurs during NREM sleep (see Figure 2.1).[13] This means that, when people walk in their sleep, they are not acting out a dream. *Sleep talking*, which is usually not considered a sleep problem, can occur during either REM sleep or NREM sleep. Occasionally, the muscles that control our speech avoid the paralysis that goes with REM sleep, and people can talk out while they are dreaming. (Both my wife and my son talk in their sleep—an indication of the genetic nature of this behavior—and on rare, special occasions, they would talk at the same time in what seemed like a dialogue!) Sleepwalking will typically occur during the first few hours of sleep when the person is in sleep's deepest stages (Stage 3). Because it occurs when people are in this very deep point in sleep, it is difficult to awaken a person at this time—although despite the myth, this is not a dangerous thing to do. A second myth about sleepwalking is that the person will never do anything harmful during one of these episodes. People who sleepwalk seem generally aware of their surroundings and tend to avoid harming themselves. However, there are occasional reports of people hurting themselves or others during sleepwalking. It is also thought that *sleep eating* (fixing yourself a snack and eating while asleep) is a similar type of NREM sleep problem.

Sleepwalking is primarily a problem for children, although a small percentage continue to sleepwalk as adults. A relatively large number of children, some 15%–30%, have at least one episode of sleepwalking. Sleepwalking affects less than 1% of adults, although when it does occur, it is usually associated with other psychological problems. As with some of the other sleep problems, we do not know how prevalent this problem is among people with special needs. And we do not as yet have a clear understanding about why some people sleepwalk, although factors such as fatigue, sleep deprivation, the use of sleep-inducing drugs such as sedatives or hypnotics, or stress have been suggested. There may also be a role of heredity, given that it occurs more often in some families than in others.

Periodic Limb Movements

You have probably had the experience of being next to a person as he or she falls asleep and seeing his or her body jerk all over. We still do not understand the significance of this whole-body jerk, but it appears

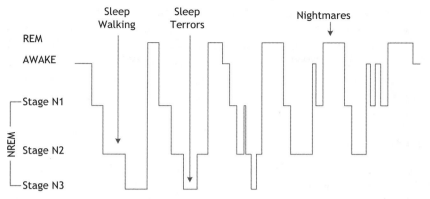

Figure 2.1. Sleep disorders.

to be unrelated to any sleep or medical problem. However, there are people whose legs or arms jerk and twitch throughout the night in a condition known as *periodic limb movements*.[14] This twitching lasts for only a few seconds and can occur every few minutes or every several hours. By themselves, these limb movements will not harm the person; however, as we saw with interrupted breathing and apnea, limb movements during sleep can interrupt the person's sleep rhythm. For some, they awaken and are therefore bothered by these frequent night wakings. If they do not fully awaken, excessive daytime sleepiness may result. We sometimes have reports of people who are tired during the day even after 8–10 hours of sleep and discover the cause to be these sleep-related body movements. One clue to whether or not a person has periodic limb movements can be the state of their bed in the morning. If a person's blankets and sheets are disheveled, it may be a sign of excessive limb movement during sleep. Being on certain medications, such as antidepressants, can cause periodic limb movements, as can attempting to stop taking other medications such as tranquilizers or sedatives.

A related sleep problem involves an unsettled feeling in a person's legs, sometimes described as a powerful urge to move. Called *restless legs syndrome,* this feeling in the legs can be most uncomfortable and usually interferes with the ability to fall asleep. Unfortunately, many people with restless legs syndrome also experience periodic limb movements and will feel exhausted during the day. Causes of both of these movement problems may be a lack of sleep or poor circulation as the result of a lack of exercise. Be warned that an increase of exercise can temporarily increase this problem, although it should resolve itself in a week or two. Too much caffeine can also cause these sleep problems, which is something that can be easily remedied. Iron supplements can sometimes be helpful for periodic limb movement problems.

Bed-Wetting

Bed-wetting (also called *enuresis*) is a common problem among children and is surprisingly common among adults as well. Between 6% and 10% of 7-year-olds wet their beds frequently.[15] Among all children with special needs, this number is generally higher. Wetting the bed is not usually considered a problem for children if it occurs during the first 4 years of development. By age 5, however, frequent bed-wetting—for example, several times per week—can be very upsetting for both the child and the family, can start to interfere with a child's sense of self-worth and self-esteem, and probably should be addressed. Bladder control problems can be part of more significant medical problems for some children with special needs, such as those who have spina bifida with myelomeningocele (defects in the spinal column producing a fluid-filled sac that is visible from birth).

Some children may go for weeks, months, or even years without bed-wetting and then relapse. This can often be a sign of some psychological distress; for example, marital problems between their parents frequently lead to bed-wetting for some children, as may the addition of a new child into the family. It can also signal the presence of a medical problem such as a urinary tract infection, diabetes, epilepsy, or a kidney disorder.

Tooth Grinding

"There it is again!" I told my wife that I heard a strange noise, and now it was happening again. Being the brave protector, I got out of bed to investigate. Following the noise into my son's room, I found that he was the source. Fast asleep, he was grinding his teeth loud enough to be heard from the other side of the house. More formally referred to as *sleep bruxism,* tooth grinding is a little-understood phenomenon that occurs with some frequency among children and adults.[16] The grinding can be related to dental problems and should be brought to the attention of a dentist if it persists. It is also believed that stress can cause tooth grinding, and stress reduction techniques are sometimes recommended.

Rhythmic Movement Problems

We often observe children who rock themselves to sleep. It is comforting for some children to rock their body or their head back and forth repeatedly just before falling asleep. As with all sleep problems, this sleep-related *rhythmic movement* is not considered a sleep problem unless it is disruptive to sleep or is a source of concern.[17] Children with visual impairments and those with ASD and other developmental disorders may sometimes use this as part of their bedtime routine. Unfortunately, this rhythmic movement can become more serious and include injurious forms such as severe head banging. The origins of these rhythmic movements are thought to involve the accidental discovery that rocking can be pleasurable, and therefore children continue to incorporate it into bedtime rituals just as you might need to read or watch television before going to sleep each night. Increased stress during the day can cause this rhythmic movement to increase. Also, it is important to rule out the possible role of seizures in chronic rhythmic movement problems.

CONCLUSION

I described a number of different sleep and sleep-related problems that affect children and adults with special needs. Despite the somewhat lengthy list described here, there are many more—although less common—specific sleep problems. Readers wanting more information about these other sleep problems should refer to the bibliography at the end of the book. I next turn to one of the most important sections of the book: how to determine what type of sleep problem a person has. Before a particular strategy can be recommended for helping a person sleep better, some information must be gathered about the nature of the problem.

Assessing
Sleep Problems

Identifying the Sleep Problem

If you have read through the first two chapters, you will have noticed that there are many reasons why a child might not go to sleep right away at bedtime, why someone else may wake up repeatedly at night, or why another person may be tired and disoriented during the day. This chapter is designed to walk you through a series of steps that will help identify the sleep problem and then point you to one or more strategies that will help address it. As you gain a better awareness of the specific type of sleep problem, I point you to other sections of the book that describe how you can implement your own plan to help solve the sleep problem. Included are descriptions of people my staff and I have worked with and how we designed plans for them. In most cases, you should be able to carry out your own "diagnosis" and design your own plan. Remember, understanding the sleep problem is the key to successful treatment.

STEPS TO UNDERSTANDING THE PROBLEM

The first tasks you would be asked to complete if you were going to any sleep center would be to keep a sleep diary or log for about a week and to answer some questions about the type of sleep problem your child (or you yourself) is experiencing. The sleep diary helps you and the sleep professional get a good picture of things such as how long the child sleeps, what is the pattern of sleep, what happens at problem times, and so forth. You may think that this step is unnecessary because you could already describe a typical week. You certainly have your hands full already without one more chore to add to the list! However, the information from such a diary can be extremely important and can save time later. Trying out a plan for several weeks only to find that it was the wrong one can be extremely frustrating and may be avoided with the right information ahead of time. Sometimes parents find the problem is worse than they thought once they look closely at sleep patterns over a week, and at other times, people discover that their child's sleep is actually not as disrupted as they thought. Even if your child's sleep problem requires further consultation with a professional, the information you collect now will be extremely helpful in discussing the difficulties with someone else. Take the time to monitor your child's sleep for a week. You will probably find that it is worth it.

SLEEP DIARY

Different sleep professionals use slightly different forms for people to fill out about sleep. We are always looking to collect the most information, but at the same time, we know people are busy; if the forms are too complicated, they will not be used. With that in mind, I have changed the forms we use over the years based on the feedback received from parents. I actually use two different forms: one form gives us information on the sleep–wake cycle, and the second form gives us more information about what happens if the child has disruptive behavior, either at bedtime or upon awakening during the night. Children with special needs often present two challenges: the sleep problem itself and the difficult behaviors they frequently display around sleep. Although many children with and without special needs can be disruptive before going to sleep or after waking, often children with special needs exhibit behaviors so extreme that they cause additional concern. I include a whole chapter on what are sometimes called *challenging behaviors,* which include hitting others (aggression), hitting themselves (self-injurious behavior), and other types of disruptive behavior. Often these behaviors are beyond the expertise of most sleep professionals and sometimes account for why children with special needs are not properly served.

At our clinic, we ask parents to complete the sleep diary each day. As you can see in the upcoming sleep diary, we want to know basic information such as the time the child was put in bed and approximately what time the child fell asleep. This gives us an idea about how long the child takes to fall asleep each night. Anywhere from 15–30 minutes is typical, although some people fall asleep right away. People who fall asleep quickly even during the day may have the problem of hypersomnia or narcolepsy, and we can use this preliminary information to follow up on this observation. If it takes a child longer than 30 minutes to fall asleep at night, we would suspect that the child was not tired at bedtime, and we would begin to look for reasons such as sleep schedule problems. There is room in the sleep diary to indicate if and how many times the child may have awakened during the night, and if this happens, we ask the parent to describe the awakening. This information reveals how much the child's sleep is disrupted and the kind of problems the parents face. If night waking or bedtime is a significant problem, we would have the parents also complete a *behavior log*, which we will describe next. Finally, information about the time the child wakes up each morning and naps tells us the total amount of sleep time, any schedule problems (for example, if the child wakes up too early), and the way sleep is or is not spread out during the day.

This page from a sleep diary describes a week of sleep for Michael, a 6-year-old boy with an intellectual disability (Figure 3.1).

Child: Michael			Week of: August 5				
Day	Time put to bed	Time fell asleep	Nighttime waking (time/ how long)	Describe nighttime waking	Time awoke	Describe any naps
Sunday	9:30 p.m.	Around 11:30 p.m.	—	—	6 a.m.	Slept in car for 30 mins.
Monday	9 p.m.	Around 12 a.m.	—	—	6 a.m.	Slept in school for 60 mins.
Tuesday	10 p.m.	Around 11:30 p.m.	—	—	6 a.m.	Slept in school for 60 mins.
Wednesday	9:15 p.m.	Around 12 a.m.	—	—	6 a.m.	Slept in school for 45 mins.
Thursday	9:30 p.m.	11 p.m.	—	—	6 a.m.	Slept in school and on bus for 60 mins.
Friday	11 p.m.	11:30 p.m.	—	—	9:30 a.m.	Slept in school for 50 mins.
Saturday	11 p.m.	11:30 p.m.	—	—	10 a.m.	No nap

Figure 3.1. Sleep diary for Michael.

Michael's parents and teacher were concerned because he was tired during the day, and he would be up most of the early evening. You can see from his sleep diary that there were several sleep habits that may have had a negative influence on his sleep. First, notice that Michael has no set bedtime, sometimes being put in bed as early as 9 p.m. and sometimes as late as 11 p.m. Many children seem to need a stable bedtime and bedtime routine, and without it they may have difficulty falling asleep. Chapter 6 (Good Sleep Habits) describes how we would establish a routine for someone such as Michael. Often this change alone is sufficient enough to help a child who has difficulty falling asleep at bedtime.

The next thing you notice from Michael's sleep diary is that he takes naps during the day. Because he is getting only about 6–6 ½ hours of sleep each night during the week, it is not surprising that he is tired during the day and that he would nap when he can. Notice too that he napped less over the weekend when he was allowed to sleep as late as he wanted. Based on this information about his sleep, we designed a new sleep schedule for Michael (along the lines of techniques described in Chapter 9) that helped him fall asleep in the evening and not nap at school.

BEHAVIOR LOG

Michael did not have any bedtime tantrums or night waking difficulties. Had his parents reported either of these problems, they would have been asked to complete a *behavior log* along with the sleep diary. The behavior log gives us information about the nature of these problems, such as how many times they occur on a typical night, how long the problem persists, and how the parents respond to their child during one of these episodes. You can see from Jodi's behavior log (an 8-year-old with ADHD) that she would throw a tantrum at bedtime as well as sometimes during a night waking. Over the course of 2 weeks, we could see a very distinct pattern of both Jodi's sleep problems and her parents' reactions. Jodi would resist going to bed each night, and her parents would respond by going into her room and calming her down until she fell asleep. Similarly, if Jodi awoke during the night, her parents would go into her room and stay with her until she fell asleep. I discussed in Chapter 1 how some children never learn to fall asleep on their own either at bedtime or after a night waking, and this contributes to their sleep difficulties.

Jodi seemed to be a classic case. We also noticed a bad pattern beginning to emerge. Her parents were obviously tired of going into her room each time she cried, so they were trying to ignore her. Unfortunately, Jodi would only scream louder or bang her head, and this forced them back into the room. We were concerned that Jodi was beginning to learn to escalate her behaviors, making more and more serious efforts to get her parents back into the room, and that she was being reinforced for these more severe outbursts because they worked—her parents returned. If left unchecked, we believed Jodi's behaviors would become even more dangerous. We assisted Jodi and her parents by helping them design a plan that still let them go into her room to check on her, which they insisted on for their own peace of mind (see Chapter 7). Again, the behavior log lets us take a peek into the nighttime world of families who have been struggling with these troublesome problems for years (Figure 3.2).

SLEEP INTERVIEW

Along with collecting information about each night's sleep, we conduct a sleep interview by asking the questions included on the Albany Sleep Problems Scale (ASPS; Appendix H and among the downloads).

Date	Time	Behavior at bedtime	What did you do to handle the problem?	Behavior during awakenings	What did you do to handle the problem?
2/6	10 p.m.	Crying and head banging	Went into her room and held her		
2/7	10:15 p.m.	Crying and head banging	Waited a few minutes but then went in and held her		
2/7	11:45 p.m.			Crying	Sat on her bed until she fell back to sleep
2/7	1 a.m.			Crying, screaming!	Sat with her until she fell asleep
2/8	10 p.m.	Screaming, whining, head banging, throwing toys at wall	Waited for a few minutes but then went in and held her		

Figure 3.2.   Behavior log for Jodi.

The ASPS is a form we use to help identify the type of sleep problem a child may be experiencing. Although we use this as a jumping-off point to further explore the nature of the sleep difficulty, the answers to these questions along with the information from the sleep diary often give us just the information we need to begin to design a plan.

Take a few minutes to answer each of the following questions. As you will see, we have combined questions that seem to point to similar sleep problems and go on to describe the implications of your answers to these questions. If your answers to one or more of these questions suggest the source of the problem, then I direct you to chapters in the next section of the book, which will help you design a plan. Think of this interview as a way to brainstorm what may be the problems and what may be contributing to these sleep difficulties. Because the majority of our recommendations are fairly easy to carry out, in most cases you should try out one or more of the suggestions. In some rare cases— such as with sleep problems related to breathing difficulties—we may suggest that you seek professional advice immediately.

Sleep Habits Questions

1. Does the person have a fairly regular bedtime and time that he or she awakens?

2. Does the person have a bedtime routine that is the same each evening?

One of the most popular clichés about raising children is that they like structure. Children like predictability and orderliness, despite the fact that they may resist such order at first. There is no time where such routines are more important than at bedtime. Structuring bedtime and time to awaken so that they occur at regular times each day can go a long way toward helping someone with sleep problems. Therefore, one of the things we emphasize for all people who are referred to us with sleep problems is the value of bedtime routines and regular sleep–wake schedules. Bedtime problems as well as night waking can be caused by or worsened by unpredictability surrounding sleep. If you answered "no" to either of these questions, you should implement a bedtime routine and regular sleep–wake cycle (see Chapter 6). This one step alone may fix the problems you are experiencing.

3. Does the person work or play in bed often right up to the time he or she goes to bed?

4. Does the person sleep poorly in his or her own bed but better away from it?

One source of difficulty for people who are trying to fall asleep at night is a bad association between the bed or bedroom and sleep. An attorney I met once described to me how she could not fall asleep at night. In discussing her problem, she revealed that she used her bedroom as an office, and her bed as her desk. She would work on case material until late at night and then try to fall asleep. When she tried to sleep, she found herself consumed with thoughts of work and could not turn them off. Her problem was that her bed became a signal for work and the problems associated with work, and she could not make the transition from work to sleep. In the case of children, oftentimes they use their bed to play and then have trouble relaxing in bed when it is time to sleep. Chapter 6 describes what is called *stimulus control*, which in this case involves retraining this connection so that only sleep and sleep-related activities and thoughts are associated with the bed. If you have answered "yes" to either of these questions, Chapter 6 may be very helpful to you and your child.

5. Does the person smoke, drink alcohol, or consume caffeine in any form?

The nicotine in cigarettes, the alcohol in certain beverages, and the caffeine in a number of foods and drinks can all disturb sleep. If you answered "yes" to this question, turn to Chapter 6 for a discussion of their effects and how to avoid their harmful effects on sleep.

6. Does the person engage in vigorous activity in the hours before bedtime?

Exercise or even "roughhousing" at the wrong times can also disturb sleep. Chapter 6 provides guidelines for making exercise work for better sleep.

Bedtime and Night Waking Questions

7. Does the person resist going to bed?

8. Does the person take more than an hour to fall asleep but does not resist bedtime?

These questions are obviously designed to identify children who have difficulties at bedtime. What we are looking for here is to first distinguish those children who fight going to bed from those who simply appear to be unable to fall asleep. If falling asleep is accompanied by tantrums, we need to help parents deal with these episodes. As I just described, the first step with any bedtime problem is to make sure there is a regular bedtime routine (see Chapter 6). Sometimes simply establishing a predictable routine for a child can be enough to solve these problems. If the problem persists, and the child is not resisting bedtime, we then look at interventions for sleep schedule problems (see Chapter 9). If the child is resisting bedtime, then we explore several possibilities for a plan (see Chapter 7). Part of what determines the plan is how parents feel about the problem, an issue we address at the end of this chapter.

9. Does the person awaken during the night but remain quiet and in bed?

10. Does the person awaken during the night, and is he or she disruptive (e.g., throwing tantrums, oppositional)?

You can see that these questions are similar to the previous two questions but instead involve whether or not the child has night waking problems. As was the case with bedtime disturbances, the issue of managing the night waking differs from child to child. Some children simply wake up, and parents find their child awake in his or her bed almost by accident. This can signal the presence of a sleep schedule problem (see Chapter 9). On the other hand, if it is accompanied by crying and tantrums, how to handle the tantrum also becomes an issue (see Chapter 7).

11. Does the person take naps during the day?

Napping, by itself, is not a problem. Many people use them quite successfully to catch up on lost sleep. However, for some people, naps are the problem. They are so tired during the day that people have a difficult time keeping them awake. Often others report that if a child is not allowed to sleep during part of the day, he or she becomes cranky and is extremely difficult to deal with. Here again we may suspect a sleep schedule problem (see Chapter 9), depending on how long the person sleeps at night. If the child or adult who is napping during the day seems to be sleeping a full night, a possibility is that they have hypersomnia or narcolepsy (see Chapter 11). Naps for someone who seems to be sleeping through the night may also be a sign of a breathing-related sleep problem such as sleep apnea (see Chapter 11), or it may be a limb movement problem (see Chapter 11)—either of which may be disturbing nighttime sleep. One other reason for daytime napping may be related to medication the person is taking. Medication for seizure problems, antihistamines, asthma medication, and even the use of medication at night to go to sleep may be causing drowsiness during the day (see Chapter 14). For anyone who appears to be getting a full night's sleep but continues to have trouble staying awake during the day, he or she should be evaluated at a sleep center (see Appendix C for a web site to help you find an accredited sleep center near you).

As I have discussed, other people find that naps are not a problem, and they fit naps in well during the day. However, if these individuals are also having difficulty sleeping at night, either resisting going to bed or waking during the night, the naps may be the cause of the problem. A reexamination of their sleep schedule may be needed for these people (see Chapter 9).

12. Does the person often feel exhausted during the day because of lack of sleep?

13. Has the person ever had an accident or near accident because of sleepiness from not being able to sleep the night before?

For many of the same reasons why daytime napping can be a problem, people who are extremely tired during the day despite a full night's rest may be suffering from a variety of difficulties. Sleepiness can be a sign of sleep schedule problems (see Chapter 9), hypersomnia or narcolepsy (see Chapter 11), breathing-related sleep problems such as sleep apnea (see Chapter 11), limb movement problems (see Chapter 11), or the use of certain medications (see Chapter 14). We are able, with help from your answers to other questions on this interview, to more closely pinpoint what the specific sleep problem may be.

14. Does the person ever use prescription drugs or over-the-counter medications to help him or her sleep?

15. Has the person found that sleep medication does not work as well as it did when he or she first started taking it?

16. If he or she takes sleep medication, does the person find that he or she cannot sleep during the night without it?

Chapter 14 describes the effects of certain medications on sleep. One important factor about using medications to sleep is that it is not usually recommended to use them for more than a few weeks. In most cases, medication is viewed by sleep professionals as a temporary measure. One of the concerns with using sleep medication for too long is mirrored in the previous questions. Used for too long, we begin to tolerate sleep medications so that we need more of them to be effective. Also, sometimes medications have negative effects on sleep when you stop taking them, a phenomenon known as *rebound insomnia*, which serves to disrupt sleep after you stop taking a medication. Chapter 14 describes these issues in more detail and provides guidelines for the safe use of sleep medications.

Sleep Schedule Questions

17. Does the person fall asleep early in the evening and awaken too early in the morning?

18. Does the person have difficulty falling asleep until a very late hour and difficulty awakening early in the morning?

Here again we see what may be a sleep schedule problem (see Chapter 9). Some children are wide awake at 5 a.m., ready to start the day. We would examine closely how much time they spend sleeping and how this sleep is distributed throughout the day to attempt to shift the child's sleep to a more acceptable pattern. Another concern that these questions may raise is the presence of certain psychological difficulties that may be interfering with sleep. Chapter 12 describes how anxiety and depression can change sleep patterns in this way and also outlines steps to help reduce these problems.

Nightmare Questions

19. Does the person wake up upset in the middle of the night?

20. Is the person relatively easy to comfort from these episodes?

It is important to differentiate nightmares—which are disturbing dreams—from sleep terrors—which do not appear to be bad dreams. If, as these questions suggest, the person is waking up after these episodes and can calm down and be comforted after such a dream, then it is likely the person is experiencing nightmares. Chapter 10 describes techniques to use to help people who are negatively affected by nightmares.

Sleep Terror Questions

21. Does the person have episodes during sleep where he or she screams loudly for several minutes but is not fully awake?

22. Is the person difficult to comfort during these episodes?

Unlike nightmares, sleep terrors will tend to be more active events that occur despite the fact that the child is still asleep. The child will be very difficult to awaken and comfort. If you answered "yes" to these questions, Chapter 10 describes an approach to helping children rid themselves of these upsetting sleep disturbances.

Hypersomnia and Narcolepsy Questions

23. Does the person experience sleep attacks (falling asleep almost immediately and without warning) during the day?

24. Does the person experience excessive daytime sleepiness that is not accounted for by an inadequate amount of sleep?

Sleep attacks (falling asleep almost immediately and without warning) that occur despite the fact that the person is sleeping a reasonable amount of time are a sign of possibly serious sleep problems such as hypersomnia or narcolepsy. If you suspect these are problems, you should refer to Chapter 11, which describes the various approaches that are used to help individuals with these problems. It is also recommended that a full sleep evaluation be conducted at a sleep center if either of these problems is suspected (see Appendix C).

Breathing-Related Questions

25. Does the person snore when asleep?

26. Does the person sometimes stop breathing for a few seconds during sleep?

27. Does the person have trouble breathing?

28. Is the person overweight?

If the person is tired during the day despite what appears to be a full night's sleep, or if the person seems to be restless during sleep, a breathing problem may be responsible for these difficulties. Answering "yes" to one or more of these questions would suggest that the person's breathing is interfering with sleep. Loud snoring is often a sign of nighttime breathing difficulties. These breathing problems also occur more often in people who are overweight. Chapter 11 describes help for breathing-related sleep problems, and as we recommended with hypersomnia and narcolepsy, if there is any hint that breathing problems may be present, the person should be evaluated by a physician or a sleep specialist (see Appendix C).

Sleepwalking and Sleep Talking Questions

29.   Has the person often walked when asleep?

30.   Does the person talk while asleep?

These sleep phenomena are often not significant problems for most people. However, if they do bother the person affected or if they cause concern for others, refer to Chapter 10 for a discussion on a variety of ways these sleep events can be helped.

Limb Movement and Rhythmic Movement Questions

31.   Are the person's sheets and blankets in extreme disarray in the morning when he or she wakes up?

32.   Does the person wake up at night because of kicking legs?

Answering "yes" to either of these questions may suggest that periodic limb movements are interfering with sleep. If the person seems tired during the day or if frequent night waking is a problem and limb movements are a suspected cause, refer to Chapter 11 for a discussion of treatments.

33.   While lying down, does the person ever experience unpleasant sensations in his or her legs?

This may be a sign that the person suffers from restless legs syndrome, which can cause insomnia for some people. Chapter 11 describes treatments for this troublesome problem.

34.   Does the person rock back and forth or bang a body part (e.g., head) to fall asleep?

These types of rhythmic movements are common, even in some adults. When these movements begin to cause injury, as with some children who bang their heads, some intervention is recommended. Chapter 11 describes how we have intervened in some of these cases.

Bed-Wetting Questions

35. Does the person wet the bed?

Up until about 5 years of age, bed-wetting is not considered a problem. However, after that age, children should be sleeping through the night without accidents. If this is not the case, refer to Chapter 12 for a discussion of approaches to help with this problem.

Tooth Grinding Questions

36. Does the person grind his or her teeth at night?

Occasional tooth grinding during sleep is common. However, if it is a regular occurrence, serious dental problems may result. Refer to Chapter 12 for a discussion of both medical and psychological approaches for helping people with this behavior.

Anxiety and Depression Questions

37. Does the person sleep well when it does not matter, such as on weekends, but sleep poorly when he or she "must" sleep well, such as when a busy day at school is ahead?

38. Does the person often have feelings of apprehension, anxiety, or dread when he or she is getting ready for bed?

39. Does the person worry in bed?

40. Does the person often have depressing thoughts, or do tomorrow's worries or plans buzz through his or her mind when he or she wants to go to sleep?

41. Does the person have feelings of frustration when he or she cannot sleep?

42. Has the person experienced a relatively recent change in eating habits?

All of these questions refer to problems of anxiety or depression, which can cause sleeping difficulties. If you cannot determine directly whether or not your child worries or is depressed by asking him or her, other signs may be used to pick up these problems. Abrupt changes in eating habits—such as eating too much or too little—may be a sign of depression. Also, if you can pinpoint through your sleep diary certain situations that reliably predict problems with sleep (e.g., difficulties the night before school but not on weekends), then this may suggest that your child is anxious. Chapter 12 discusses these problems, how they may interfere with sleep, and techniques you can use to help your child deal with these feelings.

Daytime Behavior Problem Questions

43. Does the person have behavior problems at times other than bedtime or upon awakening?

Chapter 13 discusses daytime behavior problems. I include this discussion for several reasons. First, getting a handle on daytime behavior problems can often help with bedtime problems. The way you respond to a tantrum at lunchtime, for example, may be similar to your handling of bedtime refusal. Second, daytime behavior problems and sleep problems are often related, and it is important to consider them together. Finally, we find that, if parents feel confident in how they deal with a child's daytime behavior problems, this can help them with the child's sleep problems as well.

OTHER POSSIBLE CAUSES

44. When did the person's primary difficulty with sleep begin?

45. What was happening in the person's life at that time or a few months before?

These questions can relate to any of the sleep problems we have discussed. We ask these questions in order to try to identify causes such as illness or disruption of sleep patterns (e.g., vacations) that preceded the current problems. Almost all the chapters refer back to your answers from these questions.

46. Is the person under a physician's care for any medical condition?

Finally, it is important to know if medical conditions or the treatments for these problems (e.g., medications) are contributing to the child's sleep difficulties. Chapter 14 describes how certain medications can affect sleep, and many of the other chapters rely on your answer to this question to determine possible causes of sleep problems.

A PARENT'S DILEMMA

There are few everyday experiences more frustrating than not being able to fall asleep at night. Even worse is the mix of emotions felt by a parent whose sleep is turned inside out by a child's disturbed sleep. You want to help, but you cannot help. You want to scream, but that would make things worse. You want to blame someone, but you end up blaming yourself. And the guilt sometimes prevents you from reaching out to others for help. We have worked with many families who have had serious problems with sleep for many years but have been too ashamed to seek professional help. Still others have looked to pediatricians or other nonsleep professionals for advice but have come away disappointed. It is important to be aware of how your emotions will or will not affect your ability to carry out a plan. Many times parents cannot bear to listen to their child cry for even a minute, which excludes any plans that involve ignoring these problems. Be realistic about what you can reasonably handle in the interventions we describe next. Do not be afraid to take things slowly. It is better to observe some success initially than to feel things are hopeless, so look for small signs that things are getting better. Our experience has been that most sleep problems can be helped simply by having parents change small things about the way they respond.

CONCLUSION

In the next chapter, I discuss these issues and how to identify if they apply to you. In other words, the next section is more about you than your child. The research that we conducted and that I describe in the next two chapters should provide hope for those of you who are really struggling with these child problems. Take some time to read through these sections because they may really help you better assist your child with his or her sleep problems. Good luck!

Identifying Obstacles to Successful Treatment

As promised, I am going to change the focus of the book just briefly and start to talk less about your child and more about you. Over the years, I found that many of the treatments we developed could work extremely well. However, some parents simply were not able to carry these programs out at home. In the past, my staff and I would chalk it up to parents who were not ready to make the changes necessary—saying things such as, "I guess the sleep problem isn't bad enough. When it gets worse they will come back ready to do the plan." But this rarely happened, and we did not see those families again. So we challenged ourselves. I was always taught that, if a child with special needs was not making improvements on a plan I designed, then it was not the child's fault or the fault of their special need but my fault! I must have designed the plan incorrectly. What if we applied the same logic to parents, and instead of blaming them for not following a plan, we took responsibility and admitted that we did not design the plan properly for this family?

INTERFERING THOUGHTS

I have found through research with many families that a major hurdle for about half of the mothers and fathers with whom we worked was their thoughts about themselves and their child with special needs. In other words, thinking things such as "I should be a better parent" or "My child can't do this because of his ADHD" would interfere with a program's success. No plan works perfectly or immediately. For the parents who had these interfering thoughts, as soon as there was any setback in a plan (for example, their child started waking up crying at night again), they would question themselves or their child and give up. This chapter is designed to see if you have any of these very common but interfering thoughts. I next provide a brief Thoughts Quiz we developed and will ask you to answer these questions (see Appendix D and among the downloads). I then describe each of the themes these thoughts represent and how they can defeat you and sap whatever emotional strength you have left. If you do find yourself thinking thoughts that get in your way of helping your child, the next chapter (Chapter 5—An Optimistic Approach to Improving Sleep) is designed to help you change these thoughts.[1] I have found that these interfering thoughts can be changed to be more optimistic (for example, "I am a good mother, and my son is able to fall asleep on his own if I persist") and that these changes help parents to better carry out the sleep plans. An added bonus (that I discuss in the next chapter) of this change in the way you look at yourself and your child is that it can improve your overall well-being. Now read the instructions for the Thoughts Quiz and answer the 13 questions with a recent sleep problem your child had in your mind.

How many of these thoughts did you agree you have sometimes when your child is having a problem with sleep? If it was not very many or if these thoughts do not seem to bother you too much, then you are lucky. You probably are a very confident and optimistic parent. You should be able to carry out the programs described in later chapters without questioning yourself as a parent or your child's ability to sleep better. However, if you are like me and about half of the parents we see for problems they are having with their child, you might need some help looking at these problems surrounding sleep in a different light. If you agreed with one or more of the questions on the Thoughts Quiz, I provide help in the next chapter. But first, let us review these themes as they relate to child sleep problems.

I Have Little or No Control Over This Situation

This theme of having no control over your child's sleep problems is one of the most common ones reported by parents. It is also one of the more disruptive thoughts. Feeling as if you have no control over important things in your life can lead to depression and general feelings of helplessness. It can also contribute to giving up on a plan if it does not work right away or if the problem comes back at a later time.

I'm Not Sure How Best to Handle This Situation

This is a more specific variation of feeling out of control. Rather than thinking you cannot help at all, this involves doubts about the specific problem you are facing. For example, what should you do if your child comes into your room and wants to get in bed with you? In later chapters, I outline specific plans for what to do but also help you practice thinking that you now know what to do. Just feeling that you know how to react can make you more confident.

In This Situation, Others Are Judging Me Negatively as a Parent

Here you might be second guessing yourself because you feel that other people are disagreeing with how you handle your child's sleep problem. This can come from just a look from someone else or may be more explicit (e.g., some relatives, friends, or a spouse may directly criticize you). Again, thinking these thoughts can be very anxiety-provoking for some people and can interfere with how you handle the problem.

In This Situation, Others Are Judging My Child Negatively

This type of thought occurs more frequently in situations where a child is misbehaving in front of other people—usually in public—and, thus, may be less common with home sleep problems. However, some parents worry that their child may not be able to sleep over at other people's homes because of their disruptive behavior at bedtime or when they wake up at night. They do not want their child's friends or relatives to think that their child is odd or a problem.

My Child Is Not Able to Control This Behavior

Sometimes parents give up trying to improve their child's sleep problem because they do not believe the child is able to sleep better. They may think it is "normal" to have these problems, and therefore suggesting ways to improve sleep might be met with disbelief.

My Child's Disability or Condition Is Causing or Contributing to This Problem

This is similar to the previous question, only it is the child's special need that is thought to be the source of the sleep problem. If your child has ADHD or autism spectrum disorder, for example, you might think that the sleep difficulties are being caused by these disorders, and therefore, your child will not be able to sleep in a typical fashion. Although there are cases when a specific disorder is linked to some sleep problem (e.g., autism spectrum disorder), the child will still be able to sleep better with the plans I describe later.

This Type of Situation Is Always a Problem for My Child

Although sometimes a child might have a bedtime problem every night or awaken early every morning, some situations might be better than others. There are times when we tend to *catastrophize* or see situations as much worse than they actually are. This type of thought is common in people who are more pessimistic in their thinking—something I will discuss in the next chapter—and can be a major obstacle when tackling a sleep problem.

This Will Never Get Better or May Become Worse

In the same way people who have a pessimistic way of thinking can see things as much worse than they are, they also tend to think things will never get any better. Sometimes even when a child is beginning to improve his or her sleep patterns, parents still have thoughts that it will never be resolved.

I Will Never Have Time for Just Me

After many months or years of disturbed sleep, it is natural to feel that, not only will this continue to be a problem, but it can also make a parent feel trapped. Although some parents feel guilty admitting this, they start to get depressed that they will not have time for themselves. Again, this is a self-defeating thought that can, in turn, contribute to not persisting with a sleep plan that might be helpful.

My Child Is Doing This on Purpose

This is a thought that is the opposite of thinking that the sleep problem is out of a child's control. Here, the resistance or tantrum at bedtime looks malicious, and sometimes parents feel their child is doing this just to anger them. Our research shows that these types of problems are not efforts to annoy you, but instead, the child may simply want to be with you. Other times, it may be an effort to avoid giving up some favorite activity (e.g., watching television, playing on a computer). We discuss later how to get your child into a better sleeping habit.

This Situation Is (Spouse's, Partner's, Family Member's, or Other's) Fault for Not Handling This Like I Suggested

We like to call this thought the *ex factor* ("If only my *ex* would stop spoiling her when she is at his house, she would sleep better here."). This can be a particularly troublesome way of looking at the problem because it implies that you have no control over your child's sleep problem. We saw previously that feeling like you have no control can lead to giving up and even feelings of anger and depression. The next chapter discusses this way of thinking and provides suggestions for changing this pattern of blame.

It Is My Fault that This Is a Problem

Here blame is placed on you. Parents see other families where their child with a special need seems not to have these problems, and they question themselves ("If I was a better parent, I could get my son to sleep at night."). And once again, thinking these types of thoughts not only make you feel guilty but is also a type of "feeling out of control" that is so destructive.

Why Am I Always Responsible for My Child's Behavior?

If you are the one solely responsible for bedtime or nighttime wakings, it can become a burden that turns into resentment. Being responsible may be inevitable for a single parent. However, if others are available but are not helpful, then this type of thought can be self-defeating.

CONCLUSION

If any of these thoughts sound familiar to you and if you think that they may interfere with your ability to carry out a sleep plan for your child, please read the next chapter. I go over strategies for building confidence in yourself as well as in your child. But even if these thoughts do not seem to interfere with your working on your child's sleep problems, the information in the next chapter may be helpful for other challenges you face with your child. As you will see, the work we are doing with parents is designed to make them more optimistic, and the feedback we receive from parents who go through this process is extremely positive. Give it a try!

Strategies
for Change

An Optimistic Approach to Improving Sleep

As the previous chapter describes, many parents with whom we work struggle not only with the demands presented by their child with special needs but also with nagging doubts either about their own ability to help their child or about their child's ability to sleep better. Let us take a look at one mother's efforts to improve her daughter's sleep problem and at her pessimism about any possible progress.

☆ JACKI

Jacki was a 35-year-old mother of a 4-year-old girl who had a diagnosis of ASD with a history of tantrums at bedtime and waking up at night crying. Her daughter's sleep problems were so severe that they disrupted the whole family's sleep patterns. So along with the challenges each morning and afternoon, Jacki dealt with a day that never seemed to end and rarely got enough sleep to feel refreshed and rejuvenated. We suggested several different sleep plans for her daughter's problems, but Jacki never could carry any of them out for more than 1 or 2 nights.

Finally, I suggested that, because Jacki reported that nighttime waking was the most disruptive problem, we could do something very simple to see if it made any difference. I asked that Jacki not let her daughter get in bed with her when she came into her room crying but instead take her by the hand and lead her back to her room—saying nothing. She agreed, and the next day I called her to see what happened. I could tell by her voice she was both exhausted and felt a little guilty filling me in. "I let her get in bed with me. I'm sorry." I was dumbfounded. It was such an easy thing to do that I was surprised Jacki could not follow through.

I decided that she might be a good candidate for our Optimistic Parenting program. This approach helps parents who have challenging children (not simply those with sleep problems) confront interfering thoughts. I asked her to try again that night but this time write down what she was thinking and feeling when it was time to take her daughter back to her room. I gave her a copy of the Self-Talk Journal (see Appendix E and among the downloads) we use in our work and described how to complete it. What follows is one night's journal entry. Note that we ask parents to write down the situation. During a typical week, we ask parents to write down not just problem situations (e.g., a disruptive night waking) but also if there are good things surrounding sleep (e.g., falling asleep with minimal disruption). You will see that we often have to change the way parents see both negative and positive events. In addition to the situation, we have parents practice listening to their *inner voice*. In other words, we want them to analyze what they are thinking and feeling during these situations—something that can take some practice. Let us look at one entry by Jacki in Table 5.1.

It became clear that Jacki's inability to follow through on the night waking plan had nothing to do with her not understanding the plan. Instead, she had these interfering thoughts and feelings that made her feel defeated and give up. What Jacki needed was not more "parent training" but help with looking at herself and her daughter in a different way. A different night's journal entry shows us how seeing the world through a pessimist's eyes can change the way they see not only problem situations

Table 5.1. Jacki's self-talk journal: Initial entry

Situation	Thoughts	Feelings
What happened (success or difficulty)?	What did you think or say to yourself when this happened?	What emotions did you experience, and how did you react physically when this happened?
My daughter woke up screaming at 12:30 p.m. She came into my bedroom.	*I thought, "Oh no, here we go again. She will never sleep through the night, and I won't either. Why do I always have to deal with this? If only I were a stronger person and a better parent, this wouldn't be a problem."*	*I was angry at my husband for not helping and—although I hate to say it—I was angry at my daughter. That made me feel guilty, because it's not her fault. It's the autism. I feel totally defeated.*

Table 5.2. Jacki's self-talk journal: Subsequent entry

Situation	Thoughts	Feelings
What happened (success or difficulty)?	What did you think or say to yourself when this happened?	What emotions did you experience, and how did you react physically when this happened?
My daughter woke up screaming around midnight but didn't get out of her bed. She cried for about 10 minutes and then was quiet.	*I thought, "What are we going to do about this? She's never going to sleep through the night, and we will never be able to travel with her."*	*I felt depressed because I think this will never end.*

but also good situations. This entry, Table 5.2, was reported about a week after Jacki started our sleep plan for her daughter (sleep restriction—see Chapter 8).

Does her reaction to this major improvement in her daughter's nighttime tantrums surprise you? It should not. People who look at the world more pessimistically tend to see bad situations as their fault and think that they will always be a problem. On the other hand, these individuals will see good situations—such as when Jacki's daughter had only a minor tantrum at night—as a passing phase and will downplay their role in the improvement. I will return to Jacki's case and how we helped her not only see herself and her daughter in a different light but also carry out a plan that improved her daughter's— and the rest of the family's—sleep.

The main steps in the Optimistic Parenting approach to helping parents with interfering thoughts and feelings involve first identifying the main themes that are unique to a particular parent using the Self-Talk Journal and the Thoughts Quiz outlined in the previous chapter.[1] As I suggested earlier, some parents have a difficult time getting insight into these thoughts and feelings. Practice with the Self-Talk Journal along with keeping in mind the common themes can help. If you find that you need more help after trying to examine your thoughts or if you need more guidance to carry out any other steps, more in-depth "do-it-yourself" resources are available.[2] If you feel you might need specialized assistance with this process, professionals trained in cognitive behavior therapy would be able to guide you through the steps needed to become more aware of these thoughts and how to change them. Step-by-step instructions for carrying out this process that are designed for clinicians are also available.[3]

In the previous chapter, I described the main themes that we observe among parents who struggle with their thoughts and feelings. Once we identify these thoughts, we assist parents with changing them into more positive or optimistic ways of looking at things that help rather than hinder efforts to work with their child. Three steps are followed to facilitate this change: *disputation, distraction,* and *substitution*.[4]

DISPUTATION

Disputation is a process by which you challenge the thoughts you are having by asking yourself, "Is what I am thinking *really* true?" and "Is what I am thinking helpful to me?" So, for example, if you have the very common thought that you may not be a good parent because you are not able to get your child to sleep at night when other, perhaps more competent, parents seem to handle this well, you would put this thought to the test. Is that really true? Are you truly not a good parent? Not likely. As a parent with a child who has special needs, it is likely that you are doing a tremendous amount of work and spending enormous amounts of time helping your child navigate this difficult and complex world. The fact that you are reading a book like this means you care and you are trying very hard to do even better. In Jacki's case, she had doubts about herself as a parent as well as doubts about her daughter's ability to sleep better because of her ASD. In both cases, we helped her dispute these thoughts; see that she was a good, hard-working parent; and understand that her daughter's diagnosis of ASD would not interfere with our ability to help her or her daughter sleep better.

The second question—"Is what I am thinking helpful to me?"—is equally important. Sometimes your thoughts reflect the real world. Yes, sometimes people like your mother-in-law or brother really are judging you as a parent (e.g., "If she was just stricter with their daughter at bedtime, she wouldn't be so wild!"). But does thinking about this help you deal with problem situations? Unlikely. Often these thoughts can make you anxious and start to second guess what you do as a parent. It is important to recognize that some of these thoughts are counterproductive. Next, I describe how to begin to change some of these thoughts into more positive ways of viewing these situations.

DISTRACTION

As the name suggests, this technique involves using a different thought or activity to take your mind off of unpleasant or disruptive thoughts—at least temporarily. In one case, a mother of a young boy with an intellectual disability was describing how chaotic bedtime was with her son. He would sometimes climb out of his bed and crawl under it or hide in the closet. Other times he might sneak out of his room once his mother left and try to get food from the refrigerator. She told us that this would upset her and make her feel that the situation was completely out of control. Then she would lose her temper and spank him when he did this. On her own, however, she found a way to distract herself so she would not get upset. One night she just stepped back, looked at what was going on and said to herself, "Look at how bizarre this all is! It's like a crazy house." Rather than making her upset, this simple change in the way she viewed the situation made her smile. It was absurd—but not the end of the world. The upside was that being distracted this way helped her persist with the plan we designed for how to deal with her son's bedtime problems.

Again, distraction is not usually a permanent solution to having these unpleasant thoughts. Instead, it is simply a way to get through situations that may catch you off guard. Going back to Jacki's case, she practiced counting to 10, especially when she found herself getting angry at her husband for not pitching in during the night wakings. This delay in reacting—and not ruminating on her feelings of not being supported—helped her to regroup and remind herself about what she was supposed to do with her daughter. We did eventually get her husband to help with the plan once we probed his thoughts and found that he too doubted his daughter's ability to sleep better because of her disability. He thought the plans would ultimately be unsuccessful anyway, so why even try? This helped Jacki to see that he was not being mean or a bad husband and father—he had the same struggles with his thoughts as she did.

SUBSTITUTION

It is not enough simply to understand that your thoughts are getting in the way of being better at carrying out good parenting plans. Distraction can only go so far to help you deal with these thoughts. Ultimately, you need to replace unproductive and sometimes distressing thoughts (e.g., "This will never end!") with more helpful ways of looking at these situations. We teach parents how to select

Table 5.3.   Substituting positive thoughts

How you see yourself as a parent (self-efficacy): Here parents have general thoughts about their inability to help their child sleep better. Feeling that things are "out of control" is common.

Negative thoughts	Alternate positive thoughts
Theme: *I cannot control my child's sleep problems.*	Theme: *I am usually able to handle problem situations. I have a plan for helping my child sleep better.*

How you think others see you as a parent (concern for others—self): This theme involves thoughts about being judged as a parent because of his or her child's problems surrounding sleep. This can cause parents to second guess their parenting strategies.

Negative thoughts	Alternate positive thoughts
Theme: *When my child misbehaves like this at bedtime, people see me as a bad parent.*	Theme: *I work hard at this, and I know I am a good parent.*

How you think others view your child (concern for others—child): Parents sometimes express anxiety about how other children or adults view their child. They are sometimes afraid that others will see their child as strange or unusual and avoid taking their child to other people's homes (e.g., staying overnight at a relative's house).

Negative thoughts	Alternate positive thoughts
Theme: *I think that other people judge my child when he or she is acting out at night.*	Theme: *Most parents have times when their child misbehaves at bedtime.*

How you see your child's ability to control his or her behavior (child efficacy): Parents sometimes doubt whether or not their child can improve his or her sleep— whether it is due to the disorder or just a general pessimistic belief about the prospect for improvement.

Negative thoughts	Alternate positive thoughts
Theme: *My child is not capable of behaving better. My child's behavior is related to the disability.*	Theme: *Other children like my child are capable of going to bed without problems and sleeping through the night. This will get better.*

How you view the problem situation (pervasive): This aspect of the thoughts of some parents involves "catastrophizing" bad situations or seeing them as worse than they really are. This can lead to avoiding certain situations (e.g., letting your child sleep in your bed to avoid provoking a tantrum) or anxious anticipation of future problems.

Negative thoughts	Alternate positive thoughts
Theme: *All of these situations are always a major problem.*	Theme: *This particular incident was a problem.*

How you view the future (stable): The problems they are experiencing are viewed as permanent—often even when objective information suggests that the child is indeed better at night and getting more sleep.

Negative thoughts	Alternate positive thoughts
Theme: *Sleep will never get better or will get worse.*	Theme: *This can and will get better.*

Who is responsible for a problem situation (blame—child): There can be resentment that the child is acting out around bedtime to annoy the parent.

Negative thoughts	Alternate positive thoughts
Theme: *My child is doing this on purpose.*	Theme: *My child is not intentionally being disruptive. My child needs help to sleep better.*

Who is responsible for a problem situation (blame—others): In this case, the parent perseverates on how others treat his or her child and how that interferes with his or her own success at home. Conflicts arise with relatives or former spouses through disagreements over discipline around sleep.

Negative thoughts	Alternate positive thoughts
Theme: *If only others would follow my suggestions correctly, my child would be sleeping better.*	Theme: *My child can learn to sleep better with me even if it is a problem elsewhere.*

Who is responsible for a problem situation (blame—self): Many parents express feeling guilty about how their child is sleeping and look to their "mistakes" in the past and blame themselves.

Negative thoughts	Alternate positive thoughts
Theme: *It is my fault that things are going wrong.*	Theme: *I am doing the best that I can under the circumstances.*

Who should be responsible for the problem situation (self-concern): Some parents resent their role as being in charge of their child's care—including bedtime and night waking—and feel sorry for themselves.

Negative thoughts	Alternate positive thoughts
Theme: *Why am I always the one who has to be responsible for these situations?*	Theme: *Everyone is doing the best they can under the circumstances.*

Adapted from Durand, V.M. (in press). *Autism spectrum disorder: A clinical guide for general practitioners.* Washington, DC: American Psychological Association.

alternative—and more positive and optimistic—thoughts and ask them to practice substituting these thoughts when the negative ones start to creep back in. Table 5.3 includes themes I described in the last chapter and illustrative substitutions for these thoughts.

These substitutions are only examples, and parents are encouraged to create ones that fit them the best. Jacki chose to say to herself when her daughter was difficult—"I am in control. I am the parent, and I can do this." That simple change in what she said to herself helped her to be firm with her daughter. In fact, what she found was that when she stopped trying to avoid these tantrums, she became less upset when her daughter would scream. This makes great sense. Parents often avoid difficulties with their children because tantrums can make the parent anxious or angry. However, if you avoid these tantrums, simply anticipating them will continue to cause discomfort (e.g., being anxious as bedtime rolls around). However, what we know about things that make us anxious is this—the more you are exposed to them the less anxious you become. And if you do not fear these tantrums, you can follow through on plans even though at first it might be difficult.

Again, if your thoughts are interfering with your interacting with your child, these steps can help you become more confident and optimistic about things getting better. And if you have difficulty handling these changes on your own, remember there are resources available to help.

CONCLUSION

This chapter is designed to help you overcome thoughts and feelings that can interfere with your ability to carry out plans to improve your child's sleep. The next series of chapters introduce strategies that can be implemented at home and that should help you make progress with addressing your child's difficulties sleeping. The next chapter covers general strategies that can help anyone sleep better. This chapter is followed by several chapters that target very specific sleep problems (e.g., problems at bedtime, night waking, or sleeping at the wrong times).

Good Sleep Habits

We now know that what and when we eat and drink can affect our sleep and that our sleep can be affected by when we exercise, the temperature in our bedroom, any noise, and even what we do in bed. Everyday activities that we tend to take for granted can impact how well we go to sleep and if we stay asleep. Along these lines, there are a number of good sleep habits that should be followed if sleep is disturbed. Remember, what disturbs one person's sleep may not affect another's. You may be able to fall asleep with the television on, but the television in your room may be disturbing the sleep of your child in the next room. Coffee after dinner may not disrupt your friend's sleep but may keep you up long after your typical bedtime. We each react in our own way to many of the foods and activities of the day, so it is necessary to check the important ones to see if they are interfering with a good night's sleep.

Before describing some of these good sleep habits, let us first take a look at the case of a child for whom simply changing some sleep habits dramatically improved his sleep.

☆ HARRY

Harry was a 5-year-old boy who had an intellectual disability and who would resist going to bed at night. Harry's mother reported that he usually slept through the night and that he did not appear tired during the day. Unfortunately for Harry's mother, he did not appear tired in the evening either. Harry was a very likeable boy who seemed to have a great deal of energy. At bedtime, which his mother decided should be at 9 p.m., he would like to wrestle and jump on his bed. At times, his mother would try to get him to lie down, but he would bounce up immediately. On other nights, she felt that maybe she would "tire him out" by letting him be rambunctious. She would wrestle with him, chase him around the house, sit with him to have his evening snack, and on summer evenings, go for a walk or run with him. Harry's mother was astonished at her son's ability to remain awake and alert—which seemed to surpass her own ability by far. One night, they were up until 2 a.m., with Harry showing no signs of letting up.

One of the first things that was obvious to us when we consulted with Harry's mother was his activity at night. Harry was very active right up until bedtime. His mother believed that the more active she allowed her son to be, the more likely Harry would be tired at bedtime. Unfortunately, as we have discussed before, many times the opposite is true—exercise can actually interfere with sleep. Letting Harry run around the house, jump up and down on his bed, and go for evening runs may have been raising his internal body temperature, which in turn may have made him less likely to be drowsy at bedtime. Our first recommendation was to try to curtail Harry's more vigorous activities, at least for the hour before bedtime.

A second factor that may have been interfering with Harry's ability to fall asleep at bedtime was the lack of any stable bedtime routine. When 9 p.m. came around each evening, his mother would tell Harry it was time for bed. She would help him wash up, but other than this brief activity, there were no other rituals that would help Harry transition from play time to bedtime. We helped his mother design a calming bedtime routine for the 30 minutes before she wanted him to sleep in order to help Harry get ready for bed.

Another factor that we thought might be interfering with Harry's ability to fall asleep at night was his evening snack. Just before washing up for the night, Harry's mother allowed him to have a snack, which he enjoyed because he seemed hungry and it also seemed to be one of the few quiet and pleasant times they shared in the evening. Weight was not a problem for Harry; in fact, he was on the thin side, which concerned his mother, so she allowed Harry to pick his own snack each night. Harry's favorites were chocolate-covered cookies and a Coke. The problem with this snack is that both the cookies and Coke contain caffeine and may have contributed to Harry's late-night energy. Because snack time seemed to be a positive ritual for both Harry and his mother, we recommended that they keep this activity but substitute milk and nonchocolate cookies for Harry's snack.

One more factor about bedtime may have contributed to Harry's difficulty going to sleep. When he was not sleeping, Harry's bed was the wrestling ring. This is where he and his mother would good-naturedly wrestle and fool around each night. The problem with this arrangement was that Harry probably associated his bed more with fooling around than with sleeping. It may have been difficult for him to get into bed at 9 p.m. and turn it all off after an evening of fun and excitement. Again, because wrestling was something Harry and his mother both enjoyed, we recommended that they move their wrestling ring into the living room and reserve Harry's bed for his bedtime story and sleep.

After following these four simple recommendations alone—limiting activity in the hour before bedtime, creating a calming and stable bedtime routine, removing foods and drinks containing caffeine from his evening snack, and limiting activity in his bed to stories and sleep—Harry seemed more tired at bedtime, and he quickly got into the habit of falling asleep within about 15 minutes of being put into his bed. In fact, we were about to present his mother with a more elaborate plan for his bedtime problems when she called excitedly to tell us that Harry was now no trouble at bedtime.

THE GOOD SLEEP HABITS CHECKLIST

As we saw quite dramatically in the case of Harry, there are often simple things that we can change that will positively affect sleep. Figure 6.1 shows a checklist to help you identify things you or your child may be doing that interfere with bedtime or cause night waking. Regardless of the sleep problems you may be experiencing, everyone should probably check this list to see if certain habits have developed that may be contributing to the problem. We next discuss some of the factors that may be at the root of your child's sleep difficulties.[1]

BEDTIME ROUTINES

We have mentioned before that most children seem to thrive on structure and order. Whether this order includes the rules you make about how to eat at the dinner table, how to behave in public, or how to sit in a car seat when traveling, children soon learn what to expect of most situations and accept the structure—if you are consistent. This is especially important at bedtime. There are children who, when their parents say it is time for bed, kiss them goodnight, climb into bed, and fall asleep within minutes (It is true—I have seen it happen—although not with my son!). However, most children need a *wind-down time,* a time to help them with the transition to sleep. Any

---

The Good Sleep Habits Checklist

□ Establish a set bedtime routine.
□ Develop a regular bedtime and a regular time to awaken.
□ Eliminate all foods and drinks that contain caffeine 6 hours before bedtime.
□ Limit any use of alcohol.
□ Limit any use of tobacco.
□ Try drinking milk before bedtime.
□ Eat a balanced diet, limiting fat.
□ Do not exercise or participate in vigorous activities in the hours before bedtime.
□ Do include a weekly program of exercise during the day.
□ Restrict activities in bed to those that help induce sleep.
□ Reduce noise in the bedroom.
□ Reduce light in the bedroom.
□ Avoid extreme temperature changes in the bedroom (i.e., too hot or too cold).

Figure 6.1. The good sleep habits checklist.

relaxing series of activities that you and your child choose to include can be successful. For example, when my son was younger, we would have him brush his teeth, wash up, and change into pajamas. Then we would sit on his bed and read to him for 15–20 minutes. This would be followed by back scratching and kisses, and then the words, "Okay, it's time to sleep. Goodnight." We would do the same things in the same order each night. This type of routine seems to have a calming or sedating effect on most children and helps them to associate this time with sleep. We recommend some type of bedtime routine for *everyone*, including adults who have difficulty falling asleep at night. Often this one change can help someone who previously had a great deal of difficulty falling asleep.

The Dos and Don'ts of Bedtime Routines

• Do make the last 30 minutes before bedtime a regular routine.

• Do include activities such as dressing for sleep, washing, and reading.

• Do keep the order and timing of the activities about the same each night.

- Do not include activities that—for your child—could cause conflict (e.g., picking out clothes for school, organizing papers).

- Do not watch television during this time, which can interfere with sleep.

- Do not extend the time for the bedtime routine (i.e., "Just one more story? Pleeeease!").

- Remember the most important Do: DO WHAT WORKS FOR YOU.

The "Out of Control" Child   As I discussed in the previous chapters, many parents feel that things are so out of control that there is no way they can impose a bedtime routine and expect their child to accept it. These are parents who often have a great number of problems with their child and, unfortunately, in other parts of their lives and feel powerless to recapture control. These parents often say that their children are "uncontrollable" and that nothing seems to work with them. They often admit with some guilt that they have tried punishing their child, but he or she seems immune to such punishment.

I usually begin to talk to parents who feel that they have no control over what their children do by discussing their children and the things they do during the day. Often we can find any number of things that the child does when instructed, an obvious sign that the child is not uncontrollable. And, in the most difficult cases, I can point out that they, like all parents, get their children to go to school. When I point this out, the parents' demeanor often changes, and they say quite confidently, "Of course he or she goes to school each day. There is no way my child is going to miss school." This is the key. If you can get your child to do one thing consistently, then you should be able to make it two things, then three things, and so forth. For many families, the difference between getting a child to go to school and having him or her go to bed is one of personal resolve rather than ability. Our society has made it very clear that all children go to school. In fact, if a child does not go to school, the parent is viewed as irresponsible and, in extreme cases, can be sent to jail. Because we do not accept any alternatives, the rate of school refusal (the number of children who refuse to go to school) is quite low compared to other problems children experience. We have to teach parents how to have the same resolve for other essential demands that they need to place on their children and give them the techniques to help them carry this out. If you feel unable to place this structure on your child because you are concerned that he or she will become too disruptive, refer to Chapters 4 and 5 for helping change these thoughts and to Chapter 13 for some suggestions on how to deal with these problems outside of bedtime.

It is also important to point out that *you* should direct the bedtime routine. This is not to say that your child should not have a say as to what activities should be included in these routines. Your child's input is crucial. However, if you find that the bedtime routine is becoming longer and longer and more elaborate, it is time to regroup and take control. This happened to me. My son enjoyed his bedtime routine so much that he often wanted just one more minute of back scratching. Then it became one more round of kisses. He then seemed to build in an extra stop to the bathroom, followed by one more trip to get a glass of "cold water," which had to come from the refrigerator. Our routine, which previously had been about 30 minutes, now began to take almost an hour. He obviously wanted to avoid going to sleep at all costs.

If you find your routine taking on more and more activities and becoming longer and longer, you may need to consider that your child is using this to delay bedtime. If you both enjoy this time and have no problem with a bedtime routine longer than 30 minutes, there is no real need to change things. However, if this extra time is cutting into the amount of time your child sleeps and it is becoming a concern, you may need to start again with the original routine and make clear when it starts and ends. There will probably be some initial resistance to this reduction in time; however, your child should adjust within a few days or weeks.

Bedtime Routines for Children with Autism Spectrum Disorder

(ASD) One word of caution about bedtime routines should be made for children with ASD. It is frequently the case that these children latch on to routines so strongly that they become rituals. The difference here is that, for some children with ASD, if you try to vary their ritual even the slightest bit, this can result in a major tantrum. One child we worked with established his own bedtime routine. He would set up his extensive collection of stuffed animals around the bed, a task that could take 15 minutes given the large number he had to arrange. Unfortunately, if one of the animals was out of place or missing, he could not go to sleep. To complicate matters, if he happened to wake up at night and find the animals moved—which sometimes happened because of his moving around in bed during sleep—he would scream and cry until his mother came into his room to fix things.

There were a number of reasons why we did not try to get this boy to immediately give up his ritual. It was important to note that he seemed to like arranging his stuffed animals, and he had few activities that seemed to give him as much pleasure. We obviously did not want to take away what appeared to be his one pleasure in life. His mother also did not want to take on the challenge of changing this ritual (which would have resulted in weeks of severe disruption), and we all felt that any attempt to do so would probably be unsuccessful. Instead, we first taught him how to rearrange his own stuffed animals after he woke up. We taught his mother not to put back the animals herself when he woke up screaming but instead to prompt him to do it himself. Although this was at first rather difficult—he would cry longer—after a few weeks, he was doing it with his mother's prompting. Soon the boy was not crying at night at all but was presumably getting up, fixing the toys, and going back to sleep. In addition to this recommendation, we also suggested that his mother encourage new arrangements from time to time to get him to accept new variations. Two months after our initial contact with this mother, she was reporting that her son was going to bed more easily and was not waking up crying as he had for years before. Parents of children with ASD should be cautious when introducing new routines and should consider building in variation—for example, changing the order of the activities each night—from the very beginning.

Bedtime Routines for Children with Attention-Deficit/Hyperactivity Disorder (ADHD)   Parents of children who have been diagnosed with ADHD often report that one of the sleep problems their children experience is taking a long time to go to sleep. This may be related to ADHD or to the medication many of these children take each day (see Chapter 14 for a discussion of medication and sleep). Whatever the cause, bedtime routines may take much longer for these children. One recommendation we often make is to allow a longer than usual bedtime routine for children who seem to need more time to wind down. If after a few weeks of a 1-hour bedtime routine that the child seems to accept, you can decide if you want to change the time. Again, if this extra time seems to be interfering with sleep or is difficult to manage, we then help parents fade back the routine until it approximates the 30 minutes recommended. We do this slowly, by decreasing the routine from 60 to 50 minutes. If after 2 weeks the child has adapted to the 50-minute routine, we cut back the time to 40 minutes, and several weeks later if all is well, to 30 minutes. Fading back the bedtime routine often lets us avoid fighting over bedtime and lets the child slowly adapt to the restriction. It is important to note that fading routines, as with any of the recommendations made in this book, will need to be individually assessed. For example, if your child is doing well with 60 minutes but becomes difficult to manage when you move it back to 50 minutes, try 55 minutes instead. Remember that bedtime routines should be a calming time and not a time for fights. If fading the time is too disruptive no matter how you break it down, consider some other alternatives, such as those described in Chapter 9 (Sleeping at the Wrong Times).

REGULAR SLEEP TIMES

We are creatures of habit. For the most part, our bodies work best when we have a fairly regular schedule. Being irregular in our sleep–wake habits can negatively affect some people. One family we worked with completed the sleep diary for us prior to our interview. We found that their 3-year-old daughter would sometimes be put to bed at 10 p.m. and other times as late as 2 a.m. Bedtime was determined by her parents' schedule rather than when the little girl seemed tired. In fact, the parents did report that they tried to keep her up late on some nights because they wanted some alone time in the morning and hoped that keeping her awake the night before would make her sleep late the next morning. Other times when they wanted her to go to sleep, she would remain awake and would often awaken in the middle of the night. It seemed pretty clear that the girl's lack of a regular sleep–wake schedule was contributing to her disturbed sleep.

It is important to point out that in addition to a consistent bedtime routine, children and adults who have difficulties with their sleep should be sure to have consistent times that they go to bed and wake up each day. Providing your child with this structure may help prevent him or her from waking up at night and can help with bedtime problems. We typically help parents design good sleep–wake times by looking at the sleep diary and seeing how long their child typically sleeps. We then compare that time with what is typical for a child that age (see Chapter 1) and try to guess how long this child should sleep to be properly rested. Then we look at the wake time the child will need for school, or if a parent needs the child to be awake for another reason (e.g., day care) and work backwards. For example, if we find that 10 hours seems to be about the right amount of sleep time, and the child needs to be awake by 7 a.m. for school, then we suggest that bedtime (the time when the bedtime routine ends) should be no later than 9 p.m. If bedtime is a problem for this child or if he or she wakes up frequently during the night, then we often suggest sticking to this 9 p.m. to 7 a.m. schedule each day. Weekends can be varied somewhat (e.g., 10 p.m. to 8 a.m.), although you want to avoid dramatic changes. People have difficulty adjusting to new schedules, especially when the schedules require going to bed earlier than they are used to, so Sunday night may become a problem if your child stays up too late on Friday and Saturday nights.

Finding Sleep-Wake Times

- Use your sleep diary and Figure 1.1 to find the number of sleep hours your child seems to need to be rested (e.g., 10 hours).

- Determine a good wake time that fits with you and your child's schedules (e.g., 7 a.m., an hour before she needs to leave for school).

- Move backwards from your desired wake time the number of optimal sleep hours to find the best bedtime (e.g., 7 a.m. minus 10 hours = 9 p.m. bedtime).

- Try to stay with this sleep–wake schedule each day.

Although we recommend a consistent sleep–wake schedule for everyone, sometimes parents take this too seriously and become rigid in their scheduling. It is good to have fun. In fact, if life is too boring, this too can interfere with sleep. Try to keep to a regular schedule but do not be too concerned if you vary from it on occasion.

CAFFEINE

We all know that coffee contains caffeine. Caffeine is a naturally occurring chemical that acts as a stimulant to our brain. It has been used for centuries by people to give them more energy. Unfortunately for us, caffeine can also seriously interfere with our ability to fall asleep at night. What most people do not realize is that caffeine stays in our system, acting as a stimulant for up to 6 hours. This means that the cup of coffee you drink after dinner at 7 p.m. may still be affecting you at midnight. As is the case with most drugs, caffeine affects us each differently. Some are very sensitive to its effects, whereas others could fall asleep even after having two cups of coffee.

It is important to be aware of foods and drinks that contain caffeine and to try to avoid consuming them in the hours prior to bedtime. As you can see in Table 6.1, in addition to coffee, a number of other common foods and drugs have sufficient caffeine that may interfere with sleep. Tea contains less caffeine than drip coffee, but one cup has enough to keep you awake at night. Chocolate, especially the kind used in baking, contains a fair amount of caffeine, which means eating too many chocolate chip cookies before bed can be the culprit of bedtime problems. Coke and Pepsi have a fair amount of caffeine—probably enough to keep most people awake if they drink 8 ounces or more before bedtime. Other soft drinks such as 7-Up, Sprite, and Fresca are essentially caffeine-free and are therefore good substitutions for people who really enjoy sodas. Most people are unaware that certain nonprescription drugs contain significant amounts of caffeine. As you can see in the table, certain over-the-counter weight control drugs, diuretics (drugs designed to increase the discharge of urine), cold and allergy medicines, and even some pain relief drugs contain significant amounts of caffeine. You should check to see if your child is consuming caffeine in significant quantities anywhere up to about 6 hours before the desired bedtime and, if so, try to find caffeine-free substitutions.

ALCOHOL AND TOBACCO

It is midnight, and you are still wound up from a hectic day. You can already tell that you will not be able to fall asleep easily tonight, so you fix yourself a drink. Within a few minutes, the alcohol seems to work its magic—the tensions of the day are fading, and you look forward to getting into bed. You put your head down on the pillow and fall asleep within minutes. This same scenario is played out in thousands of homes each night across the United States and may describe your own occasional sleepless night. The problem is that alcohol is a wolf in sheep's clothing when it comes to sleep. Although it can relax you at bedtime and help drive out thoughts that may be interfering with your sleep, alcohol can also disrupt your sleep enough during the night to more than cancel out any helpful effects. If you think about it, this can obviously lead to a particularly vicious cycle for people who

Table 6.1. Common sources of caffeine

Item	Milligrams of caffeine
Coffee (6 fl. oz.)	
Brewed	103
Instant	57
Decaffeinated	2
Tea (6 fl. oz.)	
Black	36
Instant	31
Iced	11
Chocolate	
Chocolate chips, semisweet (6-oz. package)	105
Baker's semisweet chocolate (1 oz.)	13
Milk chocolate (1.55-oz. bar)	11
Chocolate milk (8 oz.)	8
Cocoa beverage (6 oz.)	4
Selected soft drinks (12 oz.)	
Mountain Dew	54
Coca-Cola	46
Pepsi-Cola	38
RC Cola	18
7-Up, Sprite	0+
Nonprescription drugs (standard dose)	
Weight control aids	168
Diuretics	167
Alertness tablets	150
Analgesic/pain relief tablets	41
Cold/allergy remedy	27

From Pennington, J.A.T., & Spungen, J. (2010). *Bowes' and Church's food values of portions commonly used* (19th ed., pp. 283-291). Philadelphia: Lippincott-Raven Publishers; reprinted with permission.

worry about their sleep. Consider the person who is concerned that he may not fall asleep soon enough and therefore drinks at bedtime in order to fall asleep at a good time. His sleep will be restless because of the alcohol, and it will disrupt the deep, restorative sleep. The next morning, he will not feel rested. The next evening, he will be even more concerned about his sleep because he is so tired and tense about not being rested. This will only serve to encourage him to drink again that night, which will in turn disrupt his sleep and start the cycle all over again. This vicious cycle is similar to what happens to people who use medications for sleep, sometimes resulting in dependence. The bottom line is that, despite its positive short-term effects on sleep (drowsiness), consuming alcohol within about 2 hours of bedtime can actually worsen your sleep.

Obviously, the use of alcohol is not a problem for the children who are referred to us for their sleep problems. However, alcohol and another drug we now discuss—the nicotine in tobacco—are used by some of the adults who are also referred to us for assistance. We often see adults with an intellectual disability who are living at home with their parents or who live in community residences. We have, on occasion, had to recommend that alcohol not be used as a sedative. More often, however, these individuals smoke, and the nicotine in the tobacco may be the source of their sleep problems.

Nicotine is a stimulant. Just like caffeine, nicotine serves to stimulate the nervous system. Smoking right before bedtime can result in an overstimulation of the brain, which interferes with sleep. Another problem for people who smoke is that, to maintain their "fix" of nicotine, they need to smoke fairly often throughout the day. The problem they have with sleep is that they can experience *withdrawal* during the night, and this can disrupt sleep. It is not surprising that many smokers light up almost as soon as they wake up in the morning because their brain is craving nicotine.

Remember that smoking cigarettes is not the only way of ingesting nicotine. Some people chew tobacco, and this too can act to stimulate the brain enough to disrupt sleep. The following is a description of one of our most intriguing cases that illustrates how nicotine can impair sleep.

☆ MICHAEL

Michael was an unusual individual who presented us with some unique challenges, only one of which was his sleep problem. My first contact with Michael was when he first arrived at the residential facility where I was working. He was 18 years old, had never been to school, and as far as we could tell, had spent a feral or semiwild existence in the rural mountains of Virginia. Both of his parents had some level of intellectual disability and let Michael spend his days wandering in the woods. When he came to us, he had never used utensils to eat, was unfamiliar with toilets, and had never slept in a bed. He did not speak and appeared quite nervous, which was to be expected given his new and (to him) unusual surroundings.

The staff quickly grew to like Michael, who despite his background, seemed to have a good sense of humor. The staff spent a great deal of time patiently teaching him the skills he would need to be more independent. Michael rapidly learned how to feed himself using a fork and knife, how to use the bathroom, and how to take care of many of his personal needs.

Unfortunately, however, Michael's sleep became quite disrupted shortly after his arrival. He did not seem tired at bedtime, often sitting up in bed until 1 a.m. or 2 a.m. and then was difficult to awaken in the morning. When we questioned his social worker, who had known Michael for a number of years, she indicated that sleep had never been a problem for him. At first we thought that sleeping in a bed or in a strange bedroom might be the problem, because his sleeping difficulties seemed to start in the residence, but after several months where he seemed to adjust to most other routines, his sleep remained disrupted. His physician was about to order *chloral hydrate* to help him sleep, but this drug can have serious side effects, so we asked for more time to try to find the cause of his difficulties.

One of the habits that Michael was particularly resistant to changing was *pica,* or the eating of inedible objects. When he lived at home, Michael would pick up twigs or nuts from the ground and hold them in his mouth most of the day. He would also hide some of these small objects in parts of his clothing. At around the time we became most concerned about Michael's sleep, we had found bits of tobacco in the folds of his pants. We investigated further and found that he was picking up cigarette butts off of the ground outside, sometimes putting the tobacco in his mouth and sometimes saving some in his pants.

It seemed that this tobacco could have been keeping him up at night. We were also concerned that continued ingestion of enough tobacco over time could make him ill, so we set out to try to get him to stop eating cigarette butts. Unfortunately, Michael's ingenuity got the better of us. He quickly surmised that we did not want him to pick up the cigarettes, so he would wait for some opportune time when we were not looking to bend down, pick one up, and pop it in his mouth. In fact, our efforts at surveillance seemed to make him more interested in cigarettes.

Accepting defeat, we decided to take a more thoughtful approach to this habit. Suppose we gave him chewing tobacco to keep in his pocket so that he could have tobacco whenever he wanted. If this stopped him from picking up cigarettes off the ground, it would at least be more sanitary. We found that he stopped reaching for cigarettes butts altogether and was not swallowing the tobacco we gave him. Next, we decided to try to reduce the amount of chewing tobacco we gave him and instead replace it with some candy or gum. The nicotine gums or patches were not available at this time, or we would have tried one of them with Michael. Over the course of several months, we slowly and methodically reduced the chewing tobacco we gave him and gave him substitutes. After 3 months, he had only tiny amounts of tobacco and was sleeping on a regular schedule. His sleep seemed to improve as the amount of tobacco he chewed was reduced.

We recommend that you limit drinking alcohol and smoking cigarettes in the hours before bedtime. Perhaps more important for a person's overall health would be to quit—especially smoking—altogether. Be warned that, if a person stops smoking completely, he or she may experience an increase in sleep problems initially (this is why we tried to wean Michael off of tobacco slowly, to avoid him going after cigarettes on the ground again). Worsening of sleep problems can occur because the body will go through withdrawal symptoms that will interfere with sleep. In the long run, however, sleep should be improved.

SLEEP AND DIET

Whether or not certain foods can help you sleep has been discussed for centuries. You may have your own family remedy—for example, warm milk and cookies—to bring on sleep at night. Fortunately, sleep researchers have investigated the helpful and harmful effects on our sleep of what we eat and drink. One of the traditionally recommended sleep aids—drinking milk before bedtime—seems to help bring on sleep for many people. Foods high in fat may disturb sleep, so it may be helpful to limit them. This does not mean that all fat should be eliminated, because fat can create a feeling of being full or satisfied and is necessary for proper hormone development. In addition, eating a well-balanced and healthy diet seems to assist people who have difficulty sleeping. Being healthy in general, which can be helped with a good diet, seems to be related to good sleep.

Certain foods that may bring on an upset stomach or heartburn during the night should be avoided. With this suggested avoidance, it is difficult to make specific recommendations because people have their own individual reactions to certain foods. Common problem foods include heavily spiced foods, cucumbers and beans (which can cause painful gas later in the evening), and foods with monosodium glutamate (MSG). As many of you may know, MSG is often used in Chinese food (and is in meat tenderizers), although increasingly it is being left out or some restaurants will leave it out if requested. Experiment with certain foods and use the sleep diary to see if your child seems to respond negatively to anything specific (e.g., a bad night's sleep after eating Chinese food).

Some years ago, the naturally occurring amino acid *tryptophan* was touted as a cure for insomnia. This amino acid is found in foods that are rich in protein, such as milk, cheese, eggs, beans, and meats. It is believed that tryptophan may help sleep because our bodies break down this substance into the brain chemical *serotonin,* which in turn may help slow down our nervous system. This may be especially important for parents of children with ASD, because this disorder has been linked to serotonin production and may account for the high rates of sleep problems in this group (I also discuss serotonin and sleep in Chapter 14 when I describe the use of the naturally occurring hormone *melatonin* and its relationship to sleep).[2] For a time in the late 1980s, synthetic tryptophan was sold as a supplement in health food stores. Unfortunately, because of impurities in the manufacturing of some brands of the supplements, serious side effects were observed in some people taking this substance (e.g., blood disorders, rashes, aching muscles and joints), and it was removed from the market in 1989. Obviously, you can still receive the benefits from tryptophan (which tend to be mild) from eating protein-rich foods, and you may want to try assessing the effects of these foods on your sleep.

Finally, certain vitamins and minerals seem to have some limited positive effects on sleep. Vitamins such as B_3 (also known as *niacin*), B_{12}, and another of the B vitamins, *folic acid*, appear to help some people sleep better. Taking a B complex multivitamin supplement each day for at least 1 week may result in some improvements in sleep. It is believed that *calcium* and *magnesium* can also serve as sedatives (sleep-inducing substances), and some people have found that supplementing their diets with these minerals has promoted improved sleep.

With all of the diet recommendations discussed here, it is important that you monitor your child's sleep to assess if and how these foods are affecting sleep. It is also important that your physician be included in any discussions concerning changes in diet, especially if you are using supplements.

EXERCISE, ACTIVITY, AND SLEEP

Timing is everything, especially when it comes to exercise and sleep. If a person exercises too close to bedtime, he or she may have difficulty falling asleep. Engage in regular exercise earlier in the day, however, and you may find that sleep is even better. Why would the time of day matter when it comes to exercise? I described in Chapter 1 how our internal body temperature changes throughout the day and night and how a dip in temperature in the evening seems to be related to becoming drowsy, and a rise in temperature in the early morning is related to becoming more alert. Exercise or vigorous activity in general is important to this pattern because it can serve to raise our internal body temperature, therefore making us more alert. Such activity right before you want your child to sleep can be counterproductive—keeping him or her awake and alert rather than drowsy and sleepy. Fortunately, you can make exercise work *for* instead of *against* your child's sleep. Raising the body's temperature by exercise will cause a kind of temperature *catch up,* where the body compensates by subsequently lowering its temperature 4–6 hours later. If you time it right and have your child exercise 4–6 hours before bedtime, his or her body temperature will drop just at the time you want it to—in time for him or her to become drowsy for sleep.

What about exercise that occurs earlier in the day, more than 6 hours before bedtime? Unfortunately, such activity will not have a direct effect on sleep. However, it does appear that being fit in general is related to better sleep. Research suggests that "couch potatoes" are more likely to have trouble sleeping than those who engage in regular exercise.

It is recommended that the exercise you have your child attempt should be of the aerobic type in order to positively impact sleep. In other words, the child must raise his or her heartbeat such that there is heavy breathing for at least 20 minutes per day. Obviously, you should not start right into a hefty exercise plan if your child has not been active. Consult with your physician and start slowly. Injuries caused by doing too much too soon can be painful and can themselves disturb sleep.

Added caution needs to be taken for some people with special needs. For example, individuals with Down syndrome (a disorder that results from having an extra 21st chromosome and is accompanied by some level of cognitive impairment) often have cardiac problems and should be extremely careful when engaging in any exercise. Similarly, people with severe physical disabilities, such as those with cerebral palsy, should also seek the advice of a physician to determine the type and duration of any exercise. Do not be discouraged if your child is not able to engage in vigorous exercise because of physical limitations. As I discuss next, any increase in activity may help him or her with sleep.

We often encounter people who are in school or who work where the activities they engage in each day are extremely boring. For example, it is all too common for people with an intellectual disability to be provided with the same repetitive tasks day in and day out. Similarly, many children with learning disabilities are routinely drilled on academic tasks to help them with their basic skills. Unfortunately, these boring tasks can contribute to sleep problems. Research with older adults, for example, suggests that, if they lead uneventful daily lives, they are more likely to have trouble falling asleep and staying asleep. It may be valuable to reexamine the types and flow of activities that your child engages in throughout the day and recommend some changes if necessary. One 17-year-old young man we worked with who had an intellectual disability spent his whole day sitting at the same table working. We suggested that he be allowed to get up from the table to get his own work (previously his teacher would get it for him) and that he get up to put it away. Even this small change seemed to make him more alert during the day and more tired at bedtime.

Exercise and Activity Suggestions

- Try to establish a daily exercise regime for your child.

- Encourage your child to engage in aerobic exercise 4–6 hours before bedtime.

- Discourage your child from exercising or engaging in vigorous activity right before bedtime.

- Consult with a physician before starting any new exercise programs.

- Look for ways to decrease boredom and increase activity throughout the day.

THE BED AND THE BEDROOM

Many of us use our bedroom as an office, a family gathering place, a dining room, an entertainment center, and a place to plan out our futures. And, for you, this may not be a problem. However, many people come to connect their bed or bedroom with activities that interfere with sleeping. Both positive and negative associations with the bed can cause a person to have trouble falling asleep. At the beginning of this chapter, I discussed how Harry may have come to associate his bed with wrestling and roughhousing with his mother. It may have been very difficult for him to turn off these exciting times and fall asleep in the same place where, minutes before, he was so exhilarated. Other people work in bed and find it difficult to stop thinking their anxious thoughts and fall asleep. Because we often do not know if these types of associations are the problems that are causing sleep difficulties, we usually recommend that parents try to restrict the child's activities surrounding the bed to only sleeping. This technique is called *stimulus control,* meaning that the bedroom or the bed can trigger behavior that can help or hurt sleep. We try to turn around previously learned associations such as "bed = wrestling" to new associations that are more beneficial to sleep, "bed = sleep."

Another implication of this association is if your child lies awake at night in bed for too long. Typically, you would expect a child to fall asleep within 15–20 minutes of putting his or her head on the pillow. However, sometimes children will either sit in bed before falling asleep or wake up in the middle of the night and worry about things that may have happened that day or what is coming up the next day. Children with an anxiety disorder, including some with the "Asperger's type" of ASD, will perseverate in their minds and not be able to fall asleep (I discuss this issue in Chapter 12). Yet an immediate concern is that the child lies in bed for more than 20 minutes without sleeping. If this should occur, we recommend getting them out of bed and have them, perhaps, sit in a chair in the room. Once they seem sleepy, then they can go back to the bed. This is to avoid having the child connect worrying and the bed. This recommendation is also relevant if you have this difficulty. And, one more thing—do not look at your clock if you wake up at the wrong time! Many people do this and become concerned that they will not get enough sleep that night. This only increases your anxiety and interferes with falling back to sleep.

Sometimes there are practical limitations when trying to follow through on this approach. For example, in smaller homes where the bedroom may be the only place to play, we recommend that child play on the floor, restricting the bed to bedtime stories and sleep. We also work with people who live in one-room apartments and for whom the bed is a couch and the bedroom is literally the living room, dining room, or so forth. In those cases, where it is impossible to keep the bed as only a place for sleep, we rely heavily on the constant and predictable bedtime routines we described at the beginning of this chapter to help the child associate the bed with sleep, at least at night.

Lastly, we often ask parents to "sleep an hour in their children's beds." We do not mean this literally but instead want parents to focus on things in the bedroom that might be interfering with their child's sleep. Is the bedroom noisy? Can you hear conversations, the television, or a dishwasher in the next room? Any number of noises at bedtime can keep a light sleeper from falling asleep. It may be necessary for the family to be quieter at night, at least until the child is asleep. Other families have found that they can move their activities into another room that is not so close to their child's bedroom and that this reduces the noise that can be heard. Light can be another problem. A too-bright hallway light, for example, may be interfering with sleep. On one occasion, we found that a child who was waking up too early in the morning did not have any window coverings in her bedroom, and the early morning light woke her up. Even something such as a too-cold or too-warm bedroom might be a problem for your child. Spend some time in your child's bedroom at night and see if there are any common sense changes that can help the onset of sleep.

CONCLUSION

This chapter is recommended for everyone whose child is having trouble sleeping. It began with a Good Sleep Habits Checklist that we recommend everyone consult before moving on to more specific techniques. These recommendations include many of the suggestions that sleep experts collectively refer to as *sleep hygiene*. Just as good physical hygiene helps us to be healthier physically, good sleep hygiene has been found to help people sleep better. The introduction of routines was highlighted first because it can be a powerful sleep technique. Other recommendations such as limiting certain foods and drinks have helped people who were unknowingly disrupting their own sleep.

It is important to point out that your child's disturbed sleep is probably causing your own sleep to be disrupted. We often find that parents also have trouble sleeping and that the start of their troubles began when their child began having difficulty. Unfortunately, we also find that, even when we can help their child to sleep better, the parents' sleep continues to be disturbed. Recognizing this, I have made the recommendations in this book applicable to anyone who is having trouble with their sleep. It may be helpful, therefore, for you to complete the Good Sleep Habits Checklist for yourself to see if you can improve your own sleep as well.

Help for Bedtime Problems

You have spent a long day juggling the demands and needs of your active family. Now, as evening approaches, you are looking forward to the all too brief time when your child is safely and quietly asleep and when you will have a few precious moments for yourself or to share with your partner. As you begin to get your child ready for bed and the resistance begins, you remember again that tonight, like most nights, it will be the "battle at bedtime." One more night when the way your child goes to sleep will resemble combat: a skirmish here, a small victory there, and then the onslaught that characterizes most nights. And when the war is over for the night, you are so wound up that sleep will be difficult for you as well.

Bedtime resistance, or in the more extreme case *bedtime tantrums*, can be extremely upsetting to a family. In the last chapter, I described how important it is for many people to have a quiet transition to sleep, yet for many households, the time before sleep is anything but quiet. Fortunately, there are ways to deal with even the worst bedtime battles, and these techniques can lead to significant improvements in a matter of weeks. Let us begin by looking at one family who had a many-year history of bedtime troubles but who managed to successfully overcome these difficulties.

☆ DENA

Dena's parents were both college students and were concerned about their 5-year-old daughter. Dena had recently been diagnosed with ASD, in part because of her delays with language and relative lack of interest in other people. Dena knew and recognized her parents but seemed to interact with them, as her parents described, "on an angle." She would never look straight at them when she approached them and often took their hands to lead them to things she wanted. She seemed to enjoy sitting with her parents but would always face away from them and would not share toys with them like other young children do. Dena liked spinning things, especially on the hardwood floors because of the sound they made.

As her parents described, Dena had never been a good sleeper but recently was beginning to sleep through the night. Unfortunately, bedtime was still a problem. Their pediatrician had suggested they give Dena a small dose of Benadryl (the allergy medication) before bedtime to make her sleepy. For a few nights this seemed to help, but she appeared to her parents to fight off the effects of the medication in order to stay up. A typical night would begin with a good bedtime routine, which included washing up, dressing for bed, a nighttime story that Dena seemed to pay some attention to, and then a short ritual where Dena would arrange the covers of her bed before getting into it. However, as soon as her parents got up from the bed, Dena would be up too and would try to go out into the living room. If they attempted to get her to go back to bed, Dena would fall to the floor and cry. As this continued, back and forth, in and out of her room, she would cry more loudly and struggle to be let loose. Her parents had been dealing with this for the last 3 years by having Dena's mother stay in bed with her until Dena fell asleep. Her mother would be in bed with her for 15–30 minutes each night before Dena was asleep. On some nights, Dena would wake up when her mother tried to leave the bed, and this usually prolonged the ritual an additional half hour.

After Dena's parents completed our assessment procedure, we talked about how they felt about Dena crying at night. Her mother and father both admitted with some embarrassment that they could not stand to hear her cry. Perhaps because they recognized the problems she was having learning to speak and develop in a typical fashion, they felt guilty if she was upset, especially if they could prevent her distress by staying in bed with her. They told me that it was not her fault that she had ASD (as if perhaps it was their fault) and that she should not have to be so miserable over bedtime. I spent some time going over with them some of the research on ASD, which clearly shows that their early parenting could not have caused Dena's current condition. They both confessed to feeling personally guilty, as if they were responsible, and also feeling secret resentment toward the other spouse, feeling that maybe it was the other partner who was to blame. Dena's mother and father appeared greatly relieved to hear that neither one of them was the cause of their beautiful daughter's ASD. It was hoped that, if this information also made them feel less guilty about letting their daughter cry, they would be able to ignore her crying at bedtime, at least for a few minutes.

The habit of waiting for her to fall asleep started innocently enough when she was 2 years old and was ill. They stayed in the bed with her on those nights to console her because she was obviously uncomfortable. However, Dena kept them there each night even after the illness was resolved by crying plaintively if they left before she fell asleep. They now felt trapped in this pattern and were desperately seeking a solution to this problem.

Before we discuss the particular plan we designed for Dena's parents, we will describe the intervention procedure in general and how it can be used in most cases of bedtime resistance.

GRADUATED EXTINCTION

Graduated extinction involves spending increasingly longer amounts of time ignoring the cries and protestations of a child at bedtime.[1] It is a variation of the typical approach of simply ignoring the crying, an adaptation that many parents find more acceptable. Most of you who have children who have put up a struggle at bedtime have probably at some point tried to ignore it. In fact, the most common recommendation pediatricians make when asked by parents how to respond to bedtime resistance is to simply ignore the crying child. Let the child "cry it out" and eventually he or she will go to bed on his or her own. I remember quite distinctly our own attempts to ignore the crying of my infant son. Being our firstborn, we did not know if his cries meant he was hungry, thirsty, ill, in pain, wet, lonely, or so forth. Over the months we began to feel comfortable that his nightly crying was not due to some horrible plague that only showed itself at night, but we still could not ignore him when he cried. I can recall feeling the pangs of guilt physically while this poor innocent infant cried as we heartlessly left him alone at night.

Fortunately, my wife and I gathered up our courage and began a plan that has been demonstrated to be quite successful in assisting with bedtime problems as well as night waking (which I discuss more fully in the next chapter). We implemented a graduated extinction program that involved both ignoring his cries but also checking on him periodically in case there really was something wrong with him. The first step in the plan (which we had already completed) was to establish a bedtime routine (described in detail in Chapter 6). My wife and I then had to agree on what a good bedtime was for our son and stick to it. Even if he did not seem tired, or more likely, if we were not ready for the battle, we needed to put him to bed at the same time each night. Then the hard part—how long could we ignore the crying without breaking down and going into his room? We came up with 5 minutes, which first seemed like only a brief moment when we discussed it but felt like an eternity when we actually had to follow through. The first evening of the plan had us putting our son to bed at 8 p.m. after about a 30-minute bedtime routine. As usual, he cried when we left the room. We waited the full 5 minutes and then would *briefly* go into his room, see that he was all right, and then tell him to go back to bed. It is important to note that we did not pick him up as we usually did at these times, nor did we feed him or play music. It was in and out in about 15 seconds. We then had to wait another 5 minutes, listening to him cry, before we could go back and repeat the brief checkup. This continued—wait 5 minutes, check on him, wait 5 more minutes—for almost 2 hours on the first night. It was difficult for us, and I remember feeling little confidence in the plan.

Despite our reservations, we extended the time between visits to his room from 5 minutes to 7 minutes on the second night. Everything else was the same—no picking him up, rocking him, or feeding him—except that now we had to wait longer. On the second night, the crying continued again for about 2 hours until he finally fell asleep. The first sign that something good was about to happen occurred on the third night. That night we again extended the time—this time to 9 minutes between visits—keeping our checkups brief and neutral. On that night, however, he did not cry continuously between the checkups. There were seconds here and there where he stopped crying briefly. And, on that night, it only took about an hour for him to fall asleep. On the fourth night, we extended the time a bit more (to 11 minutes) and found that he whimpered more than cried and fell asleep in about 45 minutes. After that night we decided not to go into his room again once we left at bedtime, and he stopped crying in about 20 minutes and presumably fell asleep. Two weeks later he only fussed a bit at bedtime, but would not cry at all after we left the room.

Graduated extinction seems to work by forcing the child to learn how to fall asleep on his or her own. If you recall from Chapter 2, we discussed how many children never learn to fall asleep alone. Often parents are present when their children fall asleep as infants because they are feeding the children or just lying next to them when they fall asleep. There is nothing more special than holding a sleeping infant. However, if this is the only situation in which their child falls asleep, then parents run the risk of creating a situation such as the one I found myself in with my son, where their child needs someone physically present to sleep. Graduated extinction requires the child to learn to fall asleep alone, because you will not be present and because other sleep-inducing factors such as the music parents sometimes play are not available. As cruel as this may feel at the time, children do need to learn how to fall asleep on their own. Fortunately, graduated extinction does allow for periodic checks on the child, which seem to serve to reassure parents that everything is all right. As the time lengthens between visits to the child's room, and these visits bring very little to the child (only brief attention from parents, no holding, no feeding, no music), children learn to comfort themselves. Research using infrared video of children going through graduated extinction (so you can see them in the dark) shows these children rearranging blankets or pillows or cuddling stuffed animals and finding their own comfort prior to sleep. Treatment research has shown that many children can benefit from this approach to dealing with bedtime problems.

What follows are the steps to use when implementing a graduated extinction procedure.

Graduated Extinction

- Follow the procedures for establishing a bedtime routine.

- Establish and be firm about a bedtime.

- Determine how long you are able to wait before checking on your child.

- Pick the night to begin the plan, assuming no one will have a good night's sleep that evening—most people begin on a Friday night.

- *On the first night*—put your child to bed, leave the room, and then wait the agreed-on time (e.g., 3 minutes). If after 3 minutes your child is still crying, go into the room (do not pick up your child, do not give him or her food or a drink, and do not engage in extensive conversation), tell him or her to go to bed, and then leave. Wait another 3 minutes and then go back into the room if your child is still crying. Continue the pattern until your child is asleep.

- *On subsequent nights*—extend the time between visits by 2 or 3 minutes. Continue the same procedure when entering the room.

In Dena's case, we designed a plan following these guidelines. However, as is so often the case, a number of factors caused us to modify the plan somewhat. First off, her parents broke down on the first night and stayed in bed with her after only the second checkup in her room. The amount of time they selected (2 minutes) was brief for most families but was obviously too long for them to listen to Dena cry. We then modified the plan to only 30 seconds between visits, increasing the time each night by 15 seconds. Although we were not sure how well this would work, after 2 weeks, Dena began having nights where she would fall asleep on her own.

Unfortunately, several weeks after having some success, Dena became ill, which included a loud cough, and her parents felt they needed to be in her bed at bedtime to comfort her. As we expected, after her cough stopped, she again was disruptive at bedtime if her parents left the room. Our suggestion was to start again from the beginning and implement the graduated extinction program, starting at 30 seconds. Dena's parents, however, were not emotionally ready for more nights of battling and put the plans on hold for a few months. After about 3 months, they again wanted to help Dena fall asleep on her own and this time stuck with the program. After 6 days of the restarted program, Dena would fall asleep with minimal disruption, and after 6 months, she continued to have few problems at bedtime.

The problems Dena's parents experienced were not unique. Because of the issues I discussed about interfering thoughts (Chapters 4 and 5), we often have to modify the basic plan for our interventions to meet the needs of the child, the family, or the situation they find themselves in. I hope that cases such as these give you some ideas of how to adapt plans such as graduated extinction to fit your own needs. In this spirit, let us look at the case of another child we worked with using graduated extinction and for whom we needed to modify our plan.

☆ NICK

Nick was a 12-year-old boy who had received a diagnosis of ASD. He lived at home with his parents and sister and attended a regular sixth-grade class at his neighborhood school. Of most concern to his parents and school were his frequent self-injurious behaviors, which mostly involved poking himself in the eyes. He would also frequently get upset at home and at school, throwing objects and sometimes even breaking windows.

We first had contact with Nick's parents because of Nick's very disruptive and disturbing behaviors. As we talked with his family, we found that he also had difficulty at bedtime and throughout the night, and we suspected that his sleep problems may be contributing to the daytime behavior problems seen at home and at school. One of the major problems surrounding Nick's sleep was his unwillingness to go to bed at night. Often he would remain awake for up to 4 or 5 hours after he was put to bed for the night. During this time, he would frequently scream, yell, throw things around his room, and bang on the walls with his fists. And, unfortunately, this was an almost every-night event.

As happens very often in children with bedtime problems, Nick also sometimes had trouble remaining asleep at night. Several nights each month after he fell asleep, he would awaken, be unable to fall back asleep, and then become disruptive in the middle of the night. Two or three times each month he would not sleep at all and would tantrum on and off throughout the night.

Before we had contact with Nick and his family, a physician had prescribed several different medications to try to help him sleep. They tried giving him some Benadryl at bedtime to try to make him drowsy. Unfortunately, Benadryl seemed to have just the opposite effect on Nick, making him more agitated, and he stayed awake later than ever. For a short time they tried a drug called Inderal—which is used to control high blood pressure and migraine headaches and is also used sometimes to reduce anxiety—but this drug seemed to have no effect on his sleep. A third drug, Mellaril, was prescribed to be given right before bedtime, and this seemed to help Nick fall asleep more easily. The positive effects of using this drug were not without cost, however. During the first 4 months that Nick was taking Mellaril, he gained 40 pounds. One night he somehow got access to the bottle, accidentally drank a large amount of the drug, and needed emergency treatment. Because of these concerns, Nick's parents were anxious to try a different approach that did not involve the use of medication.

Nick's parents had already established a fairly stable bedtime routine. When we looked at his sleep diaries, we found that, even with the Mellaril, it would take him an average of almost 2 hours each night to fall asleep. His parents had selected an 8 p.m. bedtime, in part because they wanted him to get more sleep and also because they relished time alone at night for themselves. Our suggestion for a later bedtime (10 p.m.), which was probably more appropriate for a child his age, was met with obvious resistance. The compromise we all agreed to involved continuing to put Nick in his bedroom at 8 p.m., but instead of turning out the lights and trying to get him to sleep, he would be allowed to stay up and play in his room on the floor until 10 p.m.

Each evening, Nick's parents would begin the bedtime routine, which would end with him being in his room at 8 p.m. He could keep his light on and play until 10 p.m. If he was very disruptive, they could go into his room, but other than these times, they were to leave him alone. An alarm clock was used and was set to go off at 10 p.m. to signal to both Nick and his parents that it was time for him to get into his bed for sleep. At this time, his parents would enter his room and sit by his side for a few minutes of quiet activity (backrubs, quiet talking). After no more than 15 minutes, his parents were instructed to say goodnight, turn off the light, and leave the room.

The compromise at bedtime dramatically reduced the disruption at night. During most evenings, Nick did not fight bedtime and generally cooperated with going to sleep. However, there were still 1 or 2 nights each week when Nick was disruptive, so we designed a graduated extinction plan for these times. On nights when Nick refused to stay in his bed at 10 p.m. and go to sleep, his parents were instructed to wait 5 minutes before going into his room. We suggested that they stand by his closed bedroom door so that they could hear him and so that they could respond if he tried to leave his room. If he opened the door and tried to come out, his parents would lead him back to his bed without saying anything other than, "Go back to bed." On a few nights, they could hear him banging his head, so they calmly entered the room, placed him back into bed, and then left the room. Over the course of several weeks, the problems continued to decline, and Nick's parents were delighted with the changes.

The solution of having Nick stay in his room from 8 p.m. until 10 p.m. was obviously a compromise that was not without some risk. By letting him spend so much time playing in his bedroom at night, we were concerned that he might associate the bedroom with playing rather than sleep, and this might interfere with his sleep. Fortunately, this was not the case, and on most nights he fell asleep soon after the alarm went off. Ideally his parents would have kept him up until 10 p.m., but the needs of the family—some "mental health" time together—were important to consider when we designed the plan. Its success was welcomed by the whole family.

Again, Nick's case illustrates the need to tailor these programs for each family. When children such as Nick present multiple problems surrounding sleep, it is important that you be patient and continue to monitor your child's progress. We have parents complete the sleep diaries throughout the time of the program so that they can see whatever changes are occurring, even if progress is slow. Nick's parents were initially skeptical about the program until we showed them his improvements each week. Seeing that Nick's tantrums were becoming shorter and shorter gave them the motivation to keep going. Remember to keep monitoring your child's progress and, if you need it, use this information to help you persist.

BEDTIME FADING

Although graduated extinction can be a very effective plan for children who throw tantrums at bedtime—and it is certainly easier for most parents to implement than simply ignoring all cries—this procedure is not for all families. We have many parents who cannot tolerate the crying that occurs when using a technique such as graduated extinction. Sometimes it is because their child's cries make them feel so miserable that it is not worth even this temporary battle. Dena's parents are a good example, finding it very difficult not to respond to their daughter even after only 30 seconds of crying. Other parents are concerned about neighbors. Living in an apartment often means that you cannot allow your child to scream for hours each night. In fact, many parents fall into the trap of being in their child's bed at bedtime not because they cannot handle the crying but because they are concerned that neighbors or other family members may be too disrupted. One mother who contacted us for help told us she slept on the floor next to her son's bed so that she could respond immediately if he woke up and so that his cries would not awaken her husband and disrupt his sleep. For 7 years she slept apart from her husband in order to safeguard his sleep.

Finally, sometimes children are so disruptive at bedtime that a parent cannot allow the child to continue the tantrum for too long. Often this occurs as the child grows older and can inflict more damage on themselves, on others, or on property. One 11-year-old boy who had ADHD once bragged to us that he broke his bedroom window five times over the past few years in fights over bedtime. Obviously, this type of reaction to bedtime cannot be ignored by parents and makes implementing a plan such as graduated extinction a problem.

Fortunately, an alternate approach to responding to bedtime resistance is available that may make bedtime for some children "errorless." One strategy for trying to get a child to sleep at night might not have occurred to you: keep him or her up *later* than usual. The rationale behind what is called *bedtime fading* is to keep the child up so late that he or she falls asleep on his or her own.[2] For example, if bedtime is usually 9 p.m. but your child fights going to bed at this time, you may want to temporarily make bedtime 11:30 p.m., a time when your child may be so tired that bedtime is no longer a battle. If this new bedtime is successful (in other words, your child falls asleep with little resistance), then you can begin to fade back bedtime in small increments until the bedtime you want your child to fall asleep at is achieved. One case illustrates a particularly difficult situation where bedtime was becoming almost a life-threatening event. You will see how we were able to help this particular mother deal with a situation that was rapidly getting out of hand.

☆ GLORIA

Gloria's mom called me one afternoon after hearing that I may be able to offer some help. Listening to her exhausted voice over the phone brought back memories of my own child's bedtime difficulties and the point at which I became willing to try anything. She relayed to me some background information about her daughter and the current problems she faced when trying to get Gloria to sleep.

Gloria was a very active and generally happy 12-year-old girl who had developmental delays that caused her speech to be limited. She also needed some additional help with everyday activities such as feeding herself, bathing, and the work she was given at school. Despite the hard work, Gloria liked school a great deal and enjoyed being with other children her age. Her teachers liked her as well, enjoyed having her in class, and never suspected the problems her mother was experiencing with Gloria at home.

Gloria's mother described to me how each evening she felt a sense of dread come over her. She had learned to associate nightfall with the difficulty she was having getting Gloria to go to bed at night. Ever since Gloria was born—which she reminded me was now more than 12 years ago—she would cry and resist going to bed in the evening or even if her mother tried to get her to nap. In recent years, as Gloria had become bigger, the crying had become more intense, and she began to lash out at her mother. On one recent night, Gloria kept coming out of her room, and when her mother tried to get her to go back, Gloria kicked and slapped her mother so hard that her mother fell to the floor. She told me that she was afraid of Gloria and did not know how long she could keep her at home. Her mother told me that no one else knew what was happening at night because she was too ashamed to tell anyone but that things were becoming so out of hand that she had to admit she needed help.

Obviously, Gloria's behavior was becoming unmanageable and helping Gloria's mother with her daughter's sleep could not include any recommendations for prolonged periods of ignoring her outbursts. Her mother was already trying to ignore her tantrums at bedtime and was frightened at what might happen to her. Instead, our plan for Gloria focused on trying to come up with an arrangement that would get Gloria to sleep at night without putting her mother at risk of getting hurt. As we have already mentioned, one option was to use *bedtime fading*.

For this plan, we try to find a time at night where the child is so tired that he or she would go to bed without trouble. We do this because we want to establish a pattern where the child learns to go to bed and to fall asleep on his or her own. This should seem familiar to you if you have read Chapter 6, because it is the same rationale used in the technique known as *stimulus control*. The bed, the bedroom, and the bedtime routine should all signal sleep. In Gloria's case (and in the case of her mother), all of these *stimuli* signaled a terrible battle rather than soothing and restful sleep. Keeping Gloria up later could help to make her less resistant to bedtime and, therefore, let her see how pleasant bedtime could be.

Finding the right bedtime is one of the keys to bedtime fading. Here is where the sleep diary you completed can come in handy. Often there are times when the family has been out late at a movie or a relative's house or has stayed up late at home watching television. During these times, the child may have fallen asleep on his or her own. To be safe, we take this time and add 30 minutes to come up with the new bedtime. If you do not have a good idea about when your child might fall asleep, you can experiment by staying up late. Make sure there is little activity (in other words, make it boring) and see when your child seems to be nodding off. Again, add 30 minutes to this time and try using that as the bedtime.

An Important Note About Napping

If your child is also *napping during the day,* you should probably refer to Chapter 9 (Sleeping at the Wrong Times) as well. Sometimes bedtime resistance occurs because the child is simply not tired at the designated bedtime, and this is because the child is sleeping during the day. We describe a case such as this in Chapter 7, which first involves changing naps rather than trying to work on a bedtime. If your child is also napping, this alternative approach may help.

Once you have settled on a bedtime, use a bedtime routine for the 30 minutes or so before this new bedtime and put your child to bed. Make sure that she stays awake prior to the new bedtime. This is important. You may be tempted to let your child fall asleep earlier than the new bedtime if she seems to be nodding off and close to sleep. Resist! Remember, you want your child to fall asleep after the bedtime routine and when she is in bed. Letting your child fall asleep on the couch in front of the television and then transferring her to bed defeats the purpose of the plan. Keep your child awake until the new bedtime. Your patience will be rewarded.

If you put your child to bed at the new bedtime and she seems wide awake after about 15 minutes, have her get up and extend the bedtime for one more hour. Even if your child does not resist sleep during this time, you do not want her lying in bed awake for too long. As I have mentioned previously, the reason why you want to avoid prolonged periods in bed without sleep is that you do not want your child to begin to associate the bed with *not* sleeping. Just as we discouraged Harry in Chapter 6 from wrestling in bed at night because that might keep him up, we try to keep the time in bed when a child is awake to a minimum. Again, the bed should only be a signal for sleep.

If your child is falling asleep within about 15 minutes at the new bedtime over 2 consecutive nights, then you can begin to move up the bedtime. For each 2 nights, move up bedtime by 15 minutes. For example, if you selected 12:30 a.m. as the bedtime, move it to 12:15 a.m. after your child falls asleep successfully for 2 nights. Keep moving the time earlier (e.g., 12 a.m., 11:45 p.m., 11:30 p.m.) until you reach the bedtime you want or until your child no longer falls asleep within the first 15 minutes.

Try to remain flexible when it comes to the "ideal" bedtime. We saw in Nick's case that his parents' desired bedtime was 8 p.m., but Nick did not seem tired until about 10 p.m. Because Nick was not napping during the day and he seemed to be well rested after his 9 hours of sleep (10 p.m. to 7 a.m.), we believed that 10 p.m. was a good bedtime for him. Part of the reason he resisted going to sleep at 8 p.m. was because he was simply not ready for sleep that early in the evening. His sleep problem was, therefore, partly due to his parents' selection of a bedtime that was inappropriate for him. Use the information we provide in Chapter 1 about a child's need for sleep to give you an idea about how much sleep your child needs according to his or her age. Also keep in mind, however, that each of us has different sleep needs, so what is good for one child may not be for another child of the same age. If your child seems well rested during the day, then he probably is getting enough sleep. On the other hand, if he seems tired even after 8 hours of sleep, then that may not be enough time.

The following are some general guidelines to follow when designing a bedtime fading program. As with all programs, you may need to experiment a bit to see what works best for your child.

Bedtime Fading

- Select a bedtime when your child is likely to fall asleep with little difficulty and within about 15 minutes. To determine this bedtime, use the sleep diary to find a time when your child falls asleep if left alone (e.g., 1 a.m.), then add 30 minutes to this time (new bedtime = 1:30 a.m.).

- If your child falls asleep within 15 minutes of being put to bed at this new bedtime and without resistance for 2 successive nights, move up bedtime by 15 minutes (from 1:30 a.m. to 1:15 a.m.).

- Keep your child awake before the new bedtime even if he or she seems to want to fall asleep.

- If your child does not fall asleep within about 15 minutes after being put to bed, have him or her leave the bedroom and extend the bedtime for 1 more hour.

- Continue to move up the bedtime (e.g., from 1:15 a.m. to 1 a.m.) until the desired bedtime is reached.

Returning to Gloria's case, we found that she would reliably fall asleep at around 1 a.m. if she was left alone. Based on this information, we selected a 1:30 a.m. bedtime for Gloria and asked her mother to begin a bedtime routine at 1 a.m. As often happens when using faded bedtime, Gloria would sometimes start to fall asleep as the evening progressed but before the new 1:30 a.m. bedtime. Her mother would engage her in some activity (fixing lunch for tomorrow, folding laundry) that would keep her from falling asleep but that was not too exciting and that could possibly run the risk of keeping her from falling asleep later.

Gloria's mother was initially hesitant about this program. Anything that revolved around bedtime caused her a great deal of anxiety because of the very negative history she had with her daughter and sleep. One specific concern was when she would need to tell her daughter to go to bed. Usually, Gloria's mother would wait until Gloria looked sleepy. Previously, when Gloria looked as though she was about to fall asleep on the couch, her mother would tell her to go to bed. Unfortunately, this would usually be followed by a fight, even though Gloria was obviously tired. This is where the bedtime routine is so helpful. By building up to bedtime rather than bringing it on suddenly, you avoid the abrupt transition that can be very unpleasant for children. Gloria probably did not like to be wrenched away from her activity to be immediately put to bed. Adding the more gradual transition seemed to help her accept bedtime and helped her mother cope with this previously dreaded time of night.

COMPARING GRADUATED EXTINCTION AND BEDTIME FADING

I have described two very different ways to deal with disruption at bedtime. Graduated extinction involves letting your child get upset and waiting for progressively longer periods of time to check in. On the other hand, bedtime fading involves keeping your child up much later than usual so that the child falls asleep without incident and then gradually moving this bedtime until it matches your expected time to sleep. One of the more important questions that arises is how do you decide between the two of these plans? Which one is better for you and your child?

Fortunately, both of these approaches seem to be successful in helping many families reduce or eliminate bedtime problems. Research conducted with many children with different needs indicates that either approach can achieve your ultimate goal: having a peaceful end to the day. However, there are both pluses and minuses to each of the approaches, and families should take these factors into consideration when choosing between the plans (see Table 7.1).

For example, many families who cannot bear to listen to even a few minutes of their child's cries may not do well with graduated extinction. In addition, some children engage in behaviors that are so disruptive that you cannot ignore them. Some of the children we have worked with who have ADHD, for example, have been able to basically destroy their bedroom in a few minutes. Their parents cannot wait even a few seconds during such an episode without intervening. For these families, faded bedtime becomes a good choice because you are able, in many cases, to avoid any of the disruption at bedtime. There are tradeoffs, however, for families who choose faded bedtimes. For many, the very late night or early morning schedule is too much for them. Because someone has to stay awake, sometimes until 1 a.m. or 2 a.m., faded bedtime becomes more trouble than it is worth. Also, it often takes several weeks to fade back the bedtime until the child is going to bed at the desired time, and this too can be trying for many families. Graduated extinction can sometimes be successful within days, which can be quite appealing to many parents. As you can see, the choice between the two approaches often comes down to personal preferences (quick but disruptive in the case of graduated extinction, or slower but calmer in the case of faded bedtimes), although in cases with extreme behavioral outbursts, faded bedtime may be the only option.

COMBINING PLANS WITH MEDICATION

I will discuss in some detail the sleep medications that are available and their recommended use later in Chapter 14. However, sometimes we face decisions about the use of medication and whether or not

Table 7.1.   Graduated extinction and faded bedtime

Graduated extinction

Pluses	Minuses
Can be used at the regular bedtime rather than having to wait until late at night	Requires listening to your child's cries, which can be difficult for many families
Can check on the child for reassurance	Can result in an increase in behavior problems
Usually works within the first week	Some behaviors such as injurious ones cannot be ignored

Faded bedtime

Pluses	Minuses
Can often be "errorless" with no increase in behavior problems	Requires someone remain up late at night
Often avoids long bouts of crying	Can take several weeks before the desired bedtime is reached

to recommend to families to continue the medication their child is receiving before beginning plans that involve interventions such as graduated extinction or bedtime fading. Obviously, the decision of whether or not to use medication must be one that is made in consultation with your physician. Any change in medication, whether it is to use it or discontinue its use, should be preceded by a discussion with a medical professional about the possible consequences.

Once the child's physical health is considered, another concern is evaluating the effects of your plan on your child's sleep. The concern here is that, if you change more than one thing at a time—such as starting some medication at about the same time you begin a sleep plan—you may not be sure what caused any changes in your child's sleep. You want to be able to say whether or not your plan worked. This is more than simply something of passing interest. If you can confidently determine that your graduated extinction plan, for example, helped your daughter to go to bed at night, then if this problem ever comes back (which unfortunately can happen), you know what worked before and what should work again. However, if you started the plan at the same time you changed the use of some medication, you will not know which of these to change should the problem resurface.

Again, we will describe medication issues in Chapter 14, and you should refer to this chapter if your child is currently receiving some medication or if there are plans to start. However, at this point it is important to remember—DO NOT CHANGE MORE THAN ONE THING AT A TIME. Knowing what caused sleep to improve (or to worsen) will be of tremendous value at a later time.

WHEN SLEEP PROBLEMS REAR THEIR UGLY HEADS . . . AGAIN

It may seem very pessimistic to bring up what happens if your child's sleep problems return. Unfortunately, even with our best plans, it is often the case that sleep problems return in some form during the months or years after our initial success. This should not be completely surprising, as many children have a difficult time sleeping because they were born that way—put another way, these children appear to be biologically predisposed to sleep problems in the first place. Their tendency to be a *light sleeper* (which may have been inherited from parents or other relatives) interacts with family schedules, the way we respond to them, and other factors that cause many of the sleep problems described in this book. We therefore may not be "curing" their sleep difficulties in the traditional sense but simply making it easier for these children to adapt to regular sleep schedules.

We often see children who have done quite well with a plan such as graduated extinction, only to have their problems return after an illness, vacation, or some other change in their lives that disrupts their sleep pattern. Dena's case is a good example. Only a few weeks after her parents had successfully implemented a graduated extinction program and her bedtime problems had subsided, a cold seemed to interrupt the newly established sleep cycle, and she was resisting bedtime again. Illnesses can often disturb sleep and can therefore be responsible for interfering with the types of plans we have described. Unfortunately, even after the illness is over, your child's sleep may continue to be off.

Another very common cause of the failure of a previously successful plan is the *trip to grandma's,* which is another way of saying that changes in routines can interrupt the sleep pattern you have developed. Letting a child who has sleep problems stay up later on weekends can cause the *Sunday Night syndrome.* This is a problem going to bed Sunday night after being allowed to stay up later Friday and Saturday nights. Again, trying to recover from these changes can be surprisingly difficult.

Sometimes these changes in sleep routines are inevitable. Going on vacation, sleeping over at a relative's house for a weekend, a party that goes on past bedtime, and of course illnesses either should not be avoided or cannot be avoided. Therefore, if you anticipate some event that may potentially interfere with your child's new sleep schedule, try to lessen its impact. If you let your child stay up later on Friday night as a treat, try to cut back on Saturday evening's bedtime so that Sunday evening is not so much of a problem. Try not to disrupt the bedtime routine even if your child is ill. You want the routine to become part of sleep, and it should be an automatic part of every night. Think ahead about how you can preserve the sleep patterns you have established. This may prevent you from having to begin a plan completely from scratch after every unusual event.

BEGIN AT BEDTIME

We are often faced with children who have more than one problem with sleep. Many times children who have difficulty at bedtime also wake frequently during the night and may experience other sleep problems, such as nightmares or sleep terrors. One of the questions you face then is where to begin. Which of the sleep problems should you target first? Fortunately, some research in our lab points to some practical suggestions about where to begin your sleep plans.

Some years ago, one of my graduate students—now Professor Jodi Mindell—chose to use sleep problems in children as the topic of her doctoral dissertation.[3] In designing the study, we decided to look at children who had bedtime problems as well as problems waking up throughout the night. In order to be careful about how the study was conducted, she treated half of the children first for their bedtime problems and the other half of the children for their night waking problems first. Once these problems were brought under control, she then helped the parents treat the second sleep problem as well. The study primarily relied on graduated extinction as a treatment for both sleep problems (we will discuss how to use graduated extinction for night waking in the next chapter) and was successful for all the children. What was unexpected and surprising for us in this study was that it made a big difference which problem you started with. If you first helped children with their bedtime problems, more often than not, their night waking went away on its own! No separate plan was needed for night waking for many of the children for whom their bedtime problems were resolved with graduated extinction. On the other hand, for those children for whom night waking was selected first for treatment, achieving success with this sleep problem seemed to have no effect on bedtime problems. Parents still needed a second plan to deal with their child's disruption at bedtime.

CONCLUSION

What this study tells us is that we may be able to save a great deal of time and effort for children who have both problems—at bedtime and with waking during the night—if we first help them with their bedtime problems. The savings in parents' time and anxiety can be substantial. We do not know yet how many people are likely to benefit from treating bedtime problems first. It is important to note that we also do not know if we would find the same results with a different plan than graduated extinction. For example, if we helped children with bedtime by using faded bedtimes, would their night waking be resolved as well? We do not know. Despite these unanswered questions, the findings from this study are extremely helpful to us when we need to decide how first to begin with sleep problems. *Beginning at bedtime* may be the best sleep strategy.

Sleeping
Through the Night

I have always felt that I could handle almost anything if only I could get some closure: a point at which I could say, "I've completed this," and when I could move on to the next challenge. No matter how ambitious the goal, getting the motivation to keep going requires some small accomplishments along the way. Without these little victories, going on can be even more difficult, and your gumption can drain away until you are close to giving up. This to me is one of the most insidious consequences of the next type of sleep problem we need to discuss, night waking. After a full day of fun and play, work and demands, and even perhaps a battle at bedtime, knowing that it is over for the day can provide some comfort and the return of optimism. Unfortunately, for parents who have children who do not sleep through the night, the day never seems to end. For these families, life can sometimes seem like a never-ending struggle to catch up on all of the things you need or want to do.

Children who do not sleep through the night can often be put into one of two categories: those who wake up but are not disruptive and those whose waking includes the same type of crying and tantrums we discussed in the last chapter with bedtime problems. In some ways, helping children who wake up but who do not become disruptive can be a more difficult problem. I will begin this chapter by briefly reviewing why children may not sleep through the night and then discuss a number of treatment options for children who are disruptive as well as for those children who are not.

CAUSES OF NIGHT WAKING

In Chapter 2, I discussed how early sleep patterns set the stage for later problems children may experience sleeping through the night. As you know, many infants are put to bed each evening while they are already asleep. This can happen because the parent was feeding the infant and the baby fell asleep, or because the infant just fell asleep in a parent's arms. If it is close to bedtime, the parent will naturally put the infant into his crib. If this is the only way the infant can fall asleep—that is, with a parent present—the infant runs the risk of never learning to fall asleep independently. Now, couple this bedtime pattern of only falling asleep with a parent with a natural sleep phenomenon called *partial waking*. You may recall the description of the partial wakings we all experience—those times where we transition from dream (or REM) sleep to nondream (NREM) sleep, and we briefly awaken. This happens to everyone several times each night, but these events are very brief, and we typically have no memory of them the next morning.

One theory about why children continue to awaken in the middle of the night and cry out involves partial waking.[1] It is thought that infants who have not learned to fall asleep alone may more fully awaken during these partial wakings because they become frightened at the now-strange surroundings. Put yourself in the infant's place. You have fallen asleep in the comfort of your parent's arms, in a well-lit and safe environment. Some hours later, you awaken to find your parent gone, and it is dark and cold. Your first reaction is to become alarmed at this drastic change in the world, and you start to cry. If you are your parents' first child (who is more likely to have night waking problems, in part because of what comes next), your parents are concerned that you are crying. They may be insecure about your care, and they react to any sign of your distress. Your parents come into your room, pick you up (which wakes you up even more), and try to provide comfort by holding you, feeding you, or even singing to you. Eventually, you fall back asleep in their arms, and the pattern of not falling asleep alone is continued. Your parents' natural concern for your welfare may, in part, contribute to your inability to fall asleep alone.

In addition to possibly waking infants up more fully by attending to their cries at night, feeding at night can also be a contributory problem. Continuing to feed infants in the middle of the night can cause them to be hungry at that time each night, which in turn can cause them to wake up in the middle of the night. In our last chapter, we discuss how to handle nighttime feedings so that your child will not awaken because he or she is hungry.

A final piece to this puzzle is a child's inborn nature or tendency to be a "light" sleeper. Some children seem to be able to sleep through anything, whereas others awaken with the closing of a door on the other side of the house. We are all born with a propensity to sleep in a certain way, and when a child who is a light sleeper experiences partial wakings, he or she may be more likely to fully awaken from these events. That tendency, coupled with how parents respond to these awakenings, can result in a child who, over time, develops a long history of waking throughout the night.

WAKING WITHOUT DISRUPTION

As I mentioned before, some children awaken in the middle of the night crying and screaming. This can obviously be disruptive to the whole family, causing everyone to have their sleep interrupted, and I discuss this serious situation and how to deal with it in the next section. However, there are also children who wake up from sleep too early and who have difficulty falling back to sleep. They may lie in bed awake, read, play with toys, or even get up and wander about the house. Although this form of night waking is not as dramatic as the form that involves tantrums, it can still cause considerable daytime sleepiness for the child and can disrupt parental sleep as well. I next describe a case of a boy who experienced this problem for most of his life.

☆ CRAIG

Craig was 11 years old at the time he was first referred to us for his sleep problems. Craig had mild to moderate levels of cognitive impairments, which were probably a result of his having Down syndrome. He attended a regular fifth-grade class in his local school and could carry out many important tasks on his own. He did have some attention problems and needed help staying on task. He also had some trouble communicating with others but was making progress in this area.

Craig was not a problem at bedtime and would respond well to his parents' requests to go to sleep. The problem was that he would wake up most nights after having fallen asleep. During these times, he would get out of bed, turn on lights, play with toys, watch television, fix himself a snack, or get into bed with his parents. His parents described to us that Craig had night waking problems since birth, and that it was a constant concern for them. They worried that he was not getting enough sleep and that this might cause him to have more difficulty learning in school.

During our assessment of Craig's sleep problem, we discovered that his bedtime was highly variable: sometimes being put to bed before 8 p.m. and other times after 11 p.m. We also questioned his parents about how they responded to his nightly sojourns. They reluctantly reported that they were quite inconsistent in how they handled his waking. Sometimes his parents would ignore him (because they were so tired), and this resulted in him eventually either going back to bed or getting in bed with them. On other nights, they would get up and tell him to go back to bed, which typically resulted in his going back to sleep without trouble. They thought he might be getting up because he was hungry (because he often made himself a snack at these times) and were somewhat reluctant to prevent him from eating at night.

Craig's case describes a child who would be characterized by sleep professionals as having difficulty maintaining sleep. Bedtime posed a problem for neither him nor his parents, but several times each week he would wake up anywhere between 1:15 a.m. and 6 a.m. and stay up sometimes for more than an hour. One of the first things we look for in cases such as Craig's is total sleep time. In other words, is this child getting enough sleep? If the night waking lasts for 30 minutes or more, it can begin to cut down on the amount of sleep the child is receiving along with degrading the quality of his or her sleep. We also look to see if the child is napping during the day as a way to catch up on sleep, because this can aggravate the sleep problem by increasing the likelihood that the child will have trouble sleeping through the night. To determine if the child is getting sufficient sleep, we refer to Figure 1.1 in Chapter 1 to determine what is typical for a child of that age, bearing in mind that there is a range of sleep needs at any age. A second factor that helps determine if the child is getting enough sleep is daytime behavior. Does the child seem tired? Is the child irritable or cranky, and does he or she have trouble concentrating or have a low threshold for demands? All of these reactions can be signs of insufficient sleep. In Craig's case he was sleeping within the range of a child his age (about 9 hours, which is within the normal range for a child who is 11 years old), but he often seemed cranky (which sometimes included him hitting his teacher at school) during the day, and he usually had trouble concentrating on school work. Either of these behaviors could be irrelevant to his sleep problem, but it was worth checking to see if they improved along with his sleep. Craig did not nap during the day, so this was not of concern. Later in this chapter, we will describe our efforts to help children who have night waking and who nap during the day.

Once our assessment was complete, Craig's parents were instructed in how to establish a stable bedtime along with a routine leading up to bedtime (see Chapter 6). Ten p.m. was selected as Craig's bedtime because it was the time his parents observed that he seemed tired. This bedtime would still allow him to sleep about 9 ½ hours per night, which was judged to be sufficient for him. At his parent's suggestion, he was given a light snack approximately 1 hour before he was to go to sleep because he seemed hungry when he got up at night. The snack also let his parents feel less guilty when they had to make him go right back to sleep after an awakening.

In addition to the changes around bedtime, we helped Craig's parents design a modification of a graduated extinction plan (see Chapter 7) to help them respond when he got up at night. Whenever they heard him get up at night, his father would lead him to his room and say, "It's still time to sleep, go back to bed." Physical contact and any other conversation was to be kept to a minimum. Fortunately, this only had to occur once each night because Craig would go back to bed without difficulty and fall back to sleep. The results were quick and dramatic. Within the first week of the plan, Craig went from an average of about 3 nights each week with night waking to only 1 night with waking a week. This progress continued, and some weeks he would not have an instance of night waking; on nights when he did awaken, his parents could simply call out to him to go back to bed.

Along with the improvements in Craig's sleep, his behavior at school appeared to improve as well. Instances of hitting other people or of tantrums still occurred on occasion, but they were noticeably less frequent once he was sleeping through the night. In fact, his teachers noticed the improvement in his behavior at school even before they knew about how his sleep had improved at night, which suggested to us that his behavior must have changed considerably. Both of his parents were pleased at the improvement in Craig's sleep and with his daytime behavior, and they were astounded at how easy it had been to get him to sleep through the night.

Craig's case was a bit unusual because of the ease with which he responded to his parents' plan after such a long history of sleep problems. In some ways, however, his case was similar to a number of ones we see each day. Often parents have a good idea about what they should be doing with regard to their child's sleep but feel guilty about being too strict or appearing uncaring to their child. Often our role is to give them "permission" to go ahead and be firm about bedtime or sleep. In Craig's case, his parents would do the right thing on some nights, but other times they would feel bad for him and let him come into their bed. Letting him get up and go into their bed was probably contributing to his nightly awakenings, so when they stopped allowing it (along with a number of other changes), that was sufficient enough to significantly reduce the number of nights with waking.

Sleep Restriction for Nondisruptive Waking

In Craig's case, his awakening was obvious to his parents. He appeared to immediately come out of his room after he woke up at night, and even if he did not go into their room, they could hear him walking around in the house. Other children, however, will wake up at some point at night but not cry out, come out of their room, or in any way signal that they are awake. Some of the children we have worked with describe just being up, looking around the room, thinking about school, and so forth. For other individuals who cannot talk to us and tell us about their disturbed sleep, they have often been found lying in bed awake, and these accidental discoveries have led to sleep problem referrals. In cases such as these, using the plan that we described for Craig (a version of graduated extinction where the parents send the child back to bed and then ignore any protests for a period of time) would not be effective because parents do not know when their child is awake. Under these circumstances, we often use a plan known as *sleep restriction* to help children sleep through the night.[2]

At first glance, sleep restriction may seem counterintuitive as a way to help children sleep better. It involves restricting the amount of time a child is in bed to the total amount of time the child seems to sleep. In other words, instead of putting a child to bed earlier you may want to keep him or her up later. This procedure makes sense if you think about how you sleep after being kept up for several days. I remember a time when my son was young, and he was having frequent night wakings as well as waking up at 5 a.m. for the day. All week long my wife and I got an average of about 4 hours of sleep each night. Fortunately, we had a babysitter for that weekend, and we were able to get away for 2 nights. I remember the morning after our first night away from home, waking up close to noon and feeling as if I had slept forever. Being so sleep deprived caused us to "catch up" on some of this sleep and helped us sleep soundly. In much the same way, sleep restriction helps the child begin a pattern of sleeping through the night. Being truly tired may help the child sleep more soundly and without interruption.

Designing a sleep restriction plan first requires that you know how long your child actually sleeps each evening. The sleep diary (see Chapter 3) can be useful here. Looking at the amount of sleep time across a 2-week period can give you an "average" night—say, 8 hours. It is important that you estimate how much time your child actually sleeps as opposed to the time spent in bed. If your child takes a while to fall asleep each night, subtract that time from the sleep time. Also, subtract any time your child spends up in bed in the middle of the night during a period of awakening. For some children who do not create a problem during this time, it may be difficult to get an exact estimate of this time, so you may need to take an educated guess. The overall goal is to find out how long your child is actually sleeping each night.

Once you have an idea about how long your child sleeps each night, what you want to do is set up a schedule so that he or she will sleep somewhat less. Remember, the idea behind sleep restriction is to make the time in bed really count, so that the person sleeps soundly through the night. In this spirit, we take the number of hours the child is sleeping—say, 8 hours—and set up a schedule that restricts sleep to about 90% of that number. We use 90% of the total amount of sleep time to allow for times when the child may be awake but not reported or not known by the parents. Multiplying the number of hours asleep (8) by 0.9 will give you the new total sleep time to strive for (8 x .9 = 7.2 hours). Then you adjust either bedtime or wake time so that your child now only sleeps for the new number of hours. Shifting to a later bedtime (from 10 p.m. to 11 p.m.) or waking your child up earlier (from 7:30 a.m. to 6:30 a.m.) will create the new sleep time.

It is recommended that, if you can handle it, you adjust the schedule by waking your child up earlier in the morning. Using bedtime to adjust the schedule may work just as well, but once you try to move the bedtime to an earlier hour, you may run into some difficulty. Recall that, because of the way our biological clock works, it is always easier to stay up later than it is to fall asleep earlier. In this case, it is usually easier to let the child sleep later in the morning as you try to fade back to the previous schedule than it is to try to get the child to fall asleep earlier.

There may be times when your child is found lying in bed awake, even with this new schedule. If that ever happens, and you feel that your child is wide awake, have him or her leave the bed and do something quietly for 15–30 minutes. As I have mentioned a number of times before, we do not want the child to associate the bed with anything other than sleeping. If he or she spends too much time awake in bed—and possibly worried, thinking about school, or even thinking about not sleeping—this will interfere with your efforts to help him or her to sleep.

If your child goes for at least a week without waking in the middle of the night with this new schedule, you can begin to slowly move toward the previous sleep schedule by about 15 minutes each week. The following is a summary description of how to design and implement a sleep restriction plan.

Sleep Restriction

- Use the sleep diary to estimate the number of hours that your child sleeps, on average, each day (for example, 8 hours). Exclude any time that your child is in bed but is awake.

- Next, take the average number of hours actually asleep each night and multiply that number by 0.9 to get 90% of the time or the number of hours your child should be sleeping with this new schedule. For example, if your child is sleeping 8 hours total, 90% (8 hours x 0.9 = 7.2 hours) of that would be a little more than 7 hours. *Do not go below about 4 ½ hours when selecting a new sleep schedule.*

- Adjust your child's bedtime (e.g., from 10 p.m. to 11 p.m.) or the time your child is awakened in the morning (e.g., from 7:30 a.m. to 6:30 a.m.) to approximate the new schedule (going from 8 to 7 hours of sleep).

- If bedtime is a problem, refer to Chapter 7 and work on this sleep problem before you begin a sleep restriction plan.

- If you find your child lying in bed and apparently wide awake, have him or her leave the bed and engage in some soothing activity until he or she appears sleepy. Then return him or her to bed.

- If night waking is eliminated or significantly diminished for 1 week, you can readjust the bedtime or waking schedule by 15 minutes. This can be adjusted once per each successful week until the desired schedule has been reached.

To illustrate how we have implemented sleep restriction for a person who did not sleep through the night, we present the following case of an adult with whom we had some success.

✩ JULIE

Julie was a 55-year-old woman who lived in a group home for people with intellectual disabilities. Julie had serious daytime behavior problems such as hitting her own head with her fist, biting her hand, screaming, and hitting other people. Despite these behavioral concerns, Julie was well liked by the staff at the group home as well as her peers. She had a beautiful voice and took every opportunity to sing with groups. At times, she could be very helpful, assisting some of her housemates with bed making and cleaning up after meals.

Staff members were concerned for Julie because they often found her lying in bed awake in the middle of the night. Although she rarely got out of bed when she awoke and she did not cry or seem upset, the staff noticed that, on nights when she seemed to be up, the next day she would have more problems at work and at home. She did not appear tired at these times, but rather, she seemed very agitated and active. The group home staff were requesting help to see if they could get her to sleep better at night.

One of the first things we noticed in our assessment of Julie's sleep was her early bedtime. She was put to bed at 8 p.m. like all of the other residents in the house. The others seemed to fall asleep quickly at this time, and they appeared to sleep through the night. Julie, on the other hand, would lie in bed until 11 p.m. or 12 a.m. Again, she did not seem upset during this time, but it was clear that she was not tired. On a typical night, she would fall asleep by midnight but would awaken again somewhere between 1:30 a.m. and 3:30 a.m. and would remain awake, often until the morning. There were days that the staff let her nap in the afternoon because she seemed so tired.

One of the first recommendations was to eliminate the daytime naps, which could have obviously been interfering with her sleep. Looking at the total amount of time she slept, it seemed to average about 5½ hours per day; it was not a great deal of time, but given that she was 55 years old, it was close to the 6-hour average for someone about that age.

Using the sleep restriction formula (5.5 hours of current total sleep time x 0.9 = 4.95 hours for the new schedule), we came up with a goal of about 5 hours of sleep to start.

After eliminating the daytime naps, the next change involved bedtime, which we suggested they move to a more reasonable one (11 p.m.). The early bedtime seemed to be more of a convenience for staff than any realistic estimate of when Julie was tired, and a later bedtime would help with having Julie tired at bedtime. We then asked that they wake her at 4 a.m. each morning, which without her naps, would give her 5 hours of sleep. On the first day of the plan, Julie slept very little. She fell asleep within a reasonable amount of time (around 11:15 p.m.), but she awoke at about 2:30 a.m. and stayed up all night. The staff had her get out of bed several times so that she was not lying in bed awake all night, but this seemed to have no effect. On the day following this first night, Julie had significant behavior problems, and the staff became quite discouraged. We tried to reassure them that this was not unusual and that Julie would probably do better within a few days—if they could survive!

On the second night, Julie was exhausted and fell asleep within minutes of her bedtime. In fact, the staff had their hands full trying to keep her up until 11 p.m. That night she slept through until 4 a.m., when they woke her up. The next day her behavior was much improved. Each night thereafter, Julie had little trouble falling asleep, and with the exception of one brief waking, she slept through the night. After about a week of success with this schedule, we adjusted her morning waking from the 4 a.m. we first recommended to 4:15 a.m. After a second week, it was moved to 4:30 a.m., and then to 5 a.m. (staff were feeling quite confident at this point, so they adjusted her schedule by 30 minutes instead of the usual 15 minutes). With her 11 p.m. bedtime and a 5 a.m. awakening, this gave Julie 6 hours of fully restful sleep, which exceeded the sleep she had previously had, even if you count her daytime naps. This seemed to be a good schedule for everyone, so the staff agreed to stick to it. They also noted that Julie's behavior during the day was significantly improved, which they attributed to her improved sleep.

Julie's case was typical in one respect—we had to provide quite a bit of encouragement in the early stages to keep people motivated. Sometimes the plans we design can, at first, seem to make the situation worse, whether it is with a sleep restriction plan, where the person has a night or two where he or she may sleep very little, or with other plans such as graduated extinction, where behavior problems may escalate. It is important during these early stages to keep your goal in mind and to remain confident that, within a few nights, you will see progress.

Dangerous Behavior at Night

For some families, having a child up in the middle of the night without supervision is of great concern. These children may not cry and scream and awaken the family. In fact, parents sometimes would prefer if they did so they would know these children were up. Instead, the children quietly get out of bed and get into trouble. Some children will break toys, televisions, or computers if they are not closely monitored. For example, one boy with whom we worked was able to completely disassemble the computer in his mother's home office while his parents slept just one room away. The concern can also reach beyond family possessions. Often we are asked to design plans for children who engage in dangerous activities in the middle of the night. A mother whose young son had ASD told us of one night when her son left the house. He made his way down the block and into the home of a neighbor. Not knowing who this boy was, the neighbor called the police—who fortunately were familiar with him—and they brought him home. His mother told us she was both humiliated (because she did not even know he was missing) and frightened that he might have been seriously hurt.

The main issue for these parents is being aware that their children are awake and out of bed. In fact, quite a number of parents have difficulty sleeping because of their anxiety over their child. They lie in bed worrying what will happen if tonight is the night their child gets up, they do not hear him or her, and something terrible happens. Some parents react by locking their child's bedroom door at night so he or she cannot get out. There is a risk in doing this, however, because should something happen where you need to leave the house quickly—as with a fire—you run the risk of losing very valuable time getting your child out. Others have installed Dutch or half doors, the bottom of which is locked. This type of door can keep young children in their rooms but also allows parents to hear or see in the bedroom. Other families have installed peep holes in their child's bedroom door so that they can monitor activity without opening the door. There are a number of alarm or monitoring systems that let you know if your child leaves the bed or the bedroom. Some parents use something as simple as a bell on the child's doorknob to alert them when their child leaves the room. Any of these approaches can be used to signal parents when a child leaves the room, which in turn can help them prevent difficulties at night.

If parents know when their child leaves the room, a graduated extinction procedure (described in Chapter 7 and in the next section) can be used. The case of Craig that we described at the beginning of this chapter provides a good illustration of the use of this technique. In addition, a plan called *scheduled awakening,* which we describe in the next section, can be successful if you know the time when your child is likely to awaken at night.

DISRUPTIVE NIGHT WAKING

Unfortunately, and more often than not, the children we see who wake during the night let their parents know quite clearly that they are up. In a personal example, my infant son would begin to whine and whimper usually at about 12:30 a.m. Within minutes, this fussing would develop into full blown crying and screaming, something extremely difficult to ignore. For the longest time, my wife and I felt guilty if we did not go into his room and check on him, even though we knew this probably was not the best thing to do. It was not until he was almost 2 years old that we mustered up the courage to try to ignore his night waking on a consistent basis. We used a graduated extinction procedure, a plan that has been successful for many parents, but one that is not without its limitations. Fortunately, three techniques are available for parents to help their children with disruptive night waking—graduated extinction, sleep restriction, and scheduled awakening—and we next describe each procedure as well as their strengths and weaknesses.

Graduated Extinction

In Chapter 7, I described how graduated extinction—which involves slowly increasing the time between visits to the child's bedroom during a tantrum—could be used to reduce problems at bedtime. This technique has also been a successful tool for parents to help their children with disruptive night waking. Just as you would wait to respond to crying at bedtime, graduated extinction for night waking would involve waiting for progressively longer periods of time before checking on the crying child in the middle of the night after an awakening. The next case describes the use of graduated extinction for the frequent night waking of one young girl. Important for this case, the mother's sleep was also disrupted by her daughter, and I describe our efforts to help her mother sleep better as well.

☆ MARNIE

Marnie was 5 years old when we first met her. Several years before, she had received a diagnosis of an intellectual disability. Her speech was delayed as were some of her other skills, although she was doing well in her first-grade class. Marnie's mother told us that the advertisement that we placed in the newspaper offering help to parents whose children had trouble sleeping seemed like an answer to her prayers. Her daughter's pediatrician seemed to have run out of any acceptable suggestions to help Marnie, who had never in her 5 years slept through the night. Marnie's mother did not want to use the medication her doctor had prescribed, although she had seriously considered it of late. Marnie's mother was at her wit's end because her daughter would awaken one, two, or sometimes even three times per night, each time crying out quite plaintively. Her mother had tried everything she could think of so they could both get a good night's sleep, but nothing seemed to help.

Our initial discussions and assessment of Marnie's sleep seemed to point to a rather unremarkable sleep–wake cycle. She usually slept from between 10 and 11 hours each night, which was typical for someone her age. Marnie usually did not nap during the day, and her mother as well as her first-grade teacher reported that she did not seem tired during the day. Her mother had established a good bedtime routine and was consistent with Marnie's bedtime and the time she was awakened in the morning. In other words, nothing was unusual about Marnie's sleep except for the night waking.

Marnie's mother told us that her daughter had never had a full night's sleep. As an infant, Marnie would awaken each evening, and her mother would feed her. This went on until Marnie was 2 years old, at which time her mother decided "enough was enough," and she stopped these nightly feedings. However, this change in feeding had no noticeable effect on sleep, and each night, Marnie's mother would continue get out of bed when Marnie cried, holding and comforting her in her bed.

The distress Marnie's mother experienced because of her daughter's sleep problems was obvious. Not only did Marnie not sleep through the night, but this meant her mother was also being awakened—each and every night for 5 years! Her mother felt she was less tolerant of Marnie and everyone else because of her own lack of sleep. She even believed that her divorce from Marnie's father was partly the result of Marnie's nightly crying and her own disrupted sleep. She was quite motivated to do anything it took to get her daughter to sleep through the night.

Based on a few discussions and the results from the assessments, we recommended that Marnie's mother implement a graduated extinction plan. Because the first step in the graduated extinction plan was to assess how long Marnie's mother could wait before responding to her daughter's crying, we were concerned that this might be a problem for her and that she might resist any plan that asked her to ignore Marnie when she was upset. However, her mother said she was committed to helping Marnie sleep through the night, and she was ready for anything. We agreed on a 5-minute wait period for the first night.

The first night of the plan, Marnie awoke at about 1 a.m. Her mother told us that waiting for 5 minutes the first time was not as difficult as she expected. She went into Marnie's room, told her to go back to bed, and left the room. However, waiting the second time was more difficult. Her mother told us that Marnie seemed stunned that her mother left the room without comforting her, and she pleaded with her to come back. Marnie's mother told us she got through these subsequent waiting periods by staring at her clock, counting down how many seconds were left until she could go back into her daughter's room. The second night, which we agreed would include a 7-minute wait period, somehow seemed easier. Her mother told us that Marnie's cries seemed less intense, and they were not occurring continuously. The third night with 9-minute wait periods was even better, and by the fourth night, Marnie awoke only once, cried for less than a minute and slept the rest of the night. A month after we began the plan, Marnie was sleeping through most nights, and on those now rare evenings when she awoke, she fell back to sleep within minutes.

Marnie's success was not followed by an improvement in her mother's sleep. Her mother recalled that, before Marnie was born, she slept fairly well and only rarely woke during the night. During her pregnancy with Marnie, she experienced disrupted sleep, which is common for women during this time. After Marnie's birth, she found that her sleep was interrupted only in part because of her daughter. In fact, she observed that she often awoke minutes before her daughter would wake up and did not know if she somehow was responding to noise her daughter was making or if she too now had a pattern of night waking.

Looking at Marnie's mother's sleep patterns, we noticed nothing unusual other than the night wakings. When her sleep did not improve in the weeks following Marnie's success, we recommended a sleep restriction plan. Basically, we recommended that she set her alarm to wake up about an hour earlier than her usual schedule, go to bed at her usual time, and leave her bed if she awoke and felt that she would not go back to sleep right away. After an inconsistent 2-week period where she sometimes slept through the night and other times was up for several hours, Marnie's mother's sleep was much improved. She faded the hour that she awoke over another 2-week period until she was sleeping through most nights on her usual schedule.

The combination of Marnie's improved sleep as well as her own had a noticeable effect on Marnie's mother. She looked rested and refreshed and told us she had renewed energy. She found that she was much more patient with her daughter's many needs and was pleased that she had more interest in a social life for herself. As one sign of her improvement, she told us she did something she had wanted to do for years, which was to sign up for a gourmet cooking class.

Marnie's case was gratifying for several reasons. First, we were able to help her mother design a plan that allowed Marnie to get a full night's sleep for the first time ever. Just as significant, however, were the changes that occurred in her mother's life. Having Marnie sleep through the night was very important to her. And, finally having a full night's sleep seemed like a luxury. She told us that she felt a sense of renewed optimism, both for herself as well as for her daughter, and that she was ready to move on with their lives. A seemingly small thing like a good night's sleep was just what this family needed.

That Marnie's mother had her own sleep disrupted is a common occurrence among other families as well. Also typical is the observation that, even when we are able to help a child sleep through the night, often the parents' sleep does not immediately return to normal. Sometimes there is a carry-over effect such that the parents have difficulty going back to a normal sleep–wake cycle. Fortunately, the techniques we describe in this book for people with special needs work just as well for people without special needs. If you find that your own sleep is disrupted, you can assess your sleep patterns through the assessment procedures described in Chapter 3 and begin a plan to correct any of these difficulties.

It may be worthwhile to repeat at this point that, if you are faced with a person who has both bedtime disruption problems and night waking problems, it may be best to begin with a plan for bedtime. Our research with children with both of these sleep problems points to the value of starting at bedtime, because it is often the case that success at bedtime leads to a resolution of night waking problems without any further assistance. In other words, if we are successful in helping children go to bed without disruption at bedtime, they often begin to sleep through the night without having to develop a new plan. Again, you may want to refer back to Chapter 7 if your child has both of these sleep difficulties.

I next outline the basic ingredients of a successful graduated extinction plan. The steps are essentially the same as those used with graduated extinction for bedtime problems, which I outlined in detail in Chapter 7.

Graduated Extinction

- Determine how long you are able to wait before checking on your child.

- Pick the night to begin the plan, assuming no one will have a good night's sleep that evening—most people begin on a Friday night.

- *On the first night*—if your child awakens, wait the agreed-on time (e.g., 3 minutes). If after 3 minutes your child is still crying, go into the room (do not pick up your child, do not give him or her food or a drink, and do not engage in extensive conversation), tell him or her to go to bed, and then leave. Wait another 3 minutes and then go back into the room if your child is still crying. Continue the pattern until your child is asleep.

- *On subsequent nights*—extend the time between visits by 2 or 3 minutes. Continue the same procedure when entering the room.

As you can see, the only difference between using graduated extinction for bedtime problems, and using this plan for night waking is that you wait for your child to cry out at night and wait the prescribed time before checking on him or her. If this plan is not right for you, you can use several other techniques designed to help with disrupted night waking, which I describe next.

Sleep Restriction for Disruptive Waking

As I alluded to previously in the section on wakings that are not accompanied by disruptive behavior, you can use sleep restriction (similar to *bedtime fading* described in Chapter 7) to help reduce or hopefully eliminate the more disruptive wakings displayed by some children. Sleep restriction (and another technique known as *scheduled awakening,* which I describe later) is particularly valuable for those children who engage in very disruptive behavior when they awaken. Its value comes from the ability to help your child sleep through the night while at the same time avoiding many of the disruptive behaviors you would experience with graduated extinction. I next describe a child who had very disruptive night waking and how her mother intervened to reduce these nighttime problems. The procedures for using sleep restriction—which formed the basis for the plan—were described in the earlier section on nondisruptive night waking.

☆ SHONTELL

Shontell, a 4-year-old and very active little girl with ASD, first came to our attention through her school. She was attending a preschool program for children with developmental disabilities, and her teachers were concerned that Shontell seemed extremely tired every day. In fact, she was so tired that the staff had a difficult time keeping her awake at school. In a previous placement, they were not successful at all, and Shontell basically slept through most of the school day in the corner of her classroom. Her current program was more successful in keeping her awake most of the time, but doing so required a great deal of effort, and both her mother and the school program were looking for some relief. Her teachers noted that Shontell was extremely disruptive in school, especially on days when she was obviously tired and when they tried to keep her from falling asleep.

Shontell's home sleep schedule was particularly disturbed. She would nap for about 2 hours during the late afternoon, which her mother permitted because Shontell was clearly exhausted when she got home. The evening was usually uneventful, and her mother had a bedtime routine for all three of her children. Each night at about 11 p.m., after getting all of the children ready for sleep, she and the children would get into the one bed in their small apartment. Bedtime was so late because Shontell's mother served dinner at around 9 p.m. and needed time to get homework and other chores with her children completed. Shontell's mother also told us that her other children did not seem tired either and that 11 p.m. seemed to work well for all of them except Shontell.

On a typical evening, the other children would fall asleep within about 15 minutes, but Shontell remained awake. At times, she would jump up and down on the bed and wake her siblings, so her mother would then move with

Shontell into the living room to watch television until Shontell fell asleep. On most nights, Shontell would not fall asleep until 3:30 a.m. During this time, her mother had to remain awake for fear of what Shontell might do. One night, for example, her mother fell asleep in front of the television while Shontell was awake. Shontell went to the kitchen table, got a bottle of Pepsi, and poured it over her mother's head, presumably to wake her up!

Once Shontell fell asleep, she often awoke again. When she woke up at night, she would sometimes cry and scream, waking everyone else. Other times she would get out of bed and break toys, get into the refrigerator, or pull things off the shelves. Shontell's mother was quite depressed and at a loss about to how to handle her daughter.

Shontell's situation posed a number of challenges. Because the family lived in an apartment, it would be difficult to design any plan that involved having Shontell cry and scream for any length of time. Also, because there was only one bed for the whole family, any such disruption disturbed the sleep of everyone. It was also going to be difficult for her mother to give up the afternoon naps. When Shontell slept after school, this was literally the only time during the day when her mother could focus her attention on her other children. We posed the dilemma to her mother, basically offering a choice between a short period of time with increased disruption at night if she chooses to go with a graduated extinction program or a plan that would take a longer time and be less disruptive at night but involve decreasing naps during the day. Her mother chose the latter option, which would involve fading into a sleep restriction program.

Basically, the plan involved looking at the total amount of time Shontell slept in a typical day, including all naps. Her mother was surprised to see that her daughter actually slept for almost 10 hours each day, although there were days she slept for only about 4 hours and others where she slept 12 or more. We decided to try to achieve the goal of 9 hours (90% of her typical sleep time) by reducing nap time. We hoped that this would at first eliminate the problem of night waking and then allow us to move her bedtime from 3:30 a.m. to something more manageable.

On the first day of the plan, her mother woke her up early from her afternoon nap just as we had planned. Again, the goal was to reduce the time she slept during the day and restrict sleep to only at night in bed. Her mother told us that Shontell was cranky that night and never fell asleep, remaining awake all night. The next day at school was a disaster! Her teacher told us that Shontell spent the day crying and hitting everyone in school. To everyone's credit, however, despite the problem-filled day, everyone was still committed to making the plan work. On subsequent days, Shontell's mother continued to wake her about 30 minutes early from her nap, and Shontell began to fall asleep earlier at night. After the first week, her mother reported that Shontell had no night waking episodes and that she was falling asleep at about 2:30 a.m., an hour earlier than usual. The plan then called for decreasing nap time by 30 minutes for each subsequent successful week—defined as no night wakings and an improvement in her bedtime.

The weekend brought one more obstacle. Her mother reminded us that on Sundays she would take Shontell and her other children to her church in the afternoon for several hours. Typically, Shontell would sleep during this time because it was during her usual nap time. Her mother was obviously concerned about this. What if she did not let Shontell sleep and she disrupted services? Her mother did not want to give up one of the few things in her life that provided her with comfort—the community of friends and neighbors who gathered together each week to pray. In discussing the problem together, we decided to try to keep Shontell awake and provide her with some activity that would occupy her time. Shontell's mother did not feel that she could keep her awake, especially during the relatively quiet services that seemed to trigger Shontell's sleep. We suggested that Shontell's mother may want to give her something that contained caffeine right before services as a way to keep her awake. Armed with a favorite doll and a can of Coke, her mother was ready to tackle church services. Fortunately, the services went well. The other members were very helpful and forgiving for any brief disruptions, and Shontell spent most of the time quietly playing on the floor.

As the weeks passed, Shontell's sleep continued to improve. She rarely had a night waking anymore, and her bedtime progressed to about the 11 p.m. time that the rest of the family used. Her teachers reported that she seemed rested when she came to school on most days and that she was much easier to work with, especially compared to before her sleep had improved. Shontell's sleep occasionally was disrupted (for example, if she was allowed to nap on days she seemed tired), but her mother knew how to recover from these episodes—by reinstituting the plan—and now felt that she had control over this once vexing problem.

Shontell's case provided us with a number of challenges that seem to characterize our work with most children with special needs. Often we cannot use the most time-efficient techniques we have to offer because of practical considerations. Shontell, for example, might have had significantly improved sleep and a better bedtime within a few nights if we had used a graduated extinction program. However, as I pointed out, the noise and disruption that this would have caused would have been intolerable for Shontell's family and neighbors. We also have to consider the needs of parents in these cases as well. Shontell's mother needed some time to get used to the idea of not having that quiet time when her daughter would nap, so instead of recommending that she eliminate naps altogether, we designed a fading plan that would let both Shontell and her mother adjust to the new schedule. Again, this delayed the improvements in Shontell's sleep but seemed worth the time to her mother. Finally, attending church services was a potential major obstacle to the plan but was also a priority for her mother, so it required that we adjust our procedures accordingly. The success of this case should serve as note of optimism to parents in similar situations. The techniques to improve sleep that we are describing in this book appear to be quite robust—meaning that they can be modified significantly and yet yield important results. I believe that, as long as you follow the basic logic of these plans, you can change them to fit most individual needs and still expect to have some success.

Scheduled Awakening

An additional technique that has been demonstrated now through a number of studies to help with night waking is called *scheduled awakening*.[3] Scheduled awakening takes a slightly different approach to dealing with nightly waking, one that may seem odd to you at first. This plan actually involves waking your child in the period before he or she usually awakens. You gently touch or shake your child to the point where he or she seems to awaken and then you let him or her fall back to sleep. This simple technique is often successful in completely eliminating night wakings—sometimes from the first night on.

One of the keys to the success of this plan is the regularity of the night wakings. In other words, your child must have fairly predictable times when he or she awakens (for example, 12:30 a.m.) so you know when to awaken him or her. Fortunately, most children who wake during the night follow a fairly regular pattern. This regularity comes from the unvarying rhythms the brain follows in the different sleep stages we described in Chapter 1. If in the unlikely event that you find that your child awakens at very different times each night (for example, midnight on one night, 2 a.m. on a second night, 12:30 a.m. on a third), you should probably try a sleep restriction plan first. Again, using the sleep diary to uncover the patterns of waking is usually the first step to the success of this approach. Once this waking time—or times, in the case of children with multiple wakings—is determined, then you will want to awaken your child about 30 minutes prior to this time. That means, if your child typically awakens at 1 a.m., you would plan to awaken your child at 12:30 a.m.

It is important, however, that you be ready to experiment with this waking time. There is no way to pick the "perfect" time to awaken your child based simply on your observing of night wakings. Sometimes 30 minutes may be too soon for it to work. How do you know if you have picked the wrong time? One way to tell is to observe how your child reacts to being awakened. In our experience, this type of plan seems to work best when the child does not awaken fully from sleep but only opens his or her eyes briefly and then immediately goes back to sleep. If you find, however, that when you awaken your child, he or she wakes up fully and does not go back to sleep, this may signal that you have picked the wrong time. In the case where your child awakens fully, move up your scheduled awakening time by 15 minutes for the next episode. If you had picked a 12:30 a.m. awakening and your child wakes up fully, the next night try 12:15 a.m. Play with the time in this way until you discover the right time to wake your child.

Just as with sleep restriction, scheduled awakening is an "errorless" procedure because it can reduce or eliminate night waking without going through disturbing or dangerous tantrums. Even on the first night that you awaken your child, you will probably find that he or she will not wake up again at his or her usual time. This is especially valuable for those families who cannot afford to have their child be so disruptive at night.

There are, as we have seen before, always trade-offs for the advantages of any particular program. In the case of scheduled awakening, one of the biggest disadvantages reported by parents is the necessity to wake themselves up in the early morning hours for their child's waking. It is obviously not a pleasant experience to be awakened by an alarm clock only an hour or so after you have fallen asleep. This may be the time when you are in a deep stage of sleep, and it may be extremely difficult to get out of bed to follow this plan. Even though the child may not be waking, the parent still needs to get up and carry out the scheduled waking. As I have mentioned before, for some of you, avoiding the disruptive night waking is worth this temporary inconvenience, and I next describe a family for whom this approach was successful.

⭐ EDDIE

Eddie was 7 years old when we first had contact with him and his family. Sometime before, he had been given the diagnosis of ADHD because of his problems with attention, his impulsiveness, and his high energy level. He was a very likeable kid, and some years of help from a therapist had proven successful in reducing some of his daytime problems, both at school and at home.

His sleep was, however, still of concern to his parents. For the most part, he would fall asleep at night with little difficulty but several nights each week would awaken in the middle of the night. Usually the night waking would be signaled by his desire to get in bed with his parents. When he was younger, he had been allowed to get into their bed whenever he woke up, but his parents had decided more than a year before that he was old enough to go back to his own bed. On a typical night, Eddie would wake up, get out of his bed, and knock on his parents' bedroom door. If they tried to ignore him, he would only knock louder. When they told him to go back to bed, he would become very upset. Eddie would cry, sometimes saying that he had a nightmare, other times saying he felt sick. His parents reported that, about half of the time, they did not give in, they refused to let him come into their bed, and he would cry and carry on for more than an hour. The other half of the time, they refused his request, and he would work himself up so much that he would get sick. Then they would have to get out of bed to help him clean up.

On most nights when he awoke, Eddie's parents let him come into bed because they could not stand these disruptions during the late evening hours. Both of his parents worked and had to be up early and dreaded the prospect of his outbursts disturbing their sleep. Recently, even these relatively uneventful episodes when they let him into their bed were upsetting them. On the one hand, they worried that he could never be separated from them at night if, for example, a friend invited him to sleep over. Because of the problems that came along with Eddie's ADHD, making friends was already difficult, and they wanted him to have every possible chance to socialize with kids his age. On the other hand, they also wanted their privacy. As Eddie was getting bigger, there was not as much room in the bed when he was there. It seemed to be time to try something to help him sleep through the night.

During our assessment discussions, it seemed as if Eddie's problem was a combination of night waking plus his tendency to escalate disruption to the point where his parents would give in to his demand to join them in bed. A graduated extinction plan did not seem feasible to Eddie's parents because they thought they would not be able to ignore his crying, especially if he made himself sick. They also worried that he might feel abandoned if they did this and were concerned that it might have a permanent effect on their relationship with him. Of the two plans that would avoid disruption (sleep restriction and scheduled awakening), his parents seemed to prefer scheduled awakening. Eddie's night waking typically occurred at about midnight, some 2 ½ hours after his 9:30 p.m. bedtime but at a time when at least one of his parents was still awake. Therefore, getting up and waking him at about 11:30 p.m. did not seem too difficult for them.

Eddie's parents began the scheduled awakening plan on the next Friday night, just in case things did not go well and they had to deal with his tantrum. His father went into his room at 11:30 p.m., and Eddie woke up even before his father got near the bed. His father stayed in the bedroom for about 30 minutes until Eddie fell back to sleep. That night Eddie did not wake up again until morning. On the second night, Eddie's father went into his room earlier (at 11:15 p.m.), and this time Eddie was fast asleep. We moved the time back because it was clear that Eddie was in a very light sleep at 11:30 p.m. His father touched his shoulder, called his son's name, and Eddie mumbled something, rolled over, and went back to sleep. Each night that week one of his parents would gently wake him at 11:15 p.m. and on none of the nights did Eddie wake up again.

For the second week of the plan, we told his parents to pick 1 night to "skip." We wanted to begin to test if Eddie could sleep through the night without all the scheduled awakenings. Unfortunately, on the night they did not wake him, Eddie awoke on his own and came to his parents' bedroom. Because it was less disruptive than fighting over his coming into their bed, his father led him back to his own room and stayed there until Eddie fell asleep. The next day at dinner time, they all discussed that he was getting too big to sleep in their bed and that a married couple needed to sleep alone together. He did not seem to fully understand why he had to sleep alone and they did not, but his parents felt it was a mature discussion that would probably be continued for some time to come.

Because the skipped night led to an awakening, we recommended that they go for 2 more weeks waking him each night, and then they could try skipping a night again. Fortunately, the second time they skipped an awakening, he slept through the night anyway. In the following weeks, we scheduled for them to skip one more night for each good week (no waking). Over several months, there were a few lapses when he woke up (once even after a scheduled awakening), but the pattern of success was established, and his parents were confident that they could continue to fade the wakings on their own. Six months after they first began the plan, they had stopped all of the scheduled awakenings, and despite a few night wakings, they were pleased with Eddie's sleep.

Why did scheduled awakening work to eliminate Eddie's night waking? Unfortunately, despite the fact that there are now a number of studies that demonstrate the success of this technique in reducing night waking, we still do not understand why it works. Some believe that the scheduled awakenings somehow interrupt a disrupted sleep–wake cycle and "kick-start" a new and better cycle. Another view is that, by waking a child when he or she is in one of the deeper stages of sleep and then letting him or her go back to sleep alone, you are giving the child practice in learning to fall back to sleep without someone else present. Learning to fall asleep alone when awakened from a deep sleep may carry over to times when the child awakens during a light sleep stage, such as in a partial waking. Perhaps researchers will soon find the clue to the success of scheduled awakenings in eliminating night waking.

A general summary of the steps to a successful scheduled awakening plan follows. Remember, however, that you may need to experiment with the scheduled waking time to find a point in the evening before a waking that seems to catch the child in a deep sleep.

Scheduled Awakening

- Use the sleep diary (see Chapter 3) to determine the time or times that your child typically awakens during the night.

- On the night you are to begin the plan, awaken your child approximately 30 minutes prior to the typical awakening time. For example, if your child usually has a night waking at 12:30 a.m., wake up your child at 12 a.m. If your child seems to awaken very easily, move up the time 15 minutes the next night and on all subsequent nights (11:45 p.m.).

- If there is a broad range in the times your child awakens (for example, from 12 a.m. to 1:30 a.m.), awaken your child about 30 minutes prior to the earliest time (in this case, 11:30 p.m.).

- Do not fully awaken your child. Gently touch and/or talk to your child until he or she opens his or her eyes, then let him or her fall back to sleep.

- Repeat this plan each night until your child goes for a full 7 nights without a waking. If your child has achieved this level of success, skip 1 night (that is, no scheduled waking) a week. If your child has awakenings, go back to every night. Slowly reduce the number of nights with scheduled wakings until your child is no longer waking during the night.

The three approaches to reducing night waking that we have described—graduated extinction, sleep restriction, and scheduled awakening—all have their own advantages and disadvantages. When trying to decide among them, it is important to consider what each plan entails for the family and, therefore, which one has the greatest likelihood of success. This is the time when you get to be selfish. Pick which one is best for *you*. You will need to carry the plan out night after night, so pick one that fits your own needs best. Obviously, if you cannot carry out the plan, it will not work, so take some time to consider what is right for you. Table 8.1 is a partial list of the pluses and minuses of each plan. Good luck!

Table 8.1.   Graduated extinction, sleep restriction, and scheduled awakening

Graduated extinction

Pluses	Minuses
Can be used at the regular bedtime rather than having to wait until late at night	Requires listening to your child's cries, which can be difficult for many families
Can check on the child for reassurance	Can result in an increase in behavior problems
Improvements usually seen within the first week	Some behaviors such as injurious ones cannot be ignored

Sleep restriction

Pluses	Minuses
Can often be "errorless" with no increase in behavior problems	Requires someone remaining up late at night or waking early in the morning
Often avoids long bouts of crying	Can take several weeks before the desired bedtime is reached

Scheduled awakening

Pluses	Minuses
Can often be "errorless" with no increase in behavior problems	Requires someone remaining up late at night
Improvements can often be observed in the first night	Requires regular and predictable waking
Often avoids long bouts of crying	Can take several weeks before the desired bedtime is reached

CONCLUSION

Keep in mind one of the "facts of life" about sleep problems. Even with the most successful plans, these problems can resurface. A bout of the flu, a weekend at a relative's house, flying across time zones, and even some particularly exciting event can cause a child who was sleeping through the night to again begin to have night wakings. The good news is that, if your plan worked before, it will likely work again—and sometimes even more quickly. Be prepared for some setbacks, and they will not make you feel discouraged. You have some good night's sleep ahead of you!

Sleeping at the Wrong Times

Humans, as a group, are meant to sleep at night and to be awake during the day. Unlike certain nocturnal animals such as owls that sleep during the daylight hours and are awake and mainly in search of food at night, we humans are designed to be active when the sun is up and to be asleep during the twilight hours. However, a handful of individuals do not fit this pattern. They may be wide awake at midnight and not feel the urge to sleep until 3 a.m. If they are forced to be up in the morning, they usually have difficulty concentrating and generally have trouble functioning until the afternoon. Although many of us have probably had the experience of having our sleep pattern be "off" for short periods of time, for some people, this is a daily (or nightly) occurrence. It is as if they are jet-lagged but without the advantage of a pleasant trip out of town. Their sleep–wake cycle has shifted from the typical phase to one where they stay awake longer and sleep later in the day than most people. We will discuss this phenomenon—known as *delayed sleep phase syndrome*—along with efforts to help these people adapt to their sleeping patterns.[1]

I discussed earlier a second group of people who also do not sleep at the times we typically expect—those whose biological clock runs on a *non-24-hour cycle*. It is important to note that people with profound visual loss or blindness are particularly vulnerable to this sleep disorder because they do not receive the usual cues about sleep and wakefulness from the light of the sun. Finally, a third group with sleep timing problems seems to have developed *poor sleeping habits*, including napping during the day, and therefore has trouble falling asleep at night and/or has difficulty waking in the morning. I next discuss all three of these types of sleep schedule problems and how the people who experience these difficulties may be helped.

DELAYED SLEEP PHASE SYNDROME

Early to bed and early to rise,
Makes a man healthy, wealthy, and wise.

Benjamin Franklin, *Poor Richard's Almanac*, 1757

We have a prejudice in our society against people whose sleep schedules favor late nights and late mornings. As Benjamin Franklin so succinctly put it, we view "early risers" as more ambitious and more motivated, as if they are more likely to accomplish important things if they focus their energies the first thing in the morning. In contrast, people who sleep late are considered to be slacking off or lazy.

Plough deep while sluggards sleep.

Benjamin Franklin, *Poor Richard's Almanac*, 1757

In fact, several famous and successful figures in history preferred late nights, including the inventor Thomas Edison and the ancient philosopher Socrates. For most of these individuals, a slight tendency to stay awake later and sleep later in the morning does not interfere with conducting a satisfying and productive life.

However, extreme *night owls,* those individuals who report not being tired at all until the early morning hours and who also tell us of being unable to wake up until the early afternoon, are fortunately a rare breed indeed. In contrast to people who have sleep cycles that are out of sync because they are not sleeping well at night, these people seem to sleep well during the early morning hours and also report feeling rested if allowed to follow their body's desire to sleep on this unusual schedule. It is as if their sleep schedule has been pushed back or *delayed,* although in all other respects, it is normal. Unfortunately, in comparison to the other sleep problems we have described, helping people with delayed sleep syndrome can sometimes be more challenging. However, before we examine some of the more complicated techniques used to assist these people, let us first look at the case of a young man for who we were able to help quite easily.

☆ PATRICK

Patrick was a young man who lived at home with his mother and who was beginning a new stage in his life with the hope of earning a modest living working in a local grocery store. He had an intellectual disability of unknown origin but worked hard. With the support of his mother, Patrick was able to graduate from high school and was just recently hired for a job. It was a worsening problem at his new workplace that first brought Patrick to our attention. His mother was concerned that his difficulty with sleep might result in his losing the job he so dearly loved.

Patrick's boss, who was the manager of the store, was extremely supportive of Patrick and went to great lengths to provide the help and guidance he needed to succeed. When Patrick first approached the manager for the job, he agreed to teach Patrick each one of the tasks he would need to complete, including bagging groceries, helping to carry packages to customers' cars, and putting price tags on cans. The manager was pleased at how well Patrick would follow instructions, and after a 2-week training period in the afternoons, he offered Patrick a full-time, 9-to-5 job.

Patrick's mother shared Patrick's elation at the news of his new job but also harbored grave doubts about his ability to hold down a full-time job. Her reservations had less to do with any inability he might have in carrying out the necessary tasks and more to do with her fear that he would not show up to work on time. All through school, and even before he entered school, Patrick had a great deal of difficulty waking up in the morning. When he was young, his mother had to literally drag him out of bed and into the shower, and even after his shower, it would take him several hours until he was fully awake. As he got older and his mother wanted him to learn more independence, she set up an elaborate alarm system that required him to get out of his bed to turn it off. In contrast, he would remain awake in the evening, past his mother's bedtime. Usually he would watch television in his room until he fell asleep, which his mother guessed was after 2 a.m. on most days. Because of his unusual sleep pattern, Patrick's mother was rightly concerned that he would not succeed at his new job.

During the first week of his full-time responsibilities, Patrick seemed to have new energy in the morning. His mother told us it was as if the anticipation of having a real job was enough to make him a little more alert in the morning, and she had less trouble getting him up and ready. Although he still looked tired in the morning, his excitement about working "revved" him up enough to get to work. However, after the first week, things seemed to go downhill. He went back to his old pattern of staying up late and being tired in the morning. Worse yet, Patrick's manager reported that he would find the young man asleep in the back of the store each morning. He felt as if Patrick was not serious about the job and felt let down, especially because he had been so flexible and accommodating. Patrick's mother was concerned that he was about to be fired.

When we discussed Patrick's sleep problem, it was clear that this was a longstanding concern. His mother told us that, when he did not have school or work and when he could sleep on his own schedule, he would usually sleep from about 3:30 a.m. until about noon. When he followed that schedule, he had no difficulty waking and seemed fully rested and happy that day. He did not have night wakings nor were there any other obvious problems with his sleep. It seemed pretty clear from this long-running pattern that Patrick had delayed sleep phase syndrome.

Although there were several options available to try to help Patrick change his sleep–wake cycle with an eye toward better matching his job, it was suggested that instead they try to have the job match his cycle. In other words, could he work from 1 p.m. until 9 p.m., a busy time for the store anyway, and maximize his peak time of alertness? When we suggested a shift change to the store manager, he was willing to give it a try for 2 weeks but warned that he could not monitor Patrick as closely during these times and that Patrick would have to demonstrate a greater degree of responsibility. Fortunately, this change in his work hours worked immediately. Patrick was allowed to follow his body's need for sleeping later in the sleep cycle and was awake and alert throughout his work shift. His boss was pleased with his performance after the first 2 weeks, and the last time we checked, he had been working there quite happily for 3 months. His mother was relieved about his job success and also about not having to drag him out of bed in the morning. It is important to note that Patrick was also pleased. He felt obvious pride in his accomplishments at work, and he also felt—for the first time—that he was not "lazy" because of his sleep pattern but, instead, could achieve a great deal.

For many people with delayed sleep phase syndrome, the easiest approach to intervention is to arrange their lives to fit their sleep needs. Changing from the day shift to the evening shift at a job, for example, can make all the difference in the world. In fact, this sleep problem can serve as an example to all of us about how to listen to our bodies when it comes to circadian rhythms. It can be very valuable to see what time of the day is best for *you* to do certain activities. For example, for those of us more on the "night owl" side of sleep—those who prefer to sleep later in the morning but remain awake later at night—arranging tasks that require heightened alertness in the later morning (about 10:30 a.m.) may result in the best performance. In contrast, for those people who tend to be *larks*—preferring earlier morning and early bedtimes—the optimal time may be several hours earlier (about 8 a.m.). In fact, if you feel particularly motivated, you could keep a diary of your own pattern of alertness to see what times of the day work best for you and then use these times for those tasks that require your best efforts. In Patrick's case, we were able to change his work schedule to meet his sleep needs and found that he could perform dramatically better on the job.

What is the difference between someone like Patrick, who has delayed sleep phase syndrome, and someone else who simply desires a later sleep schedule? In other words, can we distinguish between someone who simply likes to watch late-night television and, as a result, is tired the next day from someone who cannot control this sleep schedule? Fortunately, there are ways to tell these two different sleep patterns apart. Someone with delayed sleep phase syndrome, for example, will not be able to adjust this pattern. Even if there is a reason why the person may want to go to bed earlier, he or she cannot, even after trying for many weeks. On the other hand, someone with a desired late sleep phase (for example, the late-night television addict) can adjust the times if there is an incentive—such as going to bed earlier the night before an important meeting. Oftentimes, their weekend sleep schedule differs from their school- or work-week schedule, which is another sign that they have control over when they sleep. It may take several nights to readjust this schedule, but it can be done fairly easily. It is important to point out that telling the difference between the involuntary delayed sleep phase syndrome and the voluntary delayed sleep schedule is particularly important for a group of adolescents I will mention next—those with a problem known as *school refusal*.

Sleep and School Refusal

Some adolescents stay up late and sleep late to avoid school. Their "sleep problem" appears to be related to difficulties at school, a problem that was once known as *school phobia* but is now known by the more generic term *school refusal*. Unlike Patrick, whose sleep pattern was constant throughout his life, these individuals usually begin to have sleep difficulties after problems in school begin to develop. Unfortunately, it is very difficult to help these adolescents with their sleeping difficulties unless you simultaneously help them with their problems at school. Sometimes these students are depressed as a result of academic or social problems, and they learn to "sleep in" to temporarily avoid these problems. In fact, some of these students do not cooperate with attempts to change their sleep patterns because to do so would eliminate a way out of their difficulties during the day. If you suspect that your child is deliberately avoiding school by staying up late at night or cannot sleep because of problems with anxiety or depression, it is recommended that an outside evaluation by a school counselor or other professional be considered. You may also want to refer to Chapter 12, where we discuss problems with sleep that are related to anxiety or depression.

Let us return to the discussion of delayed sleep phase syndrome. What do you do for someone when you do not have control over his or her school or work schedule? Is it possible to change a long-established sleep pattern, one that may be seriously interfering with the way someone lives? Fortunately, there are several approaches to helping people who do not sleep in cycles that match our typical daily school or work schedules. The development of these techniques—which I discuss next—has come about as a result of the discovery of our biological clock and the way it work to help us sleep. Chapter 1 describes some of what we know about this timing device in our brains, but it may be helpful to repeat some of this newly discovered information about our biological clock at this point to help put the new sleep techniques into perspective.

You may recall that we described how, if people are kept away from cues about daytime and nighttime, such as in a cave, they tend to sleep in schedules somewhat longer than our 24-hour day. This suggests that our brain wants to awaken and sleep in cycles more like 25–27 hours per day. This is one of the reasons why it is relatively easy for us to stay awake an hour later than usual, but it is more difficult to fall asleep an hour earlier than our typical bedtime. What resets this clock so that we are in sync with nature's day and night? Remember that light plays an important role in the timing of our sleep. More specifically, the decreasing amount of light in the later afternoon and early evening triggers the pineal gland in our brain to release more of the natural hormone *melatonin*. Melatonin reaches the biological clock (in a small structure known as the *superchiasmatic nucleus*) and tells it that it is time to sleep. Our tendency to want to sleep and awaken on a 25- to 27-hour cycle is regulated by sunlight (as well as other daily cues such as regular meal times) and the release of melatonin.

Chronotherapy

This beginning information about our sleep cycles has led to the discovery of several techniques for helping people whose schedules do not fit those of the rest of society and for whom this is a problem. One of these techniques that relies on our natural tendency to want to sleep on a non-24-hour cycle is referred to as *chronotherapy*.[2] Chronotherapy essentially involves keeping the person awake later and later on successive nights, until he or she achieves the desired new sleep schedule. For example, if a child's typical delayed sleep cycle is from 2 a.m. until noon, then you would begin a chronotherapy routine by keeping the child up until 5 a.m. during the first night, then until 8 a.m. for the second night, and then continue to shift the schedule ahead by 3 hours each subsequent night. Eventually, the schedule will advance throughout the day until the desired sleep time (for example, 10 p.m.) is reached. Figure 9.1 illustrates a typical chronotherapy schedule for someone with a 2 a.m. bedtime who desires a 10 p.m. bedtime. The following are general guidelines for creating a chronotherapy plan.

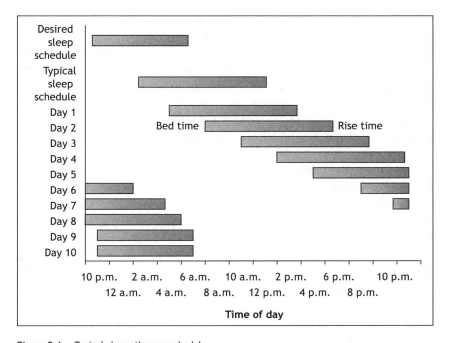

Figure 9.1. Typical chronotherapy schedule.

Chronotherapy

- Use the sleep diary (see Chapter 3) to identify the typical sleep–wake schedule for your child.

- On the night you are to begin the plan, keep your child awake approximately 3 hours after his or her typical bedtime. For example, if your child usually falls asleep at 1 a.m., keep your child up until 4 a.m.

- Do not allow your child to sleep at times other than the scheduled ones—that is, no naps.

- Each successive night, move bedtime ahead another 3 hours (for example, from 3 a.m. to 6 a.m.).

- Keep this schedule until your child's new bedtime approximates the desired bedtime (for example, 10 p.m.).

Unfortunately, what this plan offers in terms of its simplicity is usually offset by its lack of practicality. For most families, it would be extremely difficult if not impossible to adhere to this type of sleep schedule. The demands of school, work, and family would prohibit following a schedule that would, for a time, begin having the person remain awake at night and sleep during the day. For this reason, chronotherapy is not often recommended unless all other reasonable options have been tried and have failed. Even then, implementing such a plan might have to wait until an unstructured time such as a summer vacation to make it possible to begin such a strategy. Fortunately, there are other options for people who experience delayed sleep phase syndrome, which we describe next.

Bright Light Therapy   Where chronotherapy takes advantage of our non-24-hour biological clock, bright light therapy makes use of the brain's reliance on light to trigger this biological clock. Remember that decreasing light in the early evening seems to be responsible for the release of the brain hormone melatonin, which helps signal sleep. The increase in sunlight in the morning, in turn, appears to signal the decrease in production of melatonin that corresponds with our increasing alertness. Researchers have used the connection between light and sleep to develop a technique to help "jump start" the brain's sleep–wake cycle to better approximate the preferred schedule. *Bright light therapy* relies on banks of florescent light bulbs to provide a morning light boost, which for some people, helps to reset their bio-logical clock.

A typical bright light therapy plan involves having the person sit in front of a bank of lights for several hours after awaking. The lights must provide more light than is typical in a home or at school. *Light boxes* are now commercially available and usually include a series of lights. The person sits facing these lights and can work or carry on other activities at the same time. The use of these lights has helped some people regulate their sleep cycles toward ones that better match our sunrise and sundown awake and sleep preferences.

Sleep and Depression   One of the more interesting findings of recent years is the apparent interrelationship among sleep, light, and a form of depression known as *seasonal affective disorder* (SAD). I discuss sleep problems related to depression more fully in Chapter 12, but it should be pointed out here that bright light therapy is also used for people who get depressed in seasons when there is a decreased amount of light. The "winter blues" for some people can be quite debilitating, and using bright light therapy also seems to aide these individuals to bounce back from their depressive feelings.

People with delayed sleep phase syndrome can be helped with a combination of strategies, including lifestyle changes that better match their night owl preference. In addition, chronotherapy (delay-ing bedtime across the day to change their sleep pattern) and bright light therapy have proven helpful for some people whose schedules do not match the typical pattern. Several additional approaches, includ-ing the use of the hormone melatonin, have been used with this group as well as other individuals we describe next: those with non-24-hour sleep–wake cycles.

NON-24-HOUR SLEEP-WAKE CYCLES

We take for granted that we sleep and wake in cycles that correspond to the rising and setting of the sun. This type of sleep pattern has adap-tive significance—it was advantageous to the survival of our species to be awake at times when it was easiest to hunt or gather food. And it certainly makes our social and economic lives easier today that people are generally awake at similar times and feel tired and sleep at similar times. In fact, it is hard to imagine what life would be like if our sleep–wake cycle changed daily and did not necessarily correspond to those around us. This, unfortunately, is the dilemma that faces people who have *non-24-hour sleep–wake cycles*.[3]

The good news is that only a small percentage of people experience non-24-hour sleep–wake cycles, meaning that their sleep patterns are at odds with the day/night cycles most of us follow. A person with a 26-hour cycle would be sleepy at 11 p.m. on one night, would be tired at 1 a.m. on the second night, and on each successive night would fall asleep approximately 2 hours later. Although the good news is that this problem is relatively rare, the bad news is that it appears to disproportionately affect people with special needs. People with severe visual impairments and, in our experience, people with ASD appear to be at a greater risk for experiencing this sleep problem. Let us look at one person with a non-24-hour sleep–wake cycle that came to our attention.

☆ MARY

Acolleague called me one day because he was concerned about a student who had behavior problems that seemed to follow an unusual pattern. Sixteen-year-old Mary would go for days being the ideal student, being very cooperative and motivated in school. However, she would have other days where she would be very aggressive toward her teacher and sometimes to other students in her class. Mary had a severe visual impairment—so severe in fact that her doctor was not sure if she saw any light at all. Mary also had an intellectual disability, which resulted in her being very limited in her ability to communicate with others and caused her to need a great deal of help with most day-to-day activities.

Both Mary's mother and her teacher described her as going through frequent good and bad "cycles." Mary's mother told us that, in addition to these fluctuating times when she was aggressive, her sleep also seemed disrupted. During the "bad" times, Mary might not fall asleep until the early morning hours or even not at all, but then sleep at school. At these times, her teacher told us it was difficult to keep her awake in class and that Mary would lash out at others if she was awakened early. During the "good" times, Mary slept on a normal schedule and would be quite pleasant and alert in school.

We asked Mary's mother to keep a diary of Mary's sleep each night. Over about a 4-week period of time, a pattern seemed to emerge. It looked as if Mary's sleep was following a pretty regular schedule *for someone whose biological clock was not being reset each day.* In other words, Mary seemed to follow not the regular 24-hour cycle of sleep and wakefulness but an approximately 25-hour pattern. Each day she would be tired and ready for bed about an hour later than the day before. So when, on one Monday night, she fell asleep at about 9 p.m., on Tuesday it was about 10 p.m., on Wednesday it was close to 11 p.m., and by the next Monday, she was up most of the night and did not fall asleep until after 4 a.m.

Mary's typical but orderly sleep cycle was not immediately obvious to her mother or her teacher. Her sleep pattern may have been obscured because she was not allowed to follow her desired bedtime and awake time (which would have to change each day) but instead was "squeezed into" a cycle that resembled a typical one. Therefore, on days where she would have probably preferred to sleep in the late morning and afternoon, she was still required to be awake, at least part of the time. This is what led to her have periods of time when she was more irritable and aggressive.

The options for helping Mary with her sleep problem were more limited than for a person with delayed sleep phase syndrome. For one thing, it would be difficult to design a lifestyle change that could accommodate her ever-moving sleep cycles and still include educational opportunities. Secondly, bright light therapy was ruled out as an option because her visual impairment was such that the light would probably have not been processed in her brain. Chronotherapy was also not an option because her problem was a continuing delay in her sleep phase.

Given these limitations, it was recommended that several other approaches be tried at the same time. First, it was recommended that Mary's daily activities, such as meal times, be kept constant. In other words, Mary's parents were asked to try to keep to a specific schedule for when she ate, when she went out for a walk, when she bathed, and so forth. Second, Mary's parents wanted to try giving her a daily dose of melatonin because of the potential for helping her reset her biological clock. In consultation with the family's physician, they purchased melatonin in their local health food store and gave her 3 milligrams about 30 minutes prior to the desired bedtime.

This combination of routinizing Mary's daily schedule along with melatonin prior to bedtime seemed to significantly improve Mary's sleep. Although there were still nights when she did not seem tired and when she would remain awake for a number of hours, the number of these nights dropped significantly compared to before the plan. In addition, Mary's daytime behavior also improved, which included a drop in the number and intensity of her aggressive outbursts. In an interesting development, once Mary was less aggressive, her teachers at school were

less reluctant to keep her awake during the day, and this too may have helped her sleep better at night.

Daily Activity Cues

Mary's case highlights two other strategies for helping people resynchronize their biological clocks. Our recommendation for Mary's parents to keep her daily activities consistent was based on the observation that, like sunlight, certain daily activities such as eating can help signal the brain about the passage of time. Previously, because of Mary's erratic sleep–wake schedule, her parents tended to be very flexible about bedtimes, wake times on the weekends, mealtimes, and so forth. Unfortunately, these changing times for important activities could have contributed to Mary's sleep problems. Keeping to certain time-ordered routines may have helped Mary regularize her sleep cycle.

Melatonin

I discuss medical approaches for assisting with sleep problems in Chapter 14.[4] However, it is important to briefly mention the use of melatonin here in light of its use with Mary's sleep schedule problem. In recent years, the supplemental use of melatonin has been recommended for a variety of sleep problems. These recommendations are based on its *soporific effect* (the tendency of people to feel sleepy after ingesting this substance) as well as its potential for resetting the biological clock. Much still needs to be learned about taking melatonin in this way. For example, although there appears to be few, if any, short-term negative side effects, few long-term studies of its effects have been conducted. We do not know, for example, if taking melatonin night after night for months or even years will have any negative effects on sleep or any other aspect of a person's health. We do know that, like our observations with Mary, short-term use of melatonin (along with other approaches) may help with problems such as non-24-hour sleep–wake cycles.

NAPPING AND POOR SLEEP HABITS

A final consideration when faced with a person who does not sleep at regular times is the voluntary type of sleep problem that results when someone has developed poor sleep habits. I covered poor sleep habits in some detail in Chapter 6, along with specific recommendations for improving certain daily activities that can help people sleep better—and readers should refer back to that chapter for a more in-depth discussion of this issue. Looking at sleep habits is important because poor sleep habits are probably the most common explanation for sleep schedule difficulties. Delayed sleep phase syndrome and non-24-hour sleep–wake cycles are relatively rare problems for most people, whereas in contrast, many people sleep at times that are less than desirable because of other factors.

As part of the assessment process to determine the possible causes of sleeping at the wrong times, we use the Good Sleep Habits Checklist from Chapter 6. One of the more common habits that people need to address involves activities surrounding bedtime. Watching television, texting, or checking email are, for some people, counterproductive to falling asleep. Reading or other quiet activities should be substituted in the half hour or so before sleep. Snacking at night can also be a problem. Getting into the habit of eating late at night can also contribute to difficulty sleeping for some people. We often recommend delaying dessert until sometime after dinner in order to satisfy cravings and also to help people resist the urge to get up later to eat again.

Dealing with Naps

Another serious concern for people sleeping at the wrong times is daytime napping. It is important to remember that short naps for some people can be very beneficial. It can help you quickly catch up on missed sleep, and it lets many people feel refreshed in the middle of the day. Naps only become a problem when they take the place of nighttime sleeping. If you find your child, for example, napping during the day but not able to fall asleep right away at night, then you may want to try to cut back on naps. You may recall that Shontell's bedtime disturbance as well as night waking (described in Chapter 8) was helped in part by slowly fading back on her nap time and closely monitoring her nighttime sleep. Elaine's case provides another example of how napping during the day interfered with her nighttime sleep and also how we were able to help her family correct the problem.

☆ ELAINE

Elaine was 14 years old when we first met her. She was participating in a research study being conducted to assess why children engage in behavior problems such as tantrums and self-injurious behavior and how to teach them to communicate as a way to replace those behaviors. Elaine could use some words to communicate with other people, but her verbal ability was limited. During the course of our research, we were approached by Elaine's teacher and asked for help with another problem in school. Elaine came to school very tired, and her teachers would let her nap for about an hour and a half just before lunch. Her teacher knew this was not a good thing for Elaine and that her naps were cutting into the time for educational activity, but the teacher also found it almost impossible to keep Elaine awake.

It was suggested that we meet with Elaine's mother and discuss Elaine's sleep patterns both at home and at school. During this meeting, we discovered that Elaine would remain awake at night and would typically fall asleep somewhere between 1 a.m. and 3 a.m. Several times a month, Elaine would not sleep at all at night. Her mother knew that Elaine napped at school and did not object to this because she felt Elaine needed the rest. We had her mother chart the amount of sleep Elaine got, on average, each day and we found that it came to about 8 hours. We pointed out to both her mother and her teacher that her daytime naps were probably contributing to her nighttime sleep problems. Somehow Elaine started staying up later, but the naps let her compensate for this lack of sleep. As a result, Elaine was not tired on the following night, so she could stay up late again. This vicious cycle of staying up late and napping to catch up on sleep would probably not stop unless Elaine's naps were eventually reduced or eliminated.

Together we set up a plan to help fade Elaine's daytime naps. We began by cutting into her sleep in school by about 10 minutes. The plan started slowly because Elaine's teacher was very hesitant to disturb her sleep for fear that Elaine would be more disruptive in class. When she previously tried to prevent her from sleeping, Elaine would become belligerent and more aggressive. We settled on 10 minutes because this seemed like a short enough time to allow Elaine to get some sleep. The plan was to decrease her naps by 10 minutes each week until they were eliminated.

At the same time we were to reduce her naps, Elaine's mother was asked to monitor her sleep at night. More specifically, we wanted to make sure that Elaine was not spending a great deal of time in bed but not sleeping. If Elaine was associating the bed with *not* sleeping, it would be difficult for her to fall asleep right away. Her mother monitored Elaine after she was put to bed and had her get up if she did not seem to be falling asleep after 15 minutes.

Unfortunately, although her mother was putting in a great deal of time in an almost heroic effort to limit Elaine's time in bed to only sleeping, things at school were not going quite so well. In 2 weeks' time, her teacher had awakened her early from her nap only twice. On the second of these awakenings, Elaine had become quite upset, and this bad mood lasted for the rest of the day. After that incident, Elaine's teacher was reluctant to go through that bad experience again.

A closer look at Elaine's sleeping at school helped to provide a solution to her teacher's problem. Elaine was usually allowed to sleep from about 10:30 a.m. to noon, which was right before lunch. Because Elaine really enjoyed eating, she had no difficulty getting up and going to the cafeteria. When we had her teacher wake her up early, it meant that Elaine now had to wait at least 10 minutes before going to lunch. Not only was she grumpy after her nap, she was also quite upset that she could not eat right away. In retrospect, the solution should have been obvious. Instead of trying to wake her up earlier, we should have just delayed her nap by 10 minutes each week. This way she would still wake up from her nap right before lunch. This time her teacher had little difficulty following the plan, and after a few months, Elaine was no longer napping in school. At the same time, we observed a simultaneous change in her sleep at night. Over time she was able to fall asleep at an earlier and earlier time. Once we reached the point at which Elaine was no longer napping in school, she was sleeping more at night and now averaged about 8 ½ hours of sleep, 30 minutes more than before we began the plan.

Elaine's sleep problems and our quest for a solution are typical of many of our efforts. We often find that people cannot or will not follow some parts of a plan, even though they are involved in its design. It may be that some people agree to follow certain plans only because they feel pressured. Some parents, for example, feel guilty if they do not agree to a plan for fear that others will judge them as less dedicated to their child's welfare. Similarly, teachers sometimes find themselves in positions where any reluctance to participate fully might be interpreted negatively. Many times, too, people agree to a plan without knowing how much work is actually involved. Parents, for example, often overestimate their ability to listen to the cries of their own child.

Our strategy in situations where parts of a plan are not being fully carried out is *not* to place blame on the parent or teacher. Instead, we look at these situations as failures on our part to adequately design the plan. As with Elaine's plan, we probably should have recognized that waking her early from her nap but not letting her go to lunch would probably cause more problems than her teacher (who had 11

other children in her class) could handle. Therefore, rather than trying to pressure her teacher into carrying out the first version of the
plan, we reevaluated our strategy and were able to come up with an
equally effective alternative. Each obstacle is viewed as an opportunity to test the limits of our work.

CONCLUSION

People who sleep at the "wrong times" can actually have several different sleep problems, including delayed sleep phase syndrome, non-24-
hour sleep–wake cycles, or poor sleep habits. I described a number of
innovative approaches to helping these people sleep better, including
chronotherapy, bright light therapy, and even the use of melatonin.
Other approaches that can be useful have been borrowed from work
with other sleep problems and include adaptation of sleep hygiene and
stimulus control (Chapter 6) and bedtime fading (Chapter 7). There
is reason to feel optimistic about our ability to help these individuals
sleep at times that are more desirable.

10

Nightmares, Sleep Terrors, and Other Related Problems

Some of the most personally upsetting of all the sleep problems we experience are nightmares and sleep terrors. They are included together in the same chapter because these sleep problems are often confused with each other, yet you may be surprised to learn that, in some ways, they are almost mirror opposites. In addition, there are other disturbances of sleep such as sleepwalking and sleep talking that can occasionally be a source of concern. This chapter discusses these different sleep problems and efforts to help people who are troubled by these nighttime events.

We all know what it is like to experience a nightmare. Children may be dreaming that someone is chasing them, that they are lost and late for an important event, or that someone they care about has died. If the dream is frightening enough, the child may wake up in a sweat, crying, and can often remember much of what he or she has dreamed. In a similar way, the beginning of a sleep terror can resemble a nightmare. Your child may begin screaming in a terrifying way in the middle of the night, and you rush to help comfort him or her. Quickly it becomes clear, however, that this is different. Although you are able to comfort your child after a nightmare, now your child is inconsolable. And where usually a nightmare ends suddenly with the person waking up, a child having a sleep terror continues to remain asleep. What causes these two types of sleep problems, and how should we respond to them? I next discuss nightmares and sleep terrors and our own efforts to help people with special needs who are bothered by them.

NIGHTMARES

Nightmares are a near universal phenomenon. We all dream, and most people occasionally have bad or frightening dreams. In fact, somewhere between 5% and 10% of adults have frequent nightmares, and the proportion of children troubled by them is approximately 20%.[1] We know that people with special needs also experience nightmares, but exact figures on exactly how many are bothered by excessive nightmares are not yet available. One group of individuals who seem to experience more nightmares is those individuals who have been through traumatic events, including automobile accidents and instances of abuse. It is important to highlight that having nightmares does not necessarily mean that someone has been through some traumatic event. Again, almost all of us have had nightmares from time to time. Unfortunately, often people interpret a higher incidence of frightening dreams as confirmation of abuse—but the evidence for this is lacking. It may be prudent to be cautious when looking for the origins of nightmares.

Nightmares almost always occur during *rapid eye movement (REM)*, or *dream, sleep*. In fact, knowing that nightmares occur during this stage of sleep helps to explain why many people report very similar experiences during these events. For example, having a nightmare where you are trying to run toward or away from something but are having difficulty is common. Also, being frightened during a dream but not being able to scream or call out until you wake up is also something many people experience. The reason for these common nightmare experiences can be traced to the REM sleep stage. If you remember from Chapter 1, *REM sleep* is when we dream, but it also is a time when the major muscle groups in our bodies are virtually paralyzed. It is a good thing too, because if we could move our muscles when we dream, there would be a lot of running around and screaming going on each night. The muscle paralysis keeps us secure in our beds. However, the sensation of not being able to move or speak (which also involves using muscles) that comes with this temporary paralysis seems to explain why we share these feelings of powerlessness when many of us have nightmares.

Unfortunately, despite the fact that nightmares are so common, we know very little about why we have them and how to help those people who are bothered by them. Stress and upsetting or traumatic events appear to increase the chance that people will have nightmares. In Chapter 2, I described a research study on nightmares where scientists studied the sleep of people who had gone through the emotionally upsetting experience of the 9/11 attacks. If you remember, they found that going through this hellish experience caused people to have more nightmares compared to people in other parts of the country. However, the people in New York did not report having more frightening nightmares than anyone else. In other words, the larger numbers of nightmares were not necessarily more upsetting than the ones experienced by any one of us. What does this mean? This research points out that stressful events will cause more nightmares, which may be what separates most of us from people who are bothered by them. What contributes to these nightmares may be stressful events but may also include a tendency to be more anxious in general, which in turn may cause nightmares to be experienced differently by different people.

Because of the connection between stress or anxiety and nightmares, efforts to help people who are bothered by excessive nightmares have focused on decreasing their anxious feelings. A recent case may help illustrate how this can be accomplished.

☆ QUINN

Quinn was his parents' first child and was the center of their lives. They had waited until their mid-forties to have a child and were initially devastated to learn that their infant son had Down syndrome. However, shortly after his birth, it became clear that they would love their son with a depth of feeling that was unparalleled and that they could weather whatever challenges his condition might present to them. This was the family they had always dreamed of.

Quinn was generally a very good baby, and they worked hard to provide him the extra care he required. However, when he was about 5 years old, he began to wake up crying soon after bedtime. They would go into his room to find Quinn awake, sweating, and clearly upset. He would usually tell his parents that he saw a monster and that he was frightened the monster might hurt him. Quinn's parents recalled that his first nightmares may have occurred shortly after they watched a video together that may have frightened him.

Quinn's nightmares did not go away, and for 9 months, he would gen-erally awaken once per night. Because Quinn did not appear to have any other areas in his life that were unusually upsetting or stressful, we decided to try a relatively innocuous plan. The strategy was that his parents would discuss with him that the monster was only make-believe and that he was much stronger than the monster. To further bolster the plan, Quinn was allowed to sleep with his toy "power sword," which he was told would kill the monster if it bothered him. They told him that no one could hurt him in his sleep if he used his sword.

On the first night of the plan, Quinn awoke crying, and his parents went into his room to comfort him. They reminded him of the power of the sword, let him hold it next to him in his bed, and he fell back to sleep rela-tively quickly. Over the next week, he awoke only two more times, but each time he was easy to comfort, and he fell back to sleep. In the intervening months, Quinn still had occasional nightmares, but the sword story seemed to provide him with a safety signal that reduced his fear. Eventually Quinn stopped sleeping with the sword and continued to have few nightmares.

Using "Magic"

Quinn's case was a simple one. The *placebo effect* of the sword was real enough: he felt that the sword protected him and that was all that mattered. The sword, and his belief that it would help protect him, served to make him less anxious and perhaps feel more in control of the nightmares. This type of "magic" can often be very effective for children who have nightmares. Giving them something that they believe will protect them and that gives them back a sense of control can help children cope with distressful dreams.

An interesting question that is unanswered in Quinn's case is whether he incorporated the sword into his nightmare. Did he begin to see the sword when the monster approached and did he use it to ward off or kill it? Quinn was not very clear about how the sword helped him in these frightening dreams. Other children have, however, reported that similar types of sleep tools (for example, a friend's use of a "magic wand" for his daughter) do enter into the dream itself and serve a direct protective benefit. Adults have been taught to practice alternative, posi-tive endings to their nightmares (called *imagery rehearsals*), and research suggests that this can be very effective in reducing nightmares. Again, nightmares and dreams in general are still relative mysteries to us, and we as yet do not know why such treatments help some children.

Teaching Relaxation

Other children may need more or different help with their nightmare-related sleep problems. For example, some children become so distressed over their nightmares that they become afraid to go to sleep. The anxiety and tension (described in more detail in Chapter 12) that these children experience can cause bedtime problems as well as night wakings. Sometimes it is necessary to teach them skills to relax at bedtime. Like Quinn's sword, having the skills to relax can serve to help children feel less powerless over their fears. This combination of having the skill to reduce their tension as well as having a feeling of control has been helpful for many children who experience nightmares. Chapter 12 outlines the major steps necessary to teach relaxation skills, especially to children. The goal here is to have your child experience what his or her muscles feel like tensed, and it is important that they know how to make them more relaxed. Often children and adults are unaware that major muscles in their bodies are tense, and this exercise helps provide some practice at awareness of the body.

For some children, the relaxation exercises can be made part of their bedtime routine. The last thing that he or she does before going to sleep could be practicing these exercises. This may serve two very important functions. First, it can help relieve some of the muscle tension that comes along with anxiety. Second, giving your child this task at night can help keep his or her mind off of the fearful thoughts. Remind your child, however, that this relaxation skill can be used anytime—in the middle of the night if he or she awakens and is fearful or even during the day if he or she feels tense.

Another useful technique that we describe in more detail in Chapter 12 is a procedure called *paradoxical intention*. Sometimes children become anxious about not sleeping, and these thoughts alone can contribute to their difficulty going to sleep at night. Paradoxical intention involves informing a child (or an adult) that you want him or her to *try to stay awake*. While remaining in bed in the dark and being relaxed, you give them permission to stay awake. For some children, taking away the demand of having to fall asleep provides enough reassurance to help them become drowsy and sleep. Again, Chapter 12 provides a more detailed description of this technique for helping children whose own thoughts seem to interfere with their ability to sleep at night.

SLEEP TERRORS

Perhaps the most disturbing of all the sleep disorders is a problem known as *sleep terrors*.[2] This disorder is sometimes referred to as *night terrors*, although because it can occur during daytime naps as well, the term *sleep terrors* is probably more accurate. These episodes usually begin with a piercing scream, which parents find impossible to ignore. Along with screaming, the child appears extremely upset, usually with his or her heart pounding and sweating. One of the characteristics of sleep terrors that is different from a nightmare is the inability to comfort the child during these events. Holding a child who is in the middle of a sleep terror usually causes him or her to push away and sometimes to become more upset. If your child has experienced this type of problem, you know how disturbing it is, not only to see your child so distraught, but also to feel so powerless to help. On the positive side, when these episodes are over, the child usually falls back to sleep and does not have any memory of this upsetting night.

Sleep terrors differ from many of the other sleep problems because they occur from start to finish while the child is asleep. The screaming, which is sometimes accompanied by getting out of bed and wandering around the house, happens during the nondream, or NREM, sleep, which means that this upsetting time probably does not represent a bad dream, at least the way we typically think of them. The fact that they occur exclusively while the child is asleep poses a problem for some of the interventions I have described. For example, ignoring sleep terrors by using a plan such as graduated extinction would be useless because the child is unaware of whether or not someone is present in the room.

Sleep Longer

Our still limited understanding about the nature of sleep terrors suggests that having a child get more sleep may help to reduce these episodes. Sleep terrors occur during the deepest stages of sleep. If you remember, we go through four stages of NREM sleep, with Stages 1 and 2 being a time of relatively light sleep, and Stage 3 representing a deeper period of sleep. The sleep terrors a child or adult experience happen while the person is in the deep sleep of Stage 3. When we are sleep deprived, we tend to have more Stage 3, or deeper, sleep. This suggests that sleep terrors may be partly the result of a child not getting enough sleep. In contrast, sleeping more hours at night tends to decrease the amount of deep sleep. This is obviously not recommended for children who have night waking problems, because sleeping more hours will tend to produce lighter sleep and therefore can increase wakings. However, if a child has frequent sleep terrors but does not experience other sleep disturbances, it may be helpful to have the child sleep more hours at night or take a nap during the day.

Scheduled Awakening

In Chapter 8, I described the use of scheduled awakening for night waking—which involves waking the child some time prior to a typical waking. We have found that this technique may also be a valuable aid to children who have longstanding problems with sleep terrors. Before we discuss the specifics of this technique for helping children with sleep terrors, it may be useful to describe a case of a child who had a many-year history of this problem and for whom we were ultimately able to help.

☆ ALFIE

Alfie was 11 years old when we first met and had a 7-year history of sleep terrors. He was born in Jamaica and was living in the United States with an aunt. His aunt told us that he had a learning disability and that his parents sent him to school here because they felt he would receive a better education. Other than some difficulty he had remembering what he would read, Alfie did well in school both academically and socially. He had a number of friends in his suburban neighborhood and especially enjoyed playing street hockey on inline skates.

Alfie's aunt told us that he would go to bed fine at night and would usually not awaken during the night. However, about 3 nights each week, Alfie would cry out loudly. He would appear extremely upset, his heart would race as if he was running, and he would sweat profusely. At first his aunt thought he was hurt or that he was getting sick. However, when it became clear that he was fine the next day, she became more concerned. She thought that because he was separated from his parents that he was having horrifying nightmares. After our initial consultation, where I told her the incidents did not resemble nightmares, I asked that she contact Alfie's parents to see if this was something new or if he ever had these episodes before. Alfie's aunt was surprised (and a bit annoyed) to learn that Alfie had these episodes off and on for most of his life.

In order to try to help Alfie avoid these sleep terrors, we designed a plan for his aunt. After several weeks of charting when these sleep terror episodes occurred, it became clear that it usually happened at around 12:30 p.m. Based on this information, we suggested that his aunt institute a scheduled awakening plan. She was to wake up at midnight, go into his room, and gently shake him until his eyes opened. Once he briefly opened his eyes, his aunt was to let him go back to sleep. She was to repeat this pattern each night for at least 2 weeks.

On the first night of the plan, she had a little trouble waking Alfie, who appeared to be in a very deep sleep. We told her that this was probably a good sign and an indication that the midnight waking was a good one. She repeated the waking each night for 2 weeks and did not observe Alfie having any sleep terror episodes. After the first 2 weeks, we suggested that she skip 1 night the next week, 2 nights the second week, and 1 more night each subsequent week. With the exception of one instance of a sleep terror incident, Alfie was free from these nighttime problems for the next 6 months. The intervention plan seemed to help him with sleep terrors, and it did not seem to negatively affect him in any way.

Just as we saw with night waking in Chapter 8, scheduled awakening was successful in helping Alfie's aunt reduce his sleep terrors. Our experience with other children such as Alfie indicates that this may be a technique that is generally useful for children with this sleep problem. The main difficulty with scheduled awakening (which I described more thoroughly in Chapter 8) is that it can be difficult for some parents to get up at night to awaken their child. Because the wakings can usually be faded out over several weeks, it does not have to be an overwhelming burden, but depending on the timing of the waking, it still can be challenging. The following is an overview of the steps necessary to implement a scheduled awakening plan.

Scheduled Awakening

- Use the sleep diary (see Chapter 3) to determine the time or times that your child typically experiences a sleep terror during the night.

- On the night you are to begin the plan, awaken your child approximately 30 minutes prior to the typical sleep terror time. For example, if your child usually has a sleep terror episode at 12:30 a.m., wake up your child at 12 a.m. If your child seems to awaken very easily, move up the time 15 minutes the next night and on each subsequent night (11:45 p.m.).

- If there is a broad range in the times your child has sleep terrors (for example, from 12 a.m. to 1:30 a.m.), awaken your child about 30 minutes prior to the earliest time (in this case, 11:30 p.m.).

- Do not fully awaken your child. Gently touch and/or talk to your child until he or she opens his or her eyes, then let him or her fall back to sleep.

- Repeat this plan each night until your child goes for a full 7 nights without a sleep terror. If your child has achieved this level of success, skip 1 night (that is, no scheduled waking) for a week. If your child has an episode, go back to every night. Slowly reduce the number of nights with scheduled wakings until your child is no longer having sleep terrors during the night.

Why does scheduled awakening work to reduce sleep terrors? Unfortunately, we do not yet have an adequate answer to this question. One theory about the role of scheduled awakening in sleep terrors is that scheduled awakening during the deep stage of sleep may prevent the child from spending too much time in this part of sleep. Remember that sleep terrors seem to be more likely the more a person spends in deep sleep. The scheduled awakening may help the child sleep a "shallower" but more consistent sleep schedule, and that may account for the reduction in sleep terrors. Perhaps research over the next few years will help us get a better understanding of this puzzling sleep problem and will also lead to more techniques to help people who suffer from sleep terrors.

SLEEPWALKING AND SLEEP TALKING

When people walk or talk in their sleep, this usually does not occur during the time of sleep when we dream. *Sleepwalking* (also called *somnambulism*) and sleep talking are two sleep disturbances that most often occur during nondream, or NREM, sleep, usually within the first few hours after falling asleep.[3] In children, the causes of these active sleep events have been thought to include anxiety, a lack of sleep, and fatigue. They have also been linked to seizure disorders, which should be ruled out for a child who also experiences seizures.

Sleepwalking and sleep talking can be brief, lasting only for a few seconds, or can continue for 30 minutes or longer. For the most part, these sleep events should not be a source of concern. Contrary to some popular myths, it is not dangerous to awaken people who walk in their sleep, although it may be difficult because it occurs during a deep stage of sleep. The awakened sleepwalker may appear confused and disoriented at first but should have no trouble going back to sleep. Another myth about sleepwalking is that the person cannot be injured at that time. People who sleepwalk seem generally aware of their surroundings and tend to avoid harming themselves. However, there are occasional reports of people harming themselves or others during sleepwalking. For example, there was one recent report of a serious incident, a 35-year-old man who was sleepwalking who was reported to have stabbed another man. In addition, the person can be hurt by bumping into objects or falling down stairs, and therefore some precautions should be taken if this is a frequent occurrence in your home.

Although we have not been involved in trying to help children who frequently walk in their sleep, you would generally try to make sure that these individuals are fully rested and that potential sources of stress or anxiety are identified and addressed. If these efforts fail, we would recommend a trial of scheduled awakening (see previous description), especially because of the similarity between sleep terrors and these other sleep problems.

SLEEP EATING

There recently has been an increase in the number of reports of people taking another route to sleepwalking—right to the refrigerator! It appears that some people not only walk in their sleep but also prepare and consume snacks or even small meals. A number of people have observed that they were gaining weight and only later found out that they were eating at night without knowing it. Although relatively little is known about this sleep problem, it appears to be a variant of sleepwalking.[4] It may also be related to medication use such as those prescribed for depression or insomnia. The following is a case of a person who discovered after several months that she was eating while she was asleep.

☆ ☆
☆ JANINE

Janine was a very active and athletic 27-year old young woman. She was very concerned about fitness and was becoming increasingly frustrated because her efforts at dieting and exercise were not having the effect she expected. Instead of losing weight, she was gaining weight! The key to her problem was discovered one night by her husband.

Janine's husband, who was usually a very heavy sleeper, was awakened one night by a noise in the kitchen. He noticed that his wife was not beside him and got up to see if everything was all right. He found Janine at the kitchen table, consuming the last of what appeared to have been a full box of cookies. "Giving up the diet?" he quipped to his wife with a smile on his face. Strangely, she did not look up at him and continued to eat. He walked over to her, touched her on the shoulder and said, "Janine, are you okay?" With that, she stood up, walked out of the kitchen, and went to bed without ever saying a word—sending chills down her husband's spine. The next morning, he gently broached the subject of last night's binge eating episode and her strange reaction to him, but Janine looked puzzled and denied it ever happened. One night, after several of these strange events— once where his wife ate several cups of sugar—they saw a television program about a woman who ate in her sleep, and they finally concluded that Janine had the same problem.

They approached me for some advice for this sleep problem, and we discussed her sleeping habits. Other than occasionally having trouble falling asleep at night, Janine reported having few other sleep problems. She did say that both she and her father had histories of walking in their sleep, and there were a few humorous family stories about the both of them. My recommendations included having Janine eat a small snack at night before bedtime to perhaps reduce her hunger and therefore her desire to eat at night. Her husband also agreed to institute a scheduled awakening plan, whereby he would awaken Janine at about 1:15 a.m.—30 minutes before her 1:45 a.m. travels. After about 2 weeks, Janine's husband began fading out the awakenings, and he reported no obvious incidents of sleep eating. Janine's weight was beginning to stabilize at an acceptable level, and they believed that she was no longer getting up at night and bingeing on snacks.

CONCLUSION

Janine seemed to have combined her previous history of sleepwalking with an effort to satisfy cravings for "junk" food that she was having because of her diet. In fact, it is possible that increases in reports of sleep eating may be a function of increased awareness but also may be a consequence of our culture's fat-free diet craze. We await future research on sleep eating to see how frequently this occurs and who is likely to engage in this type of unusual sleep event. It may be that it disproportionately occurs among people who have a history of sleepwalking and who also have food cravings as a result of dieting. This sleep problem can be of concern if it negatively affects a person's weight. It can also cause concern because of the increased risk of injury by choking or when cooking or cutting food at a time when the person is not fully aware. Finally, these events can disrupt a person's sleep, and may contribute to daytime drowsiness.

Excessive Sleepiness

Most of us have experienced times when—despite having a reasonable number of hours of sleep—we still feel tired throughout the day. This experience of daytime sleepiness is, unfortunately for some, a chronic and obviously frustrating problem. School or work can be negatively affected, and daytime accidents are common among these individuals. Although at first it does not appear that the sleep of these people is disrupted (they usually do not have any recollection of waking during the night), often at the root of this problem is an interrupted sleep cycle. In other words, people who are excessively tired during the day after what seems to be a full night's sleep may be having their sleep interrupted without knowing it. In other cases, some individuals may have rare but very specific sleep problems that lead to daytime sleepiness or, in the extreme, involuntary attacks of sleep. This chapter will cover the different types of sleep and sleep-related problems that can lead to excessive sleepiness, along with a description of treatment approaches aimed at helping people with these problems. Unfortunately, we know very little about the sleep problems associated with excessive sleepiness among people with special needs. It is hoped that more attention will focus on these individuals to determine if they have more specific treatment needs.

HYPERSOMNIA

If *insomnia* involves not getting enough sleep (the root word *in-* means lacking or without), *hypersomnia* is a problem of sleeping too much (*hyper-* refers to having a great amount or abnormal excess).[1] Despite getting a full night's sleep each evening, some people find themselves falling asleep several times each day. One young woman whom I met through my teaching represents someone who had battled hypersomnia for many years.

☆ ANN

Ann was a college student who came by my office during office hours to discuss her progress in class. We discussed the last exam and several questions that she missed. As she was about to leave, she said that she never fell asleep during my class. This seemed like faint praise, but I thanked her for the feedback. "No," she said, "you don't understand. I usually fall asleep in *all* of my classes, but not in yours." Again, I did not quite understand what she was trying to tell me and joked that she must be more careful picking out her professors. She laughed. "That's probably true. But I also have this problem with sleeping too much."

As we discussed her sleeping problem (this time, a little bit more seriously), Ann told me that this had been a problem for her since her teenage years. If she was in situations that were monotonous, boring, or if she could not be active, she would find herself falling asleep. This could happen several times a day, depending on what she was doing. Recently, large lecture classes had become a problem for her unless the lecturer was particularly interesting or animated. Watching television and driving long distances along highways were also problems.

Ann reported that her father also had a problem with falling asleep, but that his problem was different and that the symptoms were more severe. He had recently been diagnosed with *narcolepsy* (a sleep problem we will describe next that can result in sudden and irresistible sleep attacks, along with disturbing sleep events such as brief paralysis and hallucinations) and was now being seen at a sleep clinic to help him deal with the problem. Both she and her brother had been diagnosed with *hypersomnia*. Ann had been prescribed Ritalin (a stimulant medication) about 4 years ago and said that it was only somewhat effective at keeping her awake during the day. She said the drug helped to reduce the attacks but did not eliminate them altogether.

When I asked her how she coped with falling asleep all of the time, she became a bit embarrassed. "I think of things," she said finally. I asked her what she meant. "Well, I can pretty much control it if I keep my mind busy. I think of exciting things." I waited, and she continued. "Sometimes I fantasize that I have great intellectual powers and that I am smarter than anyone else in class. Other times I think of winning an award, and for some reason, I don't tend to sleep. It seems to work for me."

Ann's hypersomnia was not so disruptive as to keep her from succeeding in school, but it was a daily struggle for her to stay awake in class. The stimulant medication Ritalin helped her somewhat, but she still found that some classes continued to challenge her ability to remain awake. We worked together on a plan to help her identify times when she felt herself falling asleep as well as fantasy scenarios she could practice that would help her stay awake. She reported back that practicing in boring classes was working, and she was feeling more control over her sleep.

Unfortunately for Ann, and for thousands of people like her, we still do not have treatments that can completely eliminate these urges to sleep. Often medications such as Ritalin and modafinil are pre-scribed to help keep people more alert; however, this seems to be only a partial fix for some people with hypersomnia. Other techniques, such as trying to become aware of when the attacks are coming on and using mental imagery to try to delay or prevent sleep may be of some use to people who are able to use such procedures. If you suspect that your child may have hypersomnia, we suggest that you contact one of the sleep centers mentioned in Appendix C of this book for a possible evaluation and recommendations for treatment.

NARCOLEPSY

Narcolepsy is a serious sleep problem that not only includes uncon-trollable sleep attacks (such as the ones experienced by Ann) but has a number of other disturbing sleep-related symptoms associated with it. In addition to the daytime sleepiness seen in people with hyper-somnia, people with narcolepsy also experience *cataplexy,* a sudden loss of muscle tone. These are not seizures but instead are involuntary sleep attacks. The loss of muscle tone seems to occur because, unlike most of our sleep episodes, these sleep attacks involve the immediate introduction of REM, or dream, sleep. If you remember, this phase of sleep involves not only dreaming but also muscle paralysis. This loss of muscle tone happens while the person is awake and can be as mild as a feeling of slight weakness in the facial muscles to a complete collapse to the floor. This cataplexy can last from several seconds to several minutes and is usually preceded by some strong emotion such as anger or happiness. Imagine that you have narcolepsy: in the middle of cheering for your favorite team, you might suddenly fall asleep; or while having an argument with a friend, you might collapse to the floor in a sound sleep.

Two other characteristics distinguish people who have narcolepsy. They commonly report *sleep paralysis,* a brief period of time upon awakening when the person cannot move or speak. This experience is often reported to be frightening by those going through it. Sleep paralysis is more common than you might think. Many individuals who otherwise have no other sleep problems—including narcolepsy—report having these frightening experiences in the morning. The last characteristic of narcolepsy is *hypnagogic hallucinations,* vivid experiences that begin at the start of sleep and are said to be unbelievably realistic because they include not only the visual aspects but also touch, hearing, and even the feeling of body movement. Examples of hypnagogic hallucinations, which like sleep paralysis can be quite terrifying, include the experience of being caught in a fire or flying through the air.

Narcolepsy is a genetic disorder that is relatively rare, occurring in 0.03%–0.16% of the population, with the numbers approximately equal among males and females. In most cases, it appears that there is a significant loss of a certain type of nerve cell (*hypocretin neurons*). These neurons create chemicals in the brain (*peptides*) that appear to play an important role in wakefulness, although why these individuals lack these specific neurons is not yet understood. Like hypersomnia, people with narcolepsy are often prescribed medications such as Ritalin and modafinil to help keep them alert during the day. Also, sometimes antidepressant medications are recommended, not because these individuals are more prone to depression, but because these drugs can help prevent the onset of REM sleep. This effect of antidepressant drugs can therefore help to prevent the attacks of cataplexy.

One very simple recommendation that is sometimes helpful for people with narcolepsy is the scheduling of daytime naps. A nap in the morning and again in the afternoon can help reduce the sleep attacks these individuals experience. In addition, making sure that the person has adequate sleep at night can also be helpful. Again, if your child shows the signs of having narcolepsy-like symptoms, an evaluation at a sleep center is essential.

BREATHING PROBLEMS

For some people, their sleepiness during the day or their disrupted sleep at night has a physical origin—namely, problems they have breathing while asleep. Because breathing is interrupted, it results in numerous brief arousals throughout the night, and the person does not feel rested even after 8 or 9 hours "asleep." For all of us, sleep is a time when the muscles of our upper airway relax, constricting this passageway somewhat, and it therefore makes breathing a little more difficult. Unfortunately for some, breathing is constricted a great deal, and they may have very labored breathing while they sleep (*hypoventilation*). Other people experience more extreme breathing problems while asleep, and they may have short periods (10–30 seconds) when breathing stops altogether, called *sleep apnea*.[2] Often the person affected is only minimally aware of his or her breathing difficulties and does not attribute sleep problems to breathing. However, a bed partner or relative in a nearby room will usually be aware of loud snoring (which is one sign of this problem) or will have witnessed the episodes of interrupted breathing, a frightening experience to observe. Other signs indicating that breathing difficulties may be responsible for disturbed sleep are sweating heavily during the night, morning headaches, and episodes of falling asleep during the day (called *sleep attacks*) but without the feeling of being rested after these episodes.

There are a number of types of breathing difficulties that can lead to sleep disruption. Specifically, three types of apnea are important to distinguish because they can have different causes, daytime complaints, and treatments—*obstructive, central,* and *mixed. Obstructive sleep apnea* (OSA; also referred to as *obstructive sleep apnea hypopnea syndrome*) occurs when airflow stops despite the continued activity of the respiratory system. For some people, the airway is too narrow; for others, some abnormality or damage obstructs or interferes with the ongoing effort to breathe. One hundred percent of a group of people with OSA also reported snoring at night. Being obese is sometimes associated with this problem, as is increasing age, and it is more often found among males. It is thought to occur in about 1%–2% of the general population. The second type of apnea—*central sleep apnea*—involves the complete cessation of respiratory activity for brief periods of time and is often associated with certain central nervous system disorders such as cerebral vascular disease, head trauma, and degenerative disorders. Unlike obstructive sleep apnea, people with central sleep apnea will wake up frequently during the night, but they tend not to report excessive daytime sleepiness and often are not aware that they have a serious breathing problem. Because of the lack of daytime symptoms, people tend not to seek treatment for this problem, so we know relatively little about it. The final breathing disorder—*mixed sleep apnea*—refers to a combination of both obstructive and central sleep apneas. All of these breathing difficulties interrupt sleep and result in symptoms similar to that of insomnia. One young woman with a breathing-related sleep problem who recently came to our attention provides an illustration of this problem.

☆ LINDA

I was consulting with a group of special educators one afternoon when the topic of sleep came up. One woman who worked in a group home for individuals who had intellectual disabilities asked for help with a young woman named Linda who lived in the house and who they were having a great deal of difficulty motivating. The worker reported that they had tried everything they could think of to get her interested in the activities at home or at work but that nothing seemed to interest Linda except sleep. You could tell by the worker's tone of voice that she considered Linda to be lazy and was extremely frustrated with her.

I began to ask some questions about her sleep to see if Linda was having difficulties falling asleep at night or sleeping through the night and if one of these problems was the cause of her fatigue. The worker reported that the opposite was true. Linda would fall asleep almost immediately after she got into bed, and she never came out of her room until they came to wake her up. In fact, she was difficult to awaken and was often cranky in the morning. Suspecting that a breathing problem might be the cause of her daytime sleepiness, I then asked if Linda snored. "The loudest I've ever heard!," the worker exclaimed. Before she could explain any further, I followed up with a question about Linda's weight. "She's very heavy," the worker said. It seems that Linda weighed more than 200 pounds. I recommended that they have Linda evaluated by a physician or at the local sleep center to determine if she had a breathing-related sleep problem.

What seemed clear from our brief conversation was that Linda fit the pattern of a person with obstructed nighttime breathing. The daytime sleepiness without nighttime sleep problems was the first clue. The next indication was that Linda was described as being cranky in the morning. This could have been a result of a dry mouth and headache that often follow a night of obstructed breathing. The answers to my questions about Linda's snoring and weight seemed to confirm my suspicions. Both are common signs of a person who may have a breathing problem at night. The worker later told me of Linda's high blood pressure, which they thought was only because of her weight but could have been made worse by her breathing problem.

The good news was that they were able to get Linda some help with her sleep problem, using some of the treatment suggestions we describe next. However, the sad part of the story is the many years that people believed that Linda was just a lazy person. And perhaps more tragically, it will take some time to determine how much of Linda's cognitive impairment was a function of the brain damage responsible for her intellectual disability and how much was a function of the cognitive impairments people have when they suffer from such breathing problems at night.

Again, if you believe your child has signs of a breathing difficulty, immediate medical evaluation is essential. The consequences of breathing problems at night can be severe, and you should seek medical advice as soon as possible. Some of the nonmedical recommendations made for these individuals include elevating the person's head with pillows at night to help ease breathing. Also, sleeping on the side instead of the back can be helpful to some people. Important recommendations for adults with breathing problems include avoiding sleeping pills and alcohol, both of which can make the breathing passages relax even more and cause increased breathing difficulty. It is also recommended to avoid smoking and to try to lose weight.

In severe cases, the most common recommendation currently made is the use of an instrument that provides *continuous positive airway pressure* (CPAP). A face mask is worn at night while sleeping, and slightly increased air pressure provided by a compressor helps to keep the airways open and greatly improves breathing. Obviously, such a device can only be used by a cooperative individual and can take some time to get used to. As a last resort, different surgical procedures are sometimes recommended, depending on the nature of the obstruction.

SUDDEN INFANT DEATH SYNDROME

Probably the most devastating and unthinkable event that can befall any new parents would be to experience the sudden and unexplainable death of their seemingly healthy infant. *Sudden infant death syndrome, or SIDS,* is the label given by medical professionals for these otherwise unexplainable deaths. Approximately 4,500 such deaths occur each year in the United States alone, and this syndrome strikes families from all racial, ethnic, and socioeconomic backgrounds. The exact cause, or more likely causes, of this medical mystery remain unknown, although it is believed to be a developmental problem that causes the baby to have difficulty regulating blood pressure, breathing, or temperature at night.[3] Placing an infant on his or her back at night (as opposed to sleeping on the stomach) seems to help prevent this problem.

Precautions for Sudden Infant Death Syndrome

- Stop using illicit drugs. Research suggests that about 25% of the mothers of SIDS babies had previously used illegal drugs.

- Stop smoking. SIDS has been found to be more prevalent in children whose mothers smoked during pregnancy, and recent research suggests that the rate is also higher in infants whose mothers smoked after the child was born.

- Most infants should be placed on their backs to sleep. The American Academy of Pediatrics recommends that during the first 6 months of age, healthy infants are at a lower risk for SIDS if they sleep on their backs or sides rather than on their stomachs. Parents of infants with existing breathing problems or those who tend to spit up a great deal after feeding should consult with their pediatrician.

- Have the infant sleep with firm bedding materials. Softer bedding such as beanbag cushions, foam pads, or waterbeds should be avoided.

- Avoid overheating an infant who has a cold or infection. Too much clothing, too heavy a blanket, or too warm a room can increase the risk of SIDS for an ill baby.

- Use pacifiers.

MOVEMENT-RELATED SLEEP PROBLEMS

Most of us have had the peculiar experience of drifting off to sleep, only to be briefly awakened by a sudden jerking of muscles called a *hypnic jerk*. This is a perfectly normal, but as yet not fully understood, physical reaction to the onset of sleep. Unfortunately for some people, these types of physical movements continue throughout most of the night, and they may interrupt sleep even without the person being aware that they are occurring. Two types of movement-related sleep problems are relatively common causes of daytime sleepiness: *periodic limb movements* and *restless legs syndrome*.[4]

Periodic Limb Movement Disorder

Does your child wake up in the morning with his or her blankets and sheets in a pile at the foot of the bed or on the floor? Does the bed look like a wrestling match occurred there in the middle of the night? If you have observed this on frequent occasions, it may be the result of a condition referred to as *periodic limb movement disorder:* episodes of leg and sometimes arm movements that occur throughout sleep. Sometimes these episodes of limb movements can be as brief as a few minutes, other times they can go on for hours. Often, people are not aware of these movements during sleep. However, if they occur often enough, the affected person may have his or her sleep interrupted and will feel tired throughout the day.

The causes of these limb movements are not yet clear, although they have sometimes been linked to the use of certain medications. Antidepressants, for example, can cause some people to experience periodic limb movements. If this is the case, it may be helpful to point it out to your physician, who may be able to switch the medication and help prevent this problem. When some people *stop* taking medications such as tranquilizers or sedatives, some of the side effects can include these limb movements. Also, certain medical conditions such as kidney disease, folic acid deficiency, poor circulation, or a metabolic disease have been linked to periodic limb movements.

No treatment is necessary for periodic limb movements unless they are interfering with sleep. Unfortunately, there is currently no cure for the more severe cases of periodic limb movements, although some treatments have been tried when sleep is significantly interrupted. If poor circulation is thought to be the cause of these problems, some professionals recommend vitamin E supplements because this can help improve circulation. The use of muscle relaxants are not recommended because they often only suppress the twitches without fully eliminating them, and these drugs can be habit forming. One medication that may be helpful is called Sinemet (a combination of two drugs: levodopa and carbidopa), which is used for people with Parkinson's disease. Other approaches include the use of vitamin and mineral supplements (especially iron), although it is not yet clear if this is an effective treatment for many people with periodic limb movements.

Restless Legs Syndrome

Described as the feeling of crawling, pulling, or tingling beneath the skin of the legs, *restless legs syndrome* affects some 5% of the general population. This physical problem often coexists with periodic limb movements such that, if a person experiences periodic limb movements, he or she usually (but not always) has restless legs syndrome as well. These extremely uncomfortable feelings usually come on when the person relaxes, and it can be extremely disruptive when the person tries to fall asleep at night. They can also occur when the person sits for any length of time, making traveling very difficult. Although this problem was previously believed to only occur in older adults, more recent research suggests that it can affect children and adolescents as well.

Medical treatment is usually recommended for people with restless legs syndrome, although exercising prior to bedtime can be helpful for some people who suffer from this problem. If you suspect that your child has either periodic limb movements or restless legs syndrome, it is recommended that a medical exam be conducted.

Rhythmic Movement Disorder

Some of the children who are referred to us are described as rocking back and forth in their beds before going to sleep. Sometimes this rocking includes head banging against the wall or the side of the crib. In all of these cases, parents usually report that the rocking or head banging seems to be soothing to their child and that it helps the child fall asleep. These types of behaviors are more formally referred to as *rhythmic movement disorder,* and they are fairly common (in their less injurious forms) among infants and toddlers.[5] There also appears to be a higher rate of this type of rocking among children with developmental disabilities. One young boy's case will help illustrate this problem and our efforts to help his parents intervene.

☆ VINNIE

Vinnie was an 18-month-old boy with a diagnosis of ASD whose parents contacted us because of his head banging. Vinnie would occasionally bang his head against objects such as the wall or the floor if he was left alone for long periods of time. Fortunately, he would stop this head banging if someone told him to, and he was doing it less and less during the day as he grew older. However, he would also bang his head against the wall next to his bed at night before falling asleep, and his parents found that if they told him to stop, he would continue as soon as they left the room. Although the head banging was not so severe as to do a great deal of harm to him, there was a spot on his head where his hair was thinning, and his parents were concerned that this would worsen if he was not helped soon.

In our initial discussions with Vinnie's parents, we tried to determine why he was banging his head at night. Our guess was that this had become a calming ritual for Vinnie and that he had learned to use it to help him fall asleep. We designed a plan for his parents that would hopefully reduce any damage he was doing with the head banging and that would also help him learn to fall asleep without this problem. His parents had at one point tried to put some padding up against the wall to protect him, but Vinnie always found ways to take it down. We suggested that they sacrifice several nights and that they sit in his bedroom at bedtime. If Vinnie banged his head, they were to tell him to stop, but otherwise they were instructed not to talk to him in any way. They were also to place his favorite stuffed animal in bed with him.

His parents found that, on the first night, Vinnie had a great deal of trouble falling asleep. He remained awake for 2 hours past the usual time he fell asleep, but his parents persisted with the plan. Similar results were observed on the second night, but by the third night, Vinnie fell asleep within 30 minutes. We asked that his parents continue to remain in his room at bedtime until the number of reminders for him to stop head banging was one or fewer. After that point, we asked them to sit just outside his room and listen for any head banging. If they heard him bang his head, they were to call to him to stop. After about 2 weeks, Vinnie was falling asleep within a reasonable amount of time on most nights without head banging, and his parents felt comfortable not monitoring his bedtime behavior.

We were able to design the plan we did for Vinnie because he was able to stop banging his head when he was asked. What we did was prevent him from using his typical strategy for falling asleep (head banging) and made him come up with other comforting strategies that were not potentially injurious to him. His parents noted that Vinnie seemed to ball up his pillow in a certain way that was comforting to him, and this was the way he usually fell asleep. He seemed to ignore his favorite stuffed animal yet over time was able to fall asleep without banging his head. Other children who are not so receptive to verbal instructions to stop head banging sometimes require physical intervention, such as the parent having to place a pillow in the way or prompt their child to put their head down. It is important to note in all of these plans that parents should not speak to their child during this time and should generally try to limit interactions. This is essential because you want the child not to see this as extending bedtime or as a time to get additional attention from parents. Talking, holding, or otherwise interacting with your child during this time may make him or her dependent on you being there to fall asleep—essentially substituting you for head banging as a soothing sleep inducer.

Remember, noninjurious rocking is probably not something to worry about because most children stop as they get older. If it becomes more severe, however, interventions such as the one we used with Vinnie should be helpful.

CONCLUSION

This chapter covers many ways sleep can be disrupted—that is, reasons you do not experience restorative sleep and therefore are excessively sleepy during the day. In general, if your child (or you) appear very tired even after what seems to have been an adequate amount of time asleep, this fatigue needs to be taken seriously and usually warrants a medical evaluation. The next chapter describes a number of sleep-related problems and how you can help your child with these difficulties.

Other Nighttime Difficulties

This chapter is designed to give you a brief overview of some problems surrounding sleep or bedtime that are not known specifically as sleep problems. Children who wet their beds during sleep at night, for example, are not considered as having a sleep problem, per se, and helping these children with their problem involves very different approaches than those we use with problems of sleep. Similarly, children who are anxious or who are depressed may have their sleep interrupted, and we need to help these children in a slightly different way. We next discuss bed-wetting, anxiety, and depression, along with sleep-related headaches and tooth grinding, and provide suggestions for assisting children who suffer from these difficulties.

BED-WETTING

Bed-wetting (more formally referred to as *enuresis*, pronounced *en-yur-ee-sis*) is one of those behaviors that is considered to be a problem depending on how old the person is.[1] If a 2-year-old wets the bed at night, for example, it is not considered a problem (more than 90% of 2-year-olds wet the bed). However, it is generally thought that by about age 5, children should be sleeping through the night without accidents. As a result, children ages 5 and older who are still wetting the bed regularly may need some additional help to let them have dry nights. This is not a particularly unusual problem among young children, considering that, for example, at least 7% of all 8-year-old children have occasional bed-wetting accidents at night. And although most children stop having these nighttime problems eventually, it can take a number of years for this problem to resolve itself. And unfortunately, for some children with special needs, bed-wetting may never be resolved without special help.

Professionals in this area typically break down the types of enuresis, or bed-wetting, into several groups. *Diurnal enuresis* is defined as wetting that occurs while the child is awake. Here the child has difficulty remaining dry during the daylight hours. *Primary nocturnal enuresis* is bed-wetting during sleep (*nocturnal*) in a child who has never successfully had bladder control (*primary*) at night. In contrast, *secondary nocturnal enuresis* is the loss of bladder control at night after a period of time—at least 3–6 months—when the child has successfully had dry nights. This *secondary* form of enuresis sometimes occurs as a result of some medical problem (for example, a bladder infection) or because of some emotional upset such as parents' pending divorce.

It has been traditionally thought that bed-wetting occurs among certain children because they have small bladders and that they wet their beds because they cannot hold their urine through the night. This does not seem to be the case. On the other hand, in about 10% of cases of enuresis, urinary tract infections can be present. With proper medical treatment of these infections, many children seem to resolve their problems with bed-wetting. However, sometimes the reverse is true, and bed-wetting problems may be causing the urinary tract infections instead. Either way, it is important that all children who have problems with bed-wetting be evaluated for possible medical causes of their nighttime accidents. There also appears to be a correlation between enuresis and obstructed sleep apnea in many children. Parents should alert pediatricians to this possible link because successful treatment of obstructed breathing at night can lead to improvement in enuresis as well.

The most recent thinking about the biological causes of bed-wetting includes the child's ability to produce a hormone that makes urine more concentrated and the physical ability to stop from urinating while asleep. It appears that many children with bed-wetting problems may not produce enough of this hormone called *antidiuretic hormone*, or *ADH*. ADH helps to concentrate urine during sleep so that it has less water and is therefore easier to avoid wetting accidents.[2] Without enough of this hormone, the child's urine has more volume and is therefore more difficult to hold in at night. At the same time, these children may be less skillful at using their body's hints that the bladder is full to prevent accidents. Putting these two factors together—the relative lack of ADH and problems picking up their body's cues—may contribute to why some children have this problem and others do not.

Psychological as well as biological factors can play a role in bed-wetting. It is rarely, if ever, the case that a child willfully wets the bed to "get back" at a parent or for other similar reasons. However, especially for children with the secondary type of enuresis—those who previously had good control and now do not—psychological stress and emotional upset can trigger this problem. In a recent case, a mother of an 8-year-old boy asked for my advice about her son, who had just recently begun to wet his bed. My first question was whether there was some recent, perhaps upsetting, changes going on at home, and she told me that her husband of 12 years had just moved out and that they were getting a divorce. She never thought to connect her son's bed-wetting with the obvious upheaval occurring at home. Fortunately, I was able to suggest some relatively easy things to do to help her help her son through this difficult time. Other children can react with bed-wetting to changes such as the birth of a new brother or sister or difficulties at school. For some, as of yet not fully understood, reason—and especially among boys—such changes can result in a regression in their previous toileting skills.

A variety of techniques have been used to help children learn (and sometimes relearn) how to avoid wetting the bed at night. Before any specific techniques are recommended, however, it is usually suggested that parents have their child limit fluids prior to bedtime and cut down on drinks or foods with caffeine, which can cause more urination. In addition, a stop in the bathroom right before going to sleep is also recommended. Punishment, in the form of yelling, nagging, or ridicule, should not be used for these accidents and can make the problem worse. Instead, fully waking a child at night—making sure that the child is truly awake—for several weeks to go to the bathroom may be enough to help him or her sleep through the night dry. If an accident occurs, have him or her participate in the clean-up, but again, this should not be done in a punishing way. If these small steps are not enough, then several more formal techniques are usually presented as possible aids for bed-wetting.

The Bell and Pad

A *urine alarm*, or the *bell and pad*, is one of the oldest techniques for helping children with enuresis.[3] This commercially available device consists of a pad that goes underneath the child's sheet (versions of this alarm are available online from a number of specialized sites). If the pad gets wet, it sets off an alarm that is loud enough to wake your child (and you), and the child is directed to finish urinating in the bathroom. This simple technique alone has proven helpful for up to 75% of children who participate in this type of plan. On the downside, a significant number of children who do at first succeed with the use of the bell and pad may return to their bed-wetting problems. For these children, additional procedures are sometimes added to this technique, and we describe two of these plans next.

The Bell and Pad

- Hook up the alarm yourself each night. Test it by touching the sensors (it is safe) with a wet finger.

- Listen for the alarm carefully and respond to it quickly.

- Have a nightlight or flashlight nearby so you will be able to see what you are doing when the alarm sounds.

- As soon as you hear the alarm, get out of bed and turn off the alarm.

- Have your child go to the bathroom and finish urinating.

- Help your child clean his or her clothes and bed.

- Use the alarm every night until your child goes 3 or 4 weeks without bedwetting. This can take 2–3 months, so be patient.

Dry Bed Training

Dry bed training includes the use of the bell and pad along with three other steps.[4] On the first night of dry bed training, the child is awakened each hour and brought to the bathroom. There the child is encouraged to urinate and then is given something to drink and is asked to try to hold it in until he or she is awakened again. Finally, the child is allowed to return to bed. On the second night of this plan, the child is awakened only once, 3 hours after going to bed, and is again given something to drink and returned to bed. For each subsequent night that the child succeeds in staying dry, the waking time is moved back one half hour until it reaches 1 hour after bedtime. If the child has an accident two or more times during any 1-week period, then the waking schedule is repeated. It is thought that this type of waking schedule may interrupt the child's typical sleep pattern and may help him or her learn to remain dry at night.

The second part of the plan is referred to as a *positive practice procedure*. Here the child is helped to practice how to delay urination. After waking with a wet bed and cleaning up, the child is asked to lie in bed and count to 50, then go into the bathroom to try to urinate. The child then returns to bed and repeats the training until he or she has completed 20 of these trials. The dry bed training procedure recommends that this practice routine be implemented after a wet bed and again at bedtime the next night.

After the first night of the waking schedule, the bell and pad are introduced to signal when the child has wet the bed. Each time that the alarm goes off, a *cleanliness training plan* is then followed. This basically involves having your child participate as much as possible in the clean-up after a toileting accident has occurred. The child is encouraged to take off the wet bed clothes—or prompted through it if he or she cannot do it alone—and also to change the wet bed linens. This is repeated 20 times after each instance of bed-wetting before the child is allowed to go back to sleep. This type of training may serve two purposes. First, it fully awakens the child after a bed-wetting incident. This seems to be important to the success of any of these programs because children can be prompted to get up and go to the bathroom while not being fully awake, and therefore, he or she may not learn to interrupt sleep to go to the bathroom alone at night. The second role of cleanliness training may involve its unpleasantness. Obviously your child will want to avoid going through these 20 trials of dressing and undressing, and this may provide more motivation to be aware of when he or she should go to the bathroom. The following is an overview of the steps involved in dry bed training.

Dry Bed Training

- Establish a nightly waking schedule. Upon awaking the child, the parent brings him or her to the bathroom, and the child is asked to urinate. After the bathroom trip, the child is given some fluids to drink and is asked to try to hold it in until the next waking. On the first night, the child is awakened every hour. On the second night, the child is awakened 3 hours after going to bed. If the child is dry for the remainder of that night, then the waking is moved back to

2½ hours after bedtime. The waking time continues moving up for each dry night until it is 1 hour after bedtime. If the child wets the bed two or more times in 1 week, the schedule is restarted.

- Begin a positive practice procedure. Ask your child to lie in bed, count to 50, and then get up and go into the bathroom and try to urinate. This should be repeated 20 times in order, both right after having a wet bed and again the next night at bedtime.

- Install the bell and pad. This should be started on the second night of the waking schedule.

- Introduce cleanliness training. If your child wets the bed after the first night and the alarm goes off, have your child change out of his or her wet clothes and remove the wets sheets from the bed. The child is then directed to get dressed and make the bed. This last step is repeated 20 times before the child can go back to sleep.[5]

Research that has looked at how dry bed training helps children who wet the bed suggests that it may improve the success over only using the bell and pad. The extra steps such as positive practice and cleanliness training may be helpful for some children who may not respond well to only being awakened after they wet the bed. There are, unfortunately, some negative aspects of dry bed training. One problem with this technique that some parents report is that it can be difficult and unpleasant for both the parent and the child. Repeating the steps for cleanliness training—putting on and taking off bed clothes after an accident—can sometimes turn into middle of the night struggles between parent and child. The other negative aspect is that relapse—or the return of bed-wetting sometime after the program is completed—may be as high as it is for the bell and pad alone, which is about two out of every five children. One variation of these techniques that has tried to reduce relapse in bed-wetting is known as *full-spectrum home training.*

Full-Spectrum Home Training

Full-spectrum home training (FSHT) includes two of the components of dry bed training: the bell and pad and cleanliness training.[5] In addition, it adds two additional techniques to try to help the child stay dry once the program is completed. A *retention control training procedure* is taught to the child during the day in a manner similar to the positive practice part of dry bed training. Here the child is given a large amount of fluids and then is asked to tell when he or she feels the need to urinate. The child is then requested to wait for 3 minutes before going to the bathroom in order to practice holding the urine. If the child is successful on the first day at 3 minutes, the second day the time is extended to 6 minutes. Each day, the time is increased by 3 more minutes unless the child has an accident. If that happens, the next day's time is held the same until the child is again successful at waiting before urinating. For each successful day, the child is given some reward to encourage his or her progress. This reward can be money or something else the child would be motivated to work for. The general idea behind retention training is that you are helping your child gain the ability to hold urine for longer and longer periods of time in the hope that it will carry over to nighttime.

The final part of FSHT is an *overlearning* component. This part of the plan is specifically designed to help children with the problem of relapse and begins after the child has been dry for 14 consecutive dry nights. Following this 2-week success, the child is given fluids before bedtime in order to help strengthen the ability to stay dry overnight. On the first night of overlearning, the child is given 4 ounces of water to drink in the last 15 minutes before bedtime. If the child successfully sleeps through the night with no accidents for 2 consecutive nights, the amount of water is increased by 2 ounces. The amount of water the child is given to drink before bedtime is increased this way (2 ounces for each 2 successful nights) until a maximum amount is reached. This maximum is calculated by taking the child's age in years and adding 2 ounces. A 7-year-old, for example, would have a maximum of 9 ounces, and a 10-year-old would stop at 12 ounces. If the child has an accident, cut back on the fluids by 2 ounces until success is achieved again. When the child has reached the maximum and has had 14 consecutive dry nights, the overlearning portion of the plan is completed. Next is an overview of the steps involved in full-spectrum home training.

Full-Spectrum Home Training

- Install and begin the bell and pad procedure.

- Introduce cleanliness training. If your child wets the bed after the first night and the alarm goes off, have your child change out of his or her wet clothes and remove the wets sheets from the bed. The child is then directed to get dressed and make the bed. This last step is repeated 20 times before the child can go back to sleep.

- Begin retention control training during the day. Give your child a large amount of fluids, and then when your child indicates that he or she has to urinate, ask him or her to hold it for 3 minutes. Give your child some tangible reward (such as money or some other prize) for holding urination after this time. Increase the time by 3 minutes each day until your child can hold his or her urination for 45 minutes, at which point training ends. If your child fails on one day, repeat the same time the next day.

- Include the overlearning component of training after 14 consecutive successful (dry) nights. Give your child 2 ounces of water in the 15 minutes before bedtime on the first night, and add 2 ounces for each 2 consecutive dry nights.

- If your child has an accident, cut back on the water by 2 ounces.

- Stop adding more water when the maximum for your child is reached. The maximum number of ounces is determined by taking the child's age in years and adding 2 ounces.

- Overlearning ends when the child has had 14 consecutive dry nights while drinking the maximum fluids prior to bedtime.

One advantage of the full-spectrum home training program may be its ability to reduce relapse among children. Research suggests that less than half of the children using this plan relapse as compared to those on the other plans we discussed. Again, however, it is important to remember that this plan, like dry bed training, requires a significant commitment by the family, and it can be several months before complete success is achieved.

Medical Treatments for Bed-Wetting   Medical treatments have been used over the years to help children who have difficulty with nighttime wetting. One group of these medications may surprise you—they are antidepressants, or the drugs typically used for people who suffer from severe bouts of depression. The success of antidepressants such as the drug imipramine (also called Tofranil) is *not* a sign that these children are depressed. Instead, it is thought that the drug may relax muscles around the bladder, which should help it hold more fluid for a longer period of time. Also, another effect of this drug is that it suppresses REM, or dream, sleep (as we saw in Chapter 11, when we discussed the REM sleep attacks of people with narcolepsy). This interruption of normal sleep may also help children with bladder control.

Drugs such as imipramine can be effective in initially reducing bed-wetting, although their positive effects seem to disappear when the child stops taking the medication. Antidepressants are powerful medications (see Chapter 14 for more detail), and parents are cautioned to follow their doctor's advice closely if they decide to try a medical approach with their child.

A newer medical approach to the treatment of bed-wetting involves the use of the drug desmopressin (DDAVP).[6] This drug increases the production of the body's natural antidiuretic hormone (ADH) that seems to be in short supply among many children who experience bed-wetting problems. DDAVP is given to children orally or in a nasal spray, and older children can learn to give themselves the medication when it is needed. This drug increases ADH and helps the child's body make less urine, reducing the risk of nighttime accidents.

For both of these medical treatments for bed-wetting there is a concern about side effects as well as problems with wetting returning after treatment is stopped. Sometimes parents prefer to use a combination of approaches such as a medication that stops the problem quickly along with the bell and pad or one of the other treatment packages that help the child stay dry at night once the medication is reduced and ultimately eliminated. This becomes an issue of personal preference that should be discussed frankly with your child's physician. Finally, some families turn to medication on a short-term basis to help a child who may be going to an overnight camp or for a child staying with a friend. The medication may allow the child to avoid potentially embarrassing situations if the bed-wetting problem is not yet under control.

PROBLEMS WITH ANXIETY

Being anxious or depressed can have a direct impact on how one sleeps.[7] It is probably not surprising to you that feeling tense can make it difficult to fall asleep. It is also true that feelings of anxiety or anxious thoughts can cause you to awaken in the middle of the night and disturb sleep in general. It is quite common for children to be anxious about everyday things in their lives. For example, many children are fearful of animals, strangers, or new situations. When it comes to sleep, fear of the dark or fear of monsters lurking in the closet or under the bed can interfere with a child's ability to fall asleep. Traumatic events can also trigger feelings of anxiety that can negatively affect a child's sleep. One such child recently came to our attention.

✩ RICKIE

Rickie's father called us in response to an ad in the local newspaper for children with sleep problems. Neither Rickie, who was 6 years old, nor anyone else in the family had ever had any significant sleep problems up until about 18 months before. It was a year and a half after the family was in a serious car accident that Rickie's father contacted us. Their minivan was hit on the side by a drunk driver, and everyone in the family was hurt, although fortunately not seriously. After the accident, all of the children had trouble sleeping, including not wanting to go to bed and waking up crying. Two months or so passed, and all the children except Rickie seemed to be back to normal. He continued to have trouble almost every night. He would appear quite frightened about going to sleep and would usually wake up at some point and would call out to his parents. At bedtime and upon waking, his parents would be in his room, spending a great deal of time talking about how there was nothing to be frightened about. It was suspected that these lengthy discussions may have helped contribute to Rickie's continued difficulties going to sleep and falling back to sleep after awakening.

Rickie's sleep problems seemed to be spilling over into his daytime behavior. His father told us that Rickie was much more hesitant in social situations, such as playing with friends, and also cried when he had to ride in the car. Rickie's father described these changes as daytime nightmares— episodes where he would scream and cry uncontrollably. He would only go in the car if he could sit next to his mother or father in the front seat.

Rickie's problems were most worrisome to his parents because they were so disruptive to the whole family at night, and they were concerned that their other children seemed to have recovered so nicely from the accident but that Rickie had not.

We recommended that his parents teach him relaxation exercises before bedtime to help him relax but also to help him keep his mind occupied and refocus his attention. Each night before sleep, his parents were instructed to have him lie back on his bed and practice tensing and relaxing each of his major muscles. After about 15 minutes of practice, his parents would kiss him goodnight and tell him to feel his muscles tingle, which he would do until he fell asleep. The goal was to have him be able to relax this way each night on his own. However, his parents enjoyed the positive routine each evening (especially because he was not getting upset anymore), so they stayed with him each night until he finished his exercises. From the very first night, Rickie stopped having trouble at bedtime. His parents were then instructed to tell him to practice his relaxation if he woke at night. After about 1 month, Rickie was sleeping through the night on most nights and would go to bed without difficulty. His parents also encouraged Rickie to use his relaxation skills in social situations where he felt tense and while riding in the car, and this seemed to have a positive impact on his behavior during the day as well.

Rickie responded quite well and quite quickly to the relaxation exercises. They seemed to help him relax in situations where he felt tense and also helped to refocus the discussions with his family to something more constructive and positive than simply saying that there was nothing to be afraid of. Relaxation training is one of the most often recommended treatments for children and adults who are anxious. The following are some guidelines for trying out such a plan.

Relaxation Instructions

- Have your child lie back on his or her bed. Arms and legs should be limp as well as the head. If your child is holding up his or her head, this means that the muscles of the neck are tensing and that he or she is not completely relaxed.

- For younger children, or children who seem to have a problem following directions, a simple instruction such as "act like a wet noodle" may be enough to help them visualize what you want them to do.

- Begin at the facial muscles, asking your child to slowly and carefully tense the muscles. The tension of the muscles should last for about 5 seconds.

- Following the tension of a set of muscles, have your child relax the muscles, and give him or her 10–15 seconds to experience the good feeling of relaxation.

- As you talk to your child, use a soothing and calming voice and take your time.

- Move from the facial muscles to the jaw (clenching and relaxing the jaw); then to the neck and shoulders; and then to the arms and hands, chest, stomach, thighs, legs, and feet.

- Have your child tell you if he or she experiences any pain or discomfort. You may need to instruct him or her to not tense the muscles too tightly, or you may want to avoid certain muscle groups.

- Have your child practice until he or she can run through it alone.

- Have your child use the relaxation procedure any time he or she feels tense or anxious.

These instructions should provide you with a rough outline of how to teach your child to relax, especially at bedtime. It is important to describe the technique to your child as a very powerful one, one that should be helpful in making him or her more relaxed. This is helpful because your child's expectation for the technique can be just as important as the technique itself. This is true for relaxation as well as for any of the other techniques we have described in the book. Believing something will work will help boost the power of such efforts to help children sleep.

"Reverse Psychology"   Asking a person to do one thing but expecting them to do the opposite is a pop psychology concept that has been the brunt of numerous jokes. However, this "reverse psychology," or more formally *paradoxical intention,* does have a place when trying to help people sleep. Some children and adults become extremely concerned that they will not be able to sleep. Perhaps there is an important event coming up the next day that they feel will be ruined if they do not sleep well. These anxious thoughts can, by themselves, interfere with sleep and make it a self-fulfilling prophesy. In other words, it is as if these individuals make their fear of not sleeping come true simply by worrying about it. For these individuals, using *paradoxical intention* can sometimes be useful. When we have used it for children, we go through the usual bedtime routine but tell the children that falling asleep is not that important. We want the children in bed, with the lights out, and with their eyes closed. However, we instruct them that they should try to remain awake without opening their eyes or moving around too much. If a child is becoming anxious about not being able to sleep, giving him or her permission to stay awake can help to relieve these fears and paradoxically help the child fall asleep.

Other Helpful Hints for Helping Children with Anxiety   Sometimes the solution to nighttime fears can be something as simple as providing a night-light. This is helpful for children who may be frightened by the dark. In addition, we have sometimes used "magic" to help children get control of their fears. The case of Quinn (see Chapter 10), for example, shows how we gave a child a magic wand that his parents told him would slay any monsters that may be in his room. This *power of suggestion* can be very persuasive and can be used to a family's advantage to help a child feel more in control. Self-talk, which involves having the child repeat positive sayings such as "I am a big girl and am not afraid" can also be helpful. Finally, providing children with some positive treat after a night without difficulty can be quite helpful. One girl who said she was afraid at night got to spend some extra time with her father the next morning if there were not outbursts the night before. Try to match the type of assistance with your child's preference and age to give him or her several different ways to overcome these anxious feelings or thoughts.

PROBLEMS WITH DEPRESSION

Depression—that feeling of sadness that we all experience from time to time—can also negatively affect sleep.[8] For some people who are depressed, they may awaken early in the morning and not be able to fall back asleep. For others, the problem is just the opposite. They cannot seem to get out of bed, and their lives are spent struggling to carry on even minimal daily activities. There is a *chicken and egg problem* when trying to understand how sleep and depression are related; in other words, does poor sleep make you depressed or does depression disrupt your sleep? For most people who have serious problems with depression, their condition obviously affects their sleep. On the other hand, not sleeping well can make some people depressed, in part because of their inability to control their own sleep, and in part because they cannot function as well during the day. Although we do not yet have a full understanding of *how* sleep and depression are related, it is essential that you recognize that they *are* related, at least among some people.

It is also important to point out that some of the classic signs of depression are behaviors that are commonly observed among otherwise healthy children and adolescents. In addition to changes in sleep patterns—which are normal during development—adolescents also show other typical signs of depression such as changes in eating habits and changes in their interest in activities. Observing only one of these signs in your child is not necessarily an indication that he or she is depressed. However, if your child shows several or all of these signs, it is important to take them seriously. Problems in school or with friends (for example, being bullied) may be causing your child's difficulties, and it is imperative that you talk to your child about the problems and possibly seek outside professional help.

The close relationship between sleep and depression is most obvious when you notice that one treatment used for people with depression that is related to the seasons—known as the *winter blues, cabin fever,* or more formally as *seasonal affective disorder*—is also a successful treatment for some sleep problems. The *bright light therapy* that we looked at previously for people whose biological clocks are off schedule has also helped many people who get depressed mainly during the winter months when there is less sunlight available. If your child seems to have depression-related sleep problems, using bright light therapy may prove helpful. Refer back to Chapter 9 for a more detailed discussion and description of this procedure.

There are a number of different approaches for helping people who suffer from depression, and a comprehensive description of these techniques is beyond the scope of this book. Again, if you suspect that your child is depressed, professional consultation is recommended.

SLEEP-RELATED HEADACHES

Some people suffer from headaches when they wake up in the morning. Obviously, if this occurs on a regular basis, these people are starting off each day in a negative mood that can set the tone for the rest of the day. There are several possible causes for early morning headaches—including breathing difficulties, caffeine withdrawal, or sleep deprivation—each one of which can be remedied fairly easily.

One cause of early morning headaches we discussed previously is breathing difficulties at night. When sleep is interrupted either by breathing difficulties or, in the extreme, by stopped breathing for a brief period of time (sleep apnea), the lack of oxygen received during the night can cause early morning headaches. Refer back to Chapter 11 for a detailed discussion of sleep-related breathing difficulties to see if your child's morning headaches are linked to this nighttime problem.

A common, but frequently overlooked, cause of early morning headaches is caffeine withdrawal. Withdrawal from any drug (and the caffeine in coffee, tea, soft drinks, and other sources *is* a drug) is the body's reaction to no longer having the substance available. In a cruel twist, when the brain detects a lack of the drug it was used to having, it sends out messages that result in unpleasant feelings—including headaches. Because caffeine leaves our systems in a matter of hours, going all night without having any can trigger early morning withdrawal symptoms, usually in the form of headaches. And it is more than just a little ironic that the headache medicine you might take (such as aspirin) works better if it is taken with caffeine. Makers of Excedrin, for example, can claim that it works better than other headache medications simply because they include a hefty dose of caffeine in with the aspirin and acetaminophen. The only true cure for caffeine-related headaches is to wean the person away from caffeine over a period of weeks.

Sleep deprivation can also cause a person to have headaches in the morning. Not getting enough sleep restricts NREM, or nondream, sleep and increases the proportion of REM, or dream, sleep. Because your brain needs dream sleep so much, it "catches up" on this type of sleep at the expense of nondream sleep when you go without sleep for a time. During dream sleep, the vessels in the brain tend to dilate (or become larger), which can cause morning headaches. When you do not get enough sleep, your brain's need to recover dream sleep can cause you to have headaches in the morning. The treatment here is obvious: get more sleep. Even napping during the day, if there are pressures for your evening time, can help to eliminate sleep deprivation–related headaches.

If none of these causes of headaches seem to fit your child's case, a medical exam may help rule out other possible causes of early morning headaches. As we see next, tooth grinding during sleep may also cause headaches, and a medical consultation may prove helpful in identifying these sources of your child's pain.

NIGHTTIME TOOTH GRINDING

Nighttime tooth grinding, which has the formal name *nocturnal bruxism,* includes all forms of teeth clenching and grinding that occur during sleep.[9] This does not seem to be a serious sleep concern on its own; however, the dental consequences (grinding down of the teeth) can become serious in people who frequently grind their teeth. In addition, people who grind their teeth are more likely to have jaw pain and headaches than those who do not grind their teeth. Research on adults suggests that tooth grinding can be related to daytime stress, such that having a high-stress day can lead to night-time tooth grinding. Why does not everyone who is stressed grind their teeth? It may be that people who have minor misaligned or unbalanced teeth (called *malocclusions*) are at more risk for tooth grinding and that, when these people are stressed during the day, this combination of dental and psychological factors causes tooth grinding.

One group of children with special needs that is particularly susceptible to tooth grinding is children with Rett syndrome. This is a serious neurological disorder that is found almost exclusively in girls and often includes intellectual disabilities, serious motor impairments, epileptic seizures, and difficulties with communication. This syndrome usually becomes noticeable during a child's second year of life and is estimated to occur in 1 out of every 10,000 female births worldwide. Tooth grinding appears as a common symptom of Rett syndrome.

A number of different approaches have been suggested to help children who have serious and longstanding problems with tooth grinding, although there is no current cure for this problem. The most successful treatment of tooth grinding to date, however, involves the use of dental splints. Made in consultation with a dental exam, acrylic splints are constructed to fit your child's back teeth. Many children who sleep with these splints have been successful in reducing their nighttime tooth grinding. In addition, it is important to look for sources of stress for your child that may be making this problem worse and to use the relaxation exercises we described earlier in this chapter to address these difficulties.

CONCLUSION

I describe in this chapter a number of nonsleep-related problems that can influence sleep, including bed-wetting, anxiety, depression, headaches, and tooth grinding. Fortunately, there are a number of techniques that can be used to reduce these problems and improve sleep. The next chapter covers daytime behavior problems, which as you will see, can be related to sleeping difficulties. I provide a brief overview of techniques to improve these other difficulties.

13

Daytime
Behavior Problems

You may be asking yourself why we have included a chapter on daytime behavior problems in a book that is about sleep. A child who is noncompliant or who is aggressive may not have any sleep problems at all, and these daytime difficulties may not be related to what happens at night. However, for some people, not sleeping well can contribute to daytime problems. Research that we have conducted with children with special needs demonstrates that *for people who already have behavior problems during the day,* sleep problems can make these behaviors worse. The irritability that you or I may experience when our sleep is disrupted can reveal itself as hitting other people, refusing to follow requests, or in extreme cases, even self-injurious behaviors such as face slapping or hand biting among people with special needs. It seems that poor sleep patterns do not cause daytime behavior problems, but it is clear that disrupted sleep can make these problems worse.

In addition to the possible relationship between poor sleep and daytime problems, we often find that some "sleep problems" resemble problems that parents experience with their children at times other than bedtime or in the middle of the night. The tantrums that children display at night may only differ in timing with tantrums that occur in other situations. For example, the tantrum that follows a request to go to bed may be no more a problem with sleep than the tantrum that occurs in school following a request to do work or the tantrum that occurs at mealtime at home. Because these difficulties may actually represent very similar problems, a good number of the parents we see need help with their child's behavior problems both at night and during the day.

It is the possible connection between sleep and behavior problems that, along with the all too common observation that children who tantrum at night may also present challenges during other times, prompted me to include this chapter. I begin with a brief overview focusing on *why* children might have behavior problems such as tantrums and then follow this discussion with some suggestions for parents to help reduce the behavior problems of their children. Obviously, I will not be able to present a comprehensive discussion of these issues in one short chapter. I have written two books that exclusively focus on managing these behavior problems, and readers can find references to these books in the notes at the end of this book. However, this chapter should help readers get started on the road to improved behavior.

WHY DO CHILDREN HAVE BEHAVIOR PROBLEMS?

The key to helping a child from misbehaving lies in understanding what is motivating the child at that point in time. Although there are many theories about how past events such as traumas, relationships with parents, or even problems at birth can contribute to a child's behavior problems, we often are powerless to change any of these. In other words, a past trauma may be one reason why a child throws a tantrum at a relative's house or in the car, but because we are not able to wipe away the past, we must look to the present for a practical solution to the problem. As a result, we often focus on the "here and now" to see, for example, why a boy is screaming in a supermarket or why a little girl is crying when she is asked to get dressed in the morning. I am *not* saying that past events are unimportant, only that many are difficult to identify and that most are impossible to remedy.[1]

Rule Out Medical Problems

As I did when I discussed sleep problems, we must also rule out physical causes for behavior problems. Although it is relatively rare for some medical problem to be the cause of your child's being upset, overlooking this possibility can lead you to many frustrating situations that could have been avoided. It is important to point out that, like poor sleep, medical problems can make behavior problems worse, but they usually are not the sole cause of a child's difficulties. This means that, even if you find a medical problem and can cure the illness, it may not lead to the complete elimination of the behavior that is so disruptive.

What should you look for? Any illness that causes pain, for example, can be at the bottom of an increase in problems. An ear infection, headache, or stomachache will make your child more irritable, which in turn will make him or her more likely to have problems. Children with special needs are often more prone to physical problems, and we therefore to need to be more vigilant about finding any possible medical condition contributing to misbehavior. A child in a wheelchair, for example, who cannot shift positions can be extremely uncomfortable after only a few minutes, and this can cause fussiness and anger outbursts. Simply shifting the child's physical position periodically may help reduce behavior problems. In general, children who are not verbal or who do not express themselves well can often not tell you when they are in pain, so a complete physical exam may be in order, especially if a child has a sudden increase in behavior problems.

Do Not Wait Too Long to Rule Out Medical Problems

At the same time you are having your child evaluated for a possible medical problem, you can follow the steps described in this chapter. Too many people wait for months to find the definitive medical diagnosis for their child only to find out that there is nothing they can do about it anyway. The steps described in the chapter can be followed at the same time that you are looking for or treating a medical problem and can begin to help your child within a few weeks.

Impulsivity

Although not technically a medical problem, some children are very impulsive by nature, and this can lead to a number of difficulties. Children with ADHD, for example, sometimes blurt out the first thing that comes to mind, stop playing a game in the middle to move on to something else, or do not finish cleaning their room because they are distracted by some other interesting activity. These types of behaviors can frustrate teachers, friends, and family members and can have some rather negative long-term consequences. Teachers may only give these children negative feedback ("Would you sit down!"), which can eventually make the child feel quite bad about him- or herself. Friends may reject such a child, and this can stunt the development of good social skills. Family members also can begin to see the child as only a bother and may feel too drained at the end of the day to give the child much "quality time." It is important to remember that these types of behaviors from the child are not intentional acts aimed at annoying people, but rather they are the result of the child's difficulty in reigning in his or her impulses. I will discuss later how you can help such a child get more control over these impulses.

Attention Difficulties

One area that parents often have trouble understanding is the limit of their child's attention span. What some parents consider noncompliance can sometimes be simply a difficulty on the part of the child to remember what he or she was supposed to do. For example, asking a young child in the middle of a television program to clean his room at the next commercial is an invitation for disaster. By the time the commercial rolls around, the parent's request is "out of mind," and the fact that the child did not clean his room probably is simply a difficulty with remembering rather than deliberate noncompliance. If the parent waited for the commercial to make the request ("While the commercial is on, I want you to go into your room and put your dirty clothes in the hamper"), the child is much more likely to cooperate. Again, young children are still learning how to remember things after being distracted, and some older children with special needs may also have trouble with this skill. Look to see if this is the cause of your child's "behavior problem," and if so, try to make requests that 1) are clear ("Put your shoes in your closet" versus "Clean up this mess") and that 2) can be completed immediately ("Put your dishes in the sink" versus "Put your books away when you come home from school").

What Are They Trying to Tell Us?

In addition to impulsivity and attention difficulties, behavior problems can sometimes serve a purpose for a child. One way to look at behavior problems such as tantrums, aggression, or noncompliance is as a way for children to communicate their wants and needs.[2] For example, crying is often the only way infants can let us know what they want. They cry when they are hungry, when they are cold or wet, and even if they simply want you near them. In fact, some parents are experts at reading the messages in their child's cries. At the same time, older children may use screaming in a store or hitting another child to communicate things that they cannot get any other way. Some exciting research in the field of behavior problems suggests that many of these difficulties can be looked at as a form of communication and that we can reduce behavior problems in children by teaching them better ways to communicate with us.

My research and that of others who work with people with special needs points to several common "messages" that children seem to communicate through their behavior problems (Figure 13.1). Understanding what a child is communicating with his or her behavior problem is at the heart of any treatment plan designed to help a child with this difficulty.

Attention from others is a common desire of many children. For most children, talking to a parent or friend, getting hugs, or even simply being near others is something they work hard to achieve. Although some children quickly learn the ability to get attention from others in positive ways, others take a different route and use their behavior problems. Through screaming or other behavior problems, some children are very successful at focusing attention on themselves. For example, I was once walking down the hall in a school on my way to consult in a classroom and was a little lost until one clue helped me to quickly pick out not only which classroom I needed to go in but to know that the behavior problem of the child in question was *attention-getting*. In one class, there was a teacher yelling at the top of her lungs at child who was misbehaving. The yelling directed me to where the classroom was, and the fact that the teacher was yelling made me believe that the child was being very successful at getting that teacher's attention. This is an important example because it should remind us that some children would prefer even something that seems unpleasant—such as yelling—over being ignored.

A good portion of the "terrible twos" may be explained as *attention-getting behavior*. I remember a scenario when my son was almost 2, and he was being quite fussy. I asked him what he wanted, and he told me "milk." After getting him a glass of milk, he did not look satisfied and said, "No want milk, want water!" A glass of water still did not satisfy him, and he said, "No, want milk!" Milk, water, which was it? After going through this several times, it dawned on me that he probably did not want something to drink at all but, instead, wanted to spend some time with me. He did not know how to initiate

Attention	Escape from demands	Escape from attention	Tangibles	Sensory
• "Would you come here?"	• "I don't want to do this!"	• "I want to be by myself!"	• "I want that!"	• "This feels good!"

Figure 13.1.   Common messages of children's behavior problems.

and carry on a sophisticated conversation, so he used his demanding requests to engage me. I was able to avoid tantrums during future episodes by remembering what was truly motivating him and using that as a cue to spend some time with him.

A second message that is seen quite frequently among children is *escape from demands*. In other words, some children misbehave to get out of doing things that they do not like. For example, one child with ASD that I worked with was hitting his teacher, and she asked for some advice on how to make him stop. During one class time, I watched as his teacher asked him to point to a certain picture. Instead of pointing to it, he hit her in the face. Her response was to very calmly ask him to stand up and sit alone in the corner. In her mind, she thought she was punishing him for hitting her, and in fact, she felt guilty about using this "time out" program. However, as we later found out, being allowed to stop working and instead sit away from his desk was exactly what he wanted! He learned that the way to get out of doing any school work was to hit his teacher.

Sometimes children act up to get out of doing things that are too difficult for them. Other times the requests may be for things that are too monotonous and mundane, and a child may misbehave to escape the boredom. Whatever the reason for wanting to escape, it is important to look for *escape from demands* as a message and use that to help the child with this problem.

A different child may act out to *escape from attention* rather than (or in addition to) escape from demands. In other words, the message may not be "I don't want to do that" but instead, "I want to be alone." Often we find that children with ASD will hit themselves or others to be left alone. Although we do not fully understand what makes other people sometimes unpleasant to be around for these children, it is critical to know that their behavior problems are occurring for this reason. Some children without ASD can also misbehave to avoid being around people they do not like. Knowing whether a child is acting up to get attention or to avoid attention is important for our efforts to help these children become better behaved.

Sometimes the goal of a child's misbehavior is to get some *thing*. Behavior problems that occur to get things or *tangibles* are quite common and can be seen on almost a daily basis in any supermarket or toy store. A child's crying and flailing about on the floor in the candy aisle after being told that she cannot have a Snickers bar is an example of a tangibly motivated behavior problem. In addition to toys or foods, the *thing* a child may want could be an activity. For example, being told he cannot go outside because it is raining can cause a boy to become aggressive because he is being denied this favorite activity. Why do children continue to act this way? Because, like the other messages we just mentioned, sometimes they work! Cry enough in a supermarket and your parent is likely to give in and get you what you want. This giving in obviously increases the chance that the child will cry again the next time he or she really wants something. If this sounds familiar, it may be helpful to review Chapters 4 and 5 for help dealing with the thoughts that contribute to parents giving in to these types of demands even when they know they should not. The next section will cover how to change these situations with your child.

The final message is a more private one than the messages we have just covered. Here the goal is *sensory* feedback—the child acts in a particular way because it looks, feels, tastes, or sounds good to do it. In other words, the behavior itself is pleasant in some way for the child, and he or she keeps doing it because of the way it feels. A child who rocks back and forth for hours at a time may be doing this simply because it feels good and not because of attention, escape, or tangibles. Sometimes children with severe disabilities will hit themselves lightly but constantly, and this may happen because of the sensory feedback it provides them. Knowing that a behavior is occurring for sensory reasons is important because it tells us that simply ignoring it will not work. In fact, being ignored and not having anything else to occupy them can be at the heart of why children act in ways to keep themselves stimulated. Other behavior plans such as time out (for example, removing the child to a corner of the classroom) will also be ineffective because the child is not behaving this way to get attention but rather because of the way it feels.

How Do You Know What They Are Trying to Tell You?

The obvious next question is, now that I know about these messages, how do I find out what *my child* is trying to tell me with his or her behavior? Sometimes understanding the message of a behavior problem is simple and obvious. For example, a child who screams each time a certain request is made ("Say your name") but very rarely at other times may be screaming to escape from demands. On the other hand, often the message is obscured, and it is difficult to figure out exactly what is setting off a problem. One thing that we recommend to parents is to keep a record of each time the behavior occurs, what was happening at the time it occurred (called the *antecedent*), and how they responded to it (called the *consequence*). For example, if your child hits you while you are on the phone and you say "Stop that" and explain why it is wrong to hit, you would write down what is shown in Table 13.1.

Just looking at this one interaction, can you guess what might be motivating this girl's aggression? If the mother was on the phone and not paying attention to her daughter, the daughter may be trying to get attention by hitting. Also, if the mother usually responds to this hitting by spending even a little bit of time with her, the behavior is successful, and the girl will probably hit again when she wants her mother's attention. If you observe these types of patterns, you can begin to make good educated guesses about what may be motivating your child's difficulty.

There are other, more formal ways of assessing the messages behind behavior problems, and these are usually used by professionals in psychology, education, or special education, although parents have also found them to be valuable at times. One assessment technique called a *functional analysis* uses the basic observation task we just described, but observations of the child are in situations that are purposely set up or staged. For example, if you thought your child was screaming to escape demands, you might give your child an easy task for 5 minutes followed by a more difficult task for 5 minutes and then compare how often your child misbehaved in each situation. You would have to repeat this several times in different orders to make sure that it was the type of task and not something else that was causing differences in your child's behavior. If you thought tangibles were involved, you could compare your child's behavior both with and without his or her favorite toy. You basically test out each of your guesses until you find something that regularly results in your child's misbehavior.

Because of the time and disruption involved in using a functional analysis to determine these messages, we developed an alternative to help better understand behavior problems. Called the Motivation Assessment Scale (MAS), this questionnaire can also be used to make more informed guesses about what might be causing a child's

Table 13.1. Sample antecedent-behavior-consequence chart

Antecedent	Behavior	Consequence
I was on the phone	Hitting me	Told her to "Stop that" and explained why hitting is wrong

disruptive behavior. It is filled out by a parent for behavior problems at home or by a teacher for school difficulties, and it provides information about what might be motivating a problem.

THE SEVEN "Cs" FOR CHANGING BEHAVIOR

Once you have an idea about *why* your child may be misbehaving, there are several different steps that you can take to help reduce the frequency of these problems. The following *seven Cs* should go a long way toward improving many behavior problems. However, more severe problems or problems that do not improve over several months should probably receive the attention of a professional.

Calm Yourself

This is most important! You cannot be an effective parent if you are upset. In fact, it would probably be better not to do anything while you are angry than to try to work on your child's behavior problem. The mother of one of the children I once worked with told me how she used a time out program on herself whenever she was getting upset. She would grab a glass of wine and close herself in the bathroom for a half hour until she was composed and could face the problems again. She told me that this happened only about once per week but that it really helped her not to act rashly or lash out at her child. In addition to your own version of a time out, you can use the relaxation exercises we described in Chapter 12 on yourself to calm down when you feel yourself getting upset. And the techniques for changing the way you look at these situations (described in Chapter 5) can help as well. Finally, if you cannot do it alone, the support of family, friends, or other parents in similar situations can be very helpful, and you should reach out in some way if you feel out of control.

Communication

We saw that research is uncovering the messages behind many of the behavior problems our children display. Research I have worked on for several decades now points to the ability to reduce even some of the most severe behavior problems by teaching a very specific form of communication. What we do is find the message being communicated by the behavior problem (for example, "I don't want to do this!") and then teach the child a better way to communicate this message—a technique referred to as *functional communication training*. For example, if we find that a child is screaming because his school work is too difficult, we would teach him to say "Help me" to his teacher, who in turn would give him more assistance on the task. If another child is screaming, but we find that this child's message is "Would you come here?," we then teach the child a better way to get someone's attention. It is important to point out that improving communication skills in general does not by itself lead to fewer behavior problems. It must involve teaching a better way to communicate the message being sent by the child's misbehavior. More detail about functional communication training is available in several of the references for this chapter in the notes at the end of this book.

Choices

Giving a child a choice in important situations can sometimes be a miracle cure for behavior problems. In just one example, when my son was younger, he hated taking baths. We found that if we told him, "It's time to take a bath," he would resist and find a hundred excuses to delay or avoid it. However, when we gave him the choice, "Do you want to take your bath with your He-Men or your Ninja Turtles?," he would pick one set and go off to get them to put in the bathtub. Giving him some control over the situation seemed to make taking a bath more acceptable to him, and we encountered much less resistance.

The example of my son's problems at bath time is a good one because it points out how we can give children choices even in situations where there does not seem to be room for a choice. He still had to take a bath every day, but he could at least pick the toys he would play with. One child I worked with who would refuse to go on the school bus was in a similar predicament. She had to go to school and get on the bus, but we still could provide her with some options. Each day as she was getting ready for school, her mother would ask her, "Do you want to carry your blue bag or your black bag on the bus?" After the girl picked one of the bags and the bus arrived, her mother would ask, "Do you want to sit in the front or the back?," and would lead her on the bus. Giving her these choices, along with other forms of encouragement, helped to eliminate any resistance to boarding the school bus. Try to find ways to provide choices to your child, even in these seemingly nonchoice situations.

Change Preparation

Young children especially will respond better to requests if they are told what is coming next. It seems that the more stressed and harried we are, the less time we have to prepare our children for the things they have to do. This lack of warning, even for a few seconds, can cause some children to refuse even relatively simple requests. Mealtime is a good example. Telling a child, "You have 5 more minutes, and then it's time for dinner," can help the transition from playing or television watching to the family meal. In fact, sometimes children give parents a hard time about doing something they *like* if they are rushed and not forewarned. This suggestion takes some practice. You need to plan ahead to try to avoid problems, and it takes some getting used to if you do not already do this. But for many children, a prewarning about a request can mean the difference between a smooth transition and a battle of minds and bodies.

Consequences

There are two important issues to deal with when it comes to how you respond to your child or to the *consequences*. One concern is how to react to a behavior problem at the time it occurs. The second concern is how to react when your child is being good. We often spend a great deal of time thinking about how to respond to a behavior problem and much less time on good times and how to make them more frequent. The bottom line to these issues is obvious: We want to react to behavior problems in ways that make them less likely to occur again, and we also want to respond to the child who is being good in ways that make these times more frequent. We cover the consequences for good behavior in the next section on *constructive feedback*.

Understanding the message or messages that your child is trying communicate with his or her behavior problem should help you with the *consequences*. For example, if a child is misbehaving to escape from having to brush his teeth, a parent should make an effort to be sure that the child does not completely succeed. This does not mean wrestling the child to the ground, clamping open his mouth, and forcing him to brush! Instead, it would involve being sure that the child spends at least a few seconds brushing his teeth before stopping to make the request. You can always work on increasing the amount of time brushing later, but the child needs to learn that he or she cannot completely escape if he or she resists. Knowing that the cries or tantrums are aimed at avoiding brushing his teeth would stop you from doing something that might actually cause more trouble, such as sending him to his room—which would let him escape. In other words, if you know what your child is communicating with his or her behavior problem, you want to make sure that he or she is not being very successful at it. Your response should make it clear that behavior problems will not get a child what he or she wants.

It is quite common for us to hear parents say that they punish their children in some way but that their children do not seem to mind it. This is one reason why we rarely, if ever, recommend strong punishment for behavior problems. Looking at misbehavior as communication may help explain why some children do not seem to mind being punished. In the example we just described of the boy who was screaming and crying when asked to brush his teeth, his parent thought that yelling at him and sending him to his room was a pretty severe punishment. Yet, as you can now see, in this boy's eyes, this was probably the *best* thing the parent could have done: letting the child get out of brushing his teeth. The punishment came when they instead made him brush his teeth, even if only for a few seconds. It is important to remember that what is a punishment to you may be a reward to the child. Again, understanding the message tells you what your child may like and dislike and how to respond to misbehavior.

Constructive Feedback

How you respond to good behavior could be looked at as constructive feedback. Constructive feedback implies that, not only are you encouraging good things, but you are also providing guidance for growth. Sometimes this takes the form of simple praise: "You really did a nice job on your homework!" More often, when a child has a more severe behavior problem, this feedback is provided more formally. "Star charts," for example, are charts designed to give visual feedback to a child for times of good behavior. These charts frequently find a home on the refrigerator, and parents can give paste-on "stars" each day or activity for good behavior. Older children can sometimes benefit from a more formal "contract," where both parent and child sit down and write out expectations for each other.

You may need to keep your expectations modest at first. Do not expect that any plan will produce miraculous changes. Instead, set your sights on modest goals. For example, having a child who is extremely impulsive sit for even 2 minutes might be a good goal to encourage in a child. Rewarding a child for these small steps can help the child feel that change is possible and can motivate him or her to strive for more.

We always recommend that parents *catch them being good*. In other words, look for instances when your child is behaving well and praise them. However, we are often so busy that, if our child is being good, we are physically or mentally off doing something else. We now recommend that parents practice being more *mindful* or aware of what is going on around them. Putting down the phone, spending time with your child, and noticing the good things that happen can help your child behave better and can also improve your own frame of mind.

Consider the Next Time

Can you anticipate future problem situations and change things to prevent a problem next time? For example, sometimes we have children who misbehave to escape task demands. Although we can teach them how to communicate for help or for a break, we can also look at what we are asking them to do and see if it can be improved. Breaking a task down into smaller steps can often prevent escape-motivated behavior problems. Thinking ahead and redesigning home or school situations (for example, getting the next day's clothes picked out to avoid the next day's rush) can often eliminate problems before they occur.

CONCLUSION: A CAUTION ABOUT BEHAVIOR PROBLEMS

Following these simple steps will be helpful for the majority of families who are having trouble with their child's behavior. However, in more difficult situations, outside help and assistance may be useful. Some of the techniques we described, such as finding out the message for your child's behavior and teaching alternative ways to communicate, can take considerable skill in more complicated cases. Your school or local college or university may be good places to turn to for advice. Be patient and be optimistic. We have learned a great deal of information about behavior problems and their treatment over the past decade, and valuable help is available.

Sleep and Medications

Using medication is probably the first thing people think of when it comes to sleep problems. Your local drug store has shelves of over-the-counter medicines that are marketed to help people sleep, and millions of prescriptions are written each year in the United States for sleeping pills. Why then do we not spend more time in this book on these medications? The simple answer is this: medication is not recommended as a long-term solution for the majority of sleep problems. The Food and Drug Administration (FDA) does not approve the use of sleep-inducing drugs for children. According to most sleep professionals, medication is usually recommended only as a short-term answer to a sleep problem—usually for no more than a few weeks.[1] Instead, the other nonmedical suggestions made throughout this book are what even the medical profession prefers for people who have troubled sleep. However, despite the preference for nonmedical help, there are times when medication is suggested, and this chapter describes the most common of these sleep medications and the issues surrounding their use.

What causes the wariness about medical treatments? One concern is *dependence,* a term used to refer to the possibility of people becoming addicted to their sleep medication. Addiction to sleeping pills can happen in several different ways. First, people can become *tolerant* or become used to the sleep medication, needing more and more of it over time to be able to fall asleep. As we will see, some of the older sleep medications (called *barbiturates*) were more likely to cause dependence than more recently developed drugs. Another problem with some medications is called *insomnia rebound,* where not only do the sleep problems come back after the person stops taking the medication, they come back *worse* than before. In real life, what happens is that the person tries to stop taking his or her medication, but the sleep problems return in a more severe form, so the reaction is to go back to taking medication. This vicious cycle can be extremely difficult to break out of once it has begun.

In addition to fears that people will become addicted to these medications and have a difficult time getting away from their use, there are also concerns that the sleep problems will not be "cured," even after a period of time on medication. For the most part, the effects of sleep medications last only as long as you take them, and there tends to be no lasting benefit once their use is discontinued.

There are also specific concerns with the use of sleep medications for children with special needs. It is important to note that many, if not most, sleep medications tend to reduce the amount of deep (NREM, Stage 3) sleep we experience. This deep sleep plays a restorative role for the brain and provides energy conservation and recuperation of nervous system functioning. With less of this deep sleep, you feel sluggish, and learning new things the next day may be impaired. You can see that a decision to use medication for problems surrounding sleep is not a simple one and that a number of risks are built into its use.

I next describe the different classes of medications used for problems surrounding sleep (see Table 14.1). It is important for you to be informed about the current thinking surrounding these drugs to help you judge whether or not they should be used for your child.

BARBITURATES

During the late 19th century, a group of drugs—called *barbiturates*—were created that would help people fall asleep. This family of drugs includes those called Seconal, Amytal, and Nembutal. Their discovery was important because, at the time, people regularly used alcohol and other drugs such as opium to help with difficulties falling asleep. By the 1930s, barbiturates were widely prescribed by physicians, and unfortunately, by the 1950s, they were among the drugs most abused by adults in the United States. Because of the strong addictive properties of this group of drugs, they are no longer regularly recommended for sleep problems. Barbiturates are occasionally recommended in cases where other drugs are not effective and where their use can be monitored closely.

Table 14.1. Common sleep medications

Medication[a]	Use
Barbiturates Secobarbital (Seconal) Amobarbital (Amytal) Pentobarbital (Nembutal)	An older class of "sleeping pills" that are highly addictive and that have the potential for severe harm if mixed with other medications. No longer generally recommended for sleep problems.
Benzodiazepines Triazolam (Halcion) Remazepam (Restoril) Estazolam (ProSom) Quazepam (Doral) Flurazepam (Dalmane)	A family of medications that replaced the use of barbiturates used to induce sleep. They tend to have fewer side effects and less potential for addiction than barbiturates.
Antihistamines Benadryl Over-the-counter "sleeping pills" (e.g., Sominex, Unisom, Sleep-Eze)	A class of drugs that has the effect of causing drowsiness. These drugs have been used to induce sleep, although their effectiveness is questionable.
Other sleep-inducing medications Chloral hydrate (Somnote, Aquachloral Supprettes)	A drug that helps induce sleep. No longer generally recommended because of the potential for harm if mixed with other drugs.
Zolpidem (Ambien)	A short-acting drug that leaves the body within a few hours. Useful for people who just need help falling asleep but do not have night waking problems.
Zaleplon (Sonata)	A short-acting drug that works quickly to help adults fall asleep.
Eszopiclone (Lunesta)	A sleep aid that has a rapid onset but an intermediate duration of action that can help someone both fall asleep and sleep through the night.
Melatonin	A natural brain hormone that can help people fall asleep and may help to reset the body's biological clock.
Ramelteon (Rozerem)	A drug that works on the brain cells that influence the production of naturally occurring melatonin.
Antidepressants Imipramine (Tofranil)	A drug used to induce sleep, especially in people who are depressed. This drug reduces attacks of REM sleep that cause paralysis (cataplexy) in people with narcolepsy and sometimes is given to people with breathing-related sleep problems. Also used for children with enuresis (bed-wetting) to help bladder control and as a substitute for stimulants for children with ADHD.
Stimulants Methylphenidate (Ritalin) Amphetamine and dextro-amphetamine (Adderall) Modafinil (Provigil)	A drug used for people with problems of excessive sleepiness.
Other sleep-related medication Desmopressin (DDAVP, DesmoMelt, Stimate, Minirin)	An artificial form of the body's natural antidiuretic hormone (ADH) that is used for children with bed-wetting problems.

[a] The drug's brand name is provided in parentheses.

BENZODIAZEPINES

Since the 1960s, a second group of drugs—called *benzodiazepines*—have replaced barbiturates as the drug of choice for people who have trouble falling asleep. These drugs have a number of effects on people in addition to helping them fall asleep, including the ability to act as tranquilizers to calm people who are tense or anxious and as muscle relaxants. You probably immediately recognize the common name of at least one of the benzodiazepines—Valium—which is used to help calm people who are feeling tense. Valium is not recommended as a sleep medication, and currently only five of the benzodiazepines are approved by the FDA for use for adults with insomnia (Dalmane, Restoril, Halcion, ProSom, and Doral).

Although safer and less likely to have significant side effects when compared with barbiturates, benzodiazepines, if used improperly, can still have serious consequences for people who use this medication. If used for long periods of time (for example, several months), people can still become addicted to benzodiazepines. In addition, you can experience *rebound insomnia*—the temporary worsening of sleep problems after the drug is removed—and if taken in combination with alcohol, benzodiazepines can lead to death. Taking too much of this drug can also impair a person's memory, again a particular concern for people with special needs. Finally, benzodiazepines tend to produce "lighter" sleep, which unlike our natural sleep rhythms, may paradoxically cause more night waking and may have as yet unknown negative effects if the drugs are used on a long-term or chronic basis.

Benzodiazepines are usually categorized into two different groups: those that last longer in the body (long-acting) and those that stop having an effect relatively quickly (short-acting). Longer-acting sleeping pills can cause people to feel "drugged" or "hung over" the next day because the medication is still having its sedative effect even after you want to wake up. The short-acting drugs tend to stop working at about the time or before you are ready to be awake. The downside to these short-acting drugs is that some people may experience interrupted sleep during the night or early morning waking because the medication no longer is having an effect. One of the decisions that needs to be made, then, when choosing a sleeping pill is whether sleeping through the night and/or waking too early are the problems, thus making a long-acting drug necessary, or whether initiating sleep and feeling refreshed the next day are the main concerns, thus making only a shorter-acting drug necessary.

Halcion

The benzodiazepine that stays the shortest amount of time in the body is Halcion (also called triazolam). This drug received a great deal of negative publicity in the 1990s when charges that its use led to suicidal thoughts made headlines. Today it is generally believed to be safe when used at its proper (lower) dosage and when taken for only short periods of time (several weeks to months). Because Halcion remains effective for only a few hours, it is typically recommended for people whose only sleep problem is falling asleep.

Restoril

Restoril (temazepam) is a longer-acting benzodiazepine that also takes a little more time to begin working than some of the other drugs. As a result, it is usually recommended that it be taken a half hour before you want to fall asleep and is therefore not useful for people who need a middle-of-the-night sleeping pill. Its ability to work for a longer period of time makes Restoril one of the medications given to people who have trouble staying asleep throughout the night.

ProSom

ProSom (estazolam), another of the benzodiazepines, can stay in the body for up to 24 hours, so it can cause drowsiness in some people into the next day. Like Restoril, ProSom is used for people who have trouble remaining asleep throughout the night.

Doral

An addition to the longer-acting benzodiazepines is Doral (quazepam), which is also prescribed for people with night waking problems. Because its effects last well into the next day, it is often recommended for people who have daytime anxiety as well as nighttime sleep problems.

Dalmane

The longest-acting of the benzodiazepines is Dalmane (flurazepam), which like Doral, is often recommended for people who need its effects into the next day. Some individuals may experience depression, irritability, or temper problems with its use.

ANTIHISTAMINES

Those of you who have ever taken a cold medicine that included an antihistamine know that this drug can make you drowsy. This is why Benadryl, which is primarily an allergy medication with an antihistamine, is often recommended for children who cannot fall asleep at night. Antihistamines are also the main ingredients in over-the-counter drugs such as Sominex, Unisom, and Sleep-Eze. Unfortunately, the use of all of these drugs is not generally recommended as a sleep aid. Some professionals question whether or not they are generally effective at making people fall asleep, although most agree that the side effects such as daytime grogginess may be worse than some prescription medications. And, like the other sleep medications, if these drugs are used over a long period of time, they lose their effectiveness.

OTHER SLEEP-INDUCING MEDICATIONS

In addition to barbiturates, benzodiazepines, and antihistamines, other medications have been used to help induce sleep in people with insomnia. Chloral hydrate is sometimes used to help people who have difficulty initiating sleep. However, the benefits of this drug must be weighed against the risk of serious harm that can result when people mix this drug with other drugs. For example, the "Mickey Finn cocktail," which is celebrated in movies as a knockout drink, is a combination of chloral hydrate and alcohol. Typically, chloral hydrate is only used in medically supervised settings.

Ambien

Ambien (also known as zolpidem) is a drug that, although it does not belong to the family of benzodiazepines, bears some resemblance in its effect on sleep. Like Halcion, it is a short-acting drug that leaves the body within a few hours of its ingestion. This makes it useful for people who simply need help falling asleep but do not have night waking problems and who do not want the groggy feeling the next day. Initial research on this drug suggests that it may not decrease the deep sleep that is affected by other medications and that addiction to this drug may also be less likely. In 2013, the FDA lowered the recommended dose to be taken—especially for women—because its effects seemed to last into the next day, making it less safe to do things like drive in the morning.

Sonata

Sonata (zaleplon) is a short-acting drug that works quickly to help adults fall asleep. Because it stays in the system for a short period of time, it is usually recommended for people who have trouble falling asleep but who do not have problems waking up at night. Some individuals report side effects that include headaches, drowsiness, and dizziness. Its use does not seem to lead to tolerance or rebound insomnia.

Lunesta

Lunesta (eszopiclone), like Sonata has a rapid onset, but it has an intermediate duration of action that can help someone both fall asleep and sleep through the night. It is associated with limited tolerance, withdrawal, and rebound insomnia. Side effects include an unpleasant taste, dry mouth, and headaches.

Melatonin

As I described previously, melatonin is a natural brain hormone that appears to be related to the resetting of our biological clock. Following the discovery that melatonin may play a role in our sleep, research was conducted to see if and how its use might affect the sleep of people who were experiencing problems. Melatonin has two apparent effects on sleep. For some people, it seems to be able to act as a *soporific,* or a drug that makes you tired. In addition, it seems to have the ability to reset the biological clock and help people who sleep at the wrong times. This ability to reset the brain's clock is especially important for people who are blind and who do not get light cues from the sun. Melatonin seems to be helpful for a number of people who have difficulties going to sleep at night and for those who are sleeping at the wrong times. One of the attractions of melatonin over the other sleep medications is that it is a natural substance that is already present in the brain. In addition, studies to date indicate few, if any, side effects like the ones often seen in other sleep medications.[2]

On the surface, melatonin would appear to be an ideal sleep medication with few downsides. However, the effects of melatonin, at least for some people, may be fleeting. Just as with the other sleep medications, a proportion of people seem to adjust to the levels of melatonin over time, and they may need to use higher dosages or it may stop working. This is a caution for people who are relying on melatonin as a long-term solution to a sleep problem. It is important to note that, because the use of melatonin every day over a long period of time has not been studied well, we do not know if there are any long-term, negative effects from using this substance over months or years. Compounding the concern is that the production of melatonin is not regulated by the FDA and is therefore not tested by the federal government for impurities. This issue is not an idle concern and became very serious when another supplement used for insomnia—L-tryptophan—was found in 1989 to cause a serious illness that included severe muscle pain. It is believed that substances used in the processing of L-tryptophan caused this illness, although to date no definitive evidence has surfaced. Although there have been no reports of problems with melatonin, the fact that it is not regulated opens it up to similar potential problems. Despite all of the positive signs, we recommend that you use melatonin only in conjunction with consultation from a medical professional.

Rozerem

A drug related to melatonin is called Rozerem (ramelteon). This FDA-approved medication works on the brain cells that influence the production of naturally occurring melatonin, and unlike the other drugs recommended for insomnia (e.g., benzodiazepines), it is not classified as a controlled substance and therefore is not tightly restricted by physicians. It does not appear to cause rebound insomnia but can produce headaches, dizziness, and fatigue.

ANTIDEPRESSANTS

In the 1950s, scientists were developing drugs for people with schizophrenia when they found that one of the compounds they were working with—called *tricyclic antidepressants*—seemed to make people less depressed. Imipramine (also called Tofranil) is an example of one of the tricyclic antidepressant drugs. These antidepressant medications have been very helpful for some people who have long suffered from serious depression. At the same time, these drugs also have a number of other beneficial effects that have proven useful for people with sleep and sleep-related problems. Because these drugs make people drowsy, they are often given to people who are dealing with both depression and insomnia. And it is interesting to note that, for some children with ADHD, the tricyclic antidepressants can have the same effect as drugs such as Ritalin and Adderall and can help those children focus their attention during the day. Because these drugs also help induce sleep, they are sometimes recommended for children with sleep problems *and* with ADHD in place of drugs such as Ritalin and Adderall—which, as stimulants, may interfere with a child's ability to fall asleep.

Another effect of antidepressant medication is the reduction of the amount of REM, or dream, sleep. As we mentioned earlier, this can sometimes be a problem because of the negative effects of reduced dream sleep on cognitive ability. However, some people with narcolepsy find these drugs quite helpful. If you remember, people with narcolepsy will often suffer sleep attacks with temporary paralysis (cataplexy) during the day. These sleep attacks are actually the immediate encroachment of dream sleep into a state of wakefulness. Taking antidepressants can often reduce these attacks during the day, which can significantly improve the quality of life for people with narcolepsy.

Two other groups also seem to benefit from this group of drugs. In Chapter 12, we saw how children who have trouble with bedwetting are sometimes prescribed these medications because of their ability to help children hold their urine longer. Finally, antidepressant medication is also used with people who have breathing-related sleep problems (see Chapter 11). The medication appears to be helpful in easing the breathing of these people, which in turn helps improve their sleep. As you can see, the tricyclic antidepressant medications have uses far beyond simply reducing depression.

PROMOTING WAKEFULNESS

A small group of people sleep too much, including those with hypersomnia and narcolepsy (discussed in Chapter 11). For these people, taking a stimulant during the day can be useful in keeping them more alert. Previously, drugs that we usually associate with ADHD, such as Ritalin (methylphenidate), were also prescribed for people who had a great deal of difficulty staying awake during the day. More recent research with a medication called Provigil (modafinil) suggests that it can be very helpful to these individuals. Unfortunately, the properties of both the stimulants, methylphenidate and modafinil, that assist with concentration (they are sometimes referred to as "smart drugs") have been abused by some.

CONCLUSION: WHAT DO YOU RECOMMEND?

Every child and every family is different, and their needs, desires, and difficulties must be accounted for when making decisions about using medication for sleep and sleep-related problems. There are clearly times when a short-term use of medication can be a blessing for some individuals. However, such decisions require careful consultation in partnership with a physician. All medications have their risks and negative side effects, and informed decision making is essential prior to using medications for sleep problems. I hope that the other recommendations made throughout this book provide families with alternatives to medication that may be just as effective but more acceptable for children with special needs.

15

Preventing
Sleep Problems

It is fitting that I end the book with a discussion of how to help parents prevent their young children from developing sleep problems. Using some of the techniques I have already discussed, along with important information about early child development, parents can help their children learn good sleep habits during the initial years of life. Ideally, couples who are expecting the birth of a child or who have recently gone through childbirth will use this information to inoculate their infants to potential sleep problems—much like they would inoculate their child against the measles or mumps. A second group that may find the information in this chapter helpful are those parents who already have a child with sleep problems and who are expecting the birth of another child. Preventing a repeat of the sleep problems with the next child is often high on the list of priorities. Being prepared for potential sleep problems can help ward off years of disruptive nights.

This is a good point to briefly revisit some of our previous discussion of how a child's innate bent toward having sleep problems works together with the way we react to them to cause sleep difficulties. In other words, some children will sleep well almost despite us, whereas other children are born with sleep problems and will be resistant to most efforts to help them. Children who are born with the potential for sleep problems are more likely to react negatively to changes in sleep schedules, feeding, or other irregularities. They tend not to be as adaptive to variation or unpredictability around sleep as other infants and are therefore more likely to learn bad habits regarding sleep. This chapter will discuss how parents of very young children can help them develop good sleep habits and can prevent their children from developing more serious problems related to sleep.[1]

DEVELOPMENTAL CHANGES IN SLEEP

One of the mysteries of parenthood—especially for first-time parents—is what to expect of your child in regard to sleep. On one extreme, some parents without much experience think that their newborn should fall asleep at around 8 p.m., sleep through the night, and awaken at 7 a.m. Others are frightened by stories of children who never sleep. The reality of newborns is that their sleep varies tremendously in the first weeks or months of life. Some infants miraculously sleep a solid 6–8 hours through the night almost from the day they are born. Others may awaken 3 or 4 times each night and be fully awake at 5 a.m. The only thing certain about the sleep of infants is uncertainty. All of these sleep patterns are "normal."

By about 6 months of age, however, it should be expected that a child will generally sleep through the night. If you look back at Figure 1.1 in Chapter 1, you will see that the average number of hours of sleep for a child this age is about 13 hours per day. This may mean that your child will sleep some 10–11 hours at night and then nap for the remainder of the time. Always remember that these times are approximate—some children sleep fewer and some sleep more. Whether or not the amount of sleep is a problem will be determined by the child's behavior during the day. If he or she sleeps only 10 hours per night but seems rested during the day, then it probably is not a problem. If, however, a child is sleeping 14 hours per night but still seems tired, then he or she may not be getting enough sleep.

What if a 6-month-old or older child is not sleeping through the night? Again, because this is approximately the age when you would expect a child to be getting a full night's sleep, a child of this age who wakes up one or more times each night could have the beginnings of a sleep problem. If you have a child younger than 6 months old, you can start to develop habits that will help him or her have better sleep patterns. I describe these habits later in this chapter.

Infant Personality and Sleep

In addition to developmental differences in sleep patterns—such as sleeping less as we grow older—another consideration for some sleep problems is a child's personality, which is sometimes referred to as *temperament*. Researchers (as well as most parents) have long known that children are born with different ways of dealing with the world. Some children are *easy*: they sleep and eat on regular schedules, and they adapt well to new situations or people. Other children, unfortunately, would be categorized as more *difficult*. These children, even as infants, eat and sleep erratically, and they do not adapt well to new situations, people, or changes in routines. They may be fussy or cranky if their usual order is disrupted. Researchers who study such children over long periods of time have found that many (but not all) children identified as *difficult* when they are infants are likely to have other behavior problems, even into adulthood.

When it comes to sleep, temperament or personality may play a role, especially for problems such as bedtime tantrums or disruptive night waking. The child who gives you a difficult time over meals may also protest at bedtime. The key to whether or not a child who may be difficult will also have problems sleeping depends on several factors. First, some children, by nature of their biology, will have trouble sleeping. They may not be tired enough at bedtime to fall asleep easily, or they may be "light sleepers" and easily awakened at night. Next, how we respond to their sleep problems will also affect sleep. As I discussed earlier, especially nervous parents may make sleep problems worse by giving a great deal of attention to a child who throws tantrums at bedtime or who is disruptive at night. Combine a natural tendency to sleep poorly with a difficult personality and parents who may not know how to react, and you have all the ingredients for a child with one or more sleep problems.

In this equation of

$$\text{poor sleep biology} + \text{difficulty personality} + \text{parental reaction} = \text{sleep problem},$$

we can change at least one of these factors: parental reaction. We know that a good reaction strategy to sleep problems can help children sleep better, even if we cannot change their sleep biology or their personality. And following certain guidelines very early on may help children establish better sleep habits before more serious problems begin. What follows are some suggestions for helping your child develop regular patterns that can improve sleep.

PREVENTION STRATEGIES

Helping your infant begin life with good sleep habits involves looking not only at sleep patterns but also at eating habits and other daily routines. For example, one of the more important factors in helping a child sleep through the night is proper fading of nighttime feedings. A child who continues to be fed in the middle of the night may continue to have disturbed sleep. In addition, the bedtime routines we described in the Good Sleep Habits chapter (Chapter 6) can be started early to help set the stage for better sleep later. Responding well to bedtime problems or night waking immediately can also help prevent more difficult episodes months or years later. Finally, some children may need help with reducing their naps, and we describe how to accomplish this and the rest of these prevention approaches next.

From Birth—Establishing Good Sleep Habits

Within the first few months of life, infants should start to develop their sleep–wake patterns. At first, a child may sleep for 6- to 8-hour stretches on and off throughout the day and night. You can help your child begin to spend more time sleeping at night in a number of ways. We know that daylight helps trigger our biological clock, so be sure to expose your child to morning daylight whenever possible. In contrast, a dark bedroom at night can help the natural release of melatonin that aids the onset of sleep. Daytime activity and exercise can help children sleep better and longer at night, but activity in the few hours before bedtime should be curtailed. Daytime naps that last too long can also interfere with nighttime sleep, so limit these to no more than 3 consecutive hours.

Create a bedtime routine leading up to sleep. This should be a series of activities that you and your child share and that remain the same each evening. A bath or washing followed by getting dressed for sleep is usually a good start. Then some quiet calm time such as reading a favorite book, even if for only a few minutes, can not only help your child fall asleep but have significant positive effects on development (as research suggests reading to children can). Some families incorporate prayers and/or a bedtime song into their routine. Finally, hugs and kisses can be the final signal to your child that it is time to sleep.

After your nightly routine, it is important to try to put your infant in the crib or bed *before* he or she is asleep. You do not want your child to associate falling asleep with being fed or even with falling asleep in your arms, because this will interfere with later bedtimes. It may also cause problems when your child awakens in the middle of the night and someone is not there, because now he or she has not learned to fall asleep alone. If this is already a problem, refer back to Chapters 7 or 8 for help dealing with these sleep difficulties.

At 3 Months—Fading Nighttime Feedings

A major contributor to early awakening or bedtime problems in very young children is nighttime feedings. Infants who are in the habit of feeding at night will likely have their sleep disrupted and may also have problems going to sleep on their own. This can occur for several reasons. First, infants who are fed right before bedtime often come to associate feeding with sleep. This often very pleasant time for both child and parent—feeding followed by sleep—can become a habit that is difficult for the child to break once the feedings are discontinued. The infant may not be able to fall asleep without first being fed. A second reason that sleep can be disrupted by feedings is that the child's diaper may become overly wet in the middle of the night, and this can wake some children. Finally, feeding affects our body's timing and rhythm, and late-night feeding can change it enough to disrupt sleep. Being used to these late feedings can cause the child to become hungry several hours later, and this can awaken the child in the middle of the night.

Typically, children should be able to go without being fed at bedtime or in the middle of the night by the age of 3 months. At about this age, then, you can start to teach your child to not feel hungry at night by increasing the time between feedings. Richard Ferber, a specialist in children's sleep problems, recommends a fading schedule that parents can follow to help eliminate extra feedings around sleep times. The goal is not to stop these nighttime feedings all at once but instead to reduce the time or amount of fluids the child receives each night and increase the time between feedings until you can eliminate bedtime and middle-of-the-night feedings.

On the first night of this fading schedule, you limit the number of ounces of liquid your child receives to 7 if he or she is bottle fed, or you reduce the number of minutes to 7 if your child is breast fed. At the same time, the amount of time between feedings should be at least 2 hours. On each night afterward, you decrease the number of ounces of fluid or minutes of breast feeding by one and increase the time between feedings by 30 minutes. This continues on each subsequent night until the eighth night, when the child should no longer be fed at bedtime or in the middle of the night. It is important to remember that a child of 3 months or older no longer needs these feedings to be properly nourished and that any discomfort should fade within a few days. If your child fusses at bedtime or awakens crying at night, refer to the section later in this chapter that provides help with these situations. Again, proper fading of nighttime feeding may help prevent later sleep problems.

Fading Nighttime Feedings

- On the first night—feed the child 7 ounces (if bottle fed) or 7 minutes (if breast fed) with 2 hours between feedings.

- On each subsequent night—reduce ounces or minutes by one (for example, the second night would be 6 ounces or minutes) and increase the time between feedings by 30 minutes (for example, from 2 hours to 2½ hours).

- A crying child older than 3 months may be hungry but does not *need* the nourishment.

- By the eighth night, the child should no longer be fed at bedtime or in the middle of the night.

- Any nighttime disruption can be handled as described in the next section.

At 6 Months—Sleeping Through the Night Most infants can sleep through the night without awakening when they are 6 months of age. This is important information for parents to have, because if their child is not sleeping through the night at this age, many parents feel that this is simply a typical situation. In fact, we often find that telling parents this information gives them "permission" to begin to change the nighttime problems. If your child continues to awaken one or more times at night after having fallen asleep and he or she is at least 6 months old, refer to the previous chapters (Chapters 7 or 8) for help in dealing with this problem.

The Preschool Years—Reducing Naps By age 2, children should be able to have an active morning without a nap. And somewhere between the ages of 3 and 6, most children no longer need an afternoon nap. Remember that we are all different when it comes to sleep needs. Some children and adults can nap during the day, and this does not negatively impact on their sleep. In contrast, other individuals who nap even for a short period of time can have trouble falling asleep at night or may awaken earlier than desired. If your child is still napping and this is interfering with sleep, then it may be time to begin to fade back on this daytime sleeping. Chapter 9 discusses the procedures to use if naps are a problem for your child's sleep.

CONCLUSION: THE BEGINNING OF BETTER NIGHTS AND BETTER DAYS

You can make a difference in your child's sleep. Following the guidelines I outlined in this book should help you to help your child sleep better at night and feel better during the day. But it obviously takes patience and persistence to get through the rough spots—the nights of feeling that you and your child's disrupted sleep will never end. Our experience with hundreds of families tells us that, if you stick with it and invest your time and energy on your child's sleep now, your efforts will pay off a thousandfold in the weeks and months to come. I wish you luck with your efforts and hope you and your family sleep better soon!

Notes

CHAPTER 1

1. Ruiz, F.S., Andersen, M.L., Martins, R.C.S., Zager, A., Lopes, J.D., & Tufik, S. (2012). Immune alterations after selective rapid eye movement or total sleep deprivation in healthy male volunteers. *Innate Immunity, 18*(1), 44–54.

2. Benedict, C., Brooks, S.J., O'Daly, O.G., Almèn, M.S., Morell, A., Åberg, K., . . . & Schiöth, H.B. (2012). Acute sleep deprivation enhances the brain's response to hedonic food stimuli: An fMRI study. *Journal of Clinical Endocrinology & Metabolism, 97*(3), E443–E447.

3. National Highway Traffic Safety Administration. (2011). *Traffic safety facts crash stats: Drowsy driving.* Washington, DC: U.S. Department of Transportation, National Highway Traffic Safety Administration.

4. Webb, W.B., & Bonnet, M.H. (1978). The sleep of "morning" and "evening" types. *Biological Psychology, 7*(1–2), 29–35.

5. Rowley, J.A., & Badr, M.S. (2012). Normal sleep. In M.S. Badr (Ed.), *Essentials of sleep medicine* (pp. 1–15). New York, NY: Humana Press.

6. Diomedi, M., Curatolo, P., Scalise, A., Placidi, F., Caretto, F., & Gigli, G. L. (1999). Sleep abnormalities in mentally retarded autistic subjects: Down's syndrome with mental retardation and normal subjects. *Brain and Development, 21*(8), 548–553.

   Harvey, M. T., & Kennedy, C. H. (2002). Polysomnographic phenotypes in developmental disabilities. *International Journal of Developmental Neuroscience, 20*(3), 443–448.

7. Atkinson, G., & Davenne, D. (2007). Relationships between sleep, physical activity and human health. *Physiology & Behavior, 90*(2–3), 229–235. doi:http://dx.doi.org/10.1016/j.physbeh.2006.09.015

CHAPTER 2

1. McKnight-Eily, L.R., Liu, Y., Wheaton, A.G., Croft, J.B., Perry, G.S., Okoro, C.A., & Strine, T. (2011). Unhealthy sleep-related behaviors—12 States, 2009. *MMWR, 60,* 233–238.

2. Durand, V.M. (in press). Sleep problems. In J.K. Luiselli (Ed.), *Children and youth with autism spectrum disorder (ASD): Recent advances and innovations in assessment, education, and intervention.* New York, NY: Oxford University Press.

3. Quine, L. (1992). Severity of sleep problems in children with severe learning difficulties: description and correlates. *Journal of Community & Applied Social Psychology, 2*(4), 247–268.

4. Durand, V.M. (2006). Sleep terrors. In J.E. Fisher & W.T. O'Donohue (Eds.), *Practitioner's guide to evidence-based psychotherapy* (pp. 654–660). New York, NY: Springer.
    Durand, V.M., & Christodulu, K.V. (2003). Nightmares. In T.H. Ollendick & C.S. Schroeder (Eds.), *Encyclopedia of pediatric and child psychology* (pp. 412–413). New York, NY: Kluwer Academic/Plenum Publishers.

5. Durand, V.M. (in press). Disorders of development. In D.H. Barlow (Ed.), *Oxford handbook of clinical psychology.* New York, NY: Oxford University.

6. Rowley, J.A., & Badr, M.S. (2012). Normal sleep. In M.S. Badr (Ed.), *Essentials of sleep medicine* (pp. 1–15). New York, NY: Humana Press.

7. Durand, V.M., Gernert-Dott, P., & Mapstone, E. (1996). Treatment of sleep disorders in children with developmental disabilities. *Journal of the Association for Persons with Severe Handicaps, 21,* 114–122.

8. Badr, M.S. (2012). Central sleep apnea. In M.S. Badr (Ed.), *Essentials of sleep medicine: An approach for clinical pulmonology* (pp. 219–232). New York, NY: Humana Press.

9. Ahmed, I., & Thorpy, M. (2012). Narcolepsy and idiopathic hypersomnia. In M.S. Badr (Ed.), *Essentials of sleep medicine: An approach for clinical pulmonology* (pp. 297–314). New York, NY: Humana Press.

10. Glickman, G. (2010). Circadian rhythms and sleep in children with autism. *Neuroscience and Biobehavioral Reviews, 34*(5), 755–768.
    Maaskant, M., van de Wouw, E., van Wijck, R., Evenhuis, H.M., & Echteld, M.A. (2013). Circadian sleep–wake rhythm of older adults with intellectual disabilities. *Research in Developmental Disabilities, 34*(4), 1144–1151. doi:http://dx.doi.org/10.1016/j.ridd.2012.12.009

11. Klein, T.P., Devoe, E.R., Miranda-Julian, C., & Linas, K. (2009). Young children's responses to September 11th: The New York City experience. *Infant Mental Health Journal, 30*(1), 1–22. doi:10.1002/imhj.20200

12. Howell, M. (2012). Parasomnias: An updated review. *Neurotherapeutics, 9*(4), 753–775. doi:10.1007/s13311-012-0143-8

13. Ohayon, M.M., Mahowald, M.W., Dauvilliers, Y., Krystal, A.D., & Leger, D.M. (2012). Prevalence and comorbidity of nocturnal wandering in the US adult general population. *Neurology, 78*(20), 1583–1589.

14. Aurora, R.N., Kristo, D.A., Bista, S.R., Rowley, J.A., Zak, R.S., Casey, K.R., . . . & Rosenberg, R.S. (2012). Update to the AASM Clinical Practice Guidelines: The treatment of Restless Legs syndrome and Periodic Limb Movement disorder in adults—An update for 2012: Practice parameters with an evidence-based systematic review and meta-analyses. *Sleep, 35*(8), 1037.

15. Harari, M.D. (in press). Nocturnal enuresis. *Journal of Paediatrics and Child Health.*

16. Carra, M.C., Huynh, N., & Lavigne, G. (2012). Sleep bruxism: A comprehensive overview for the dental clinician interested in sleep medicine. *Dental Clinics of North America, 56*(2), 387–413.

17. Haywood, P.M., & Hill, C.M. (2012). Rhythmic movement disorder: Managing the child who head-bangs to get to sleep. *Paediatrics and Child Health, 22*(5), 207–210.

CHAPTER 4

1. Durand, V.M. (2011). *Optimistic parenting: Hope and help for you and your challenging child.* Baltimore, MD: Paul H. Brookes Publishing Co.

CHAPTER 5

1. Durand (2011).
   Durand, V.M., Hieneman, M., Clarke, S., Wang, M., & Rinaldi, M. (2013). Positive family intervention for severe challenging behavior I: A multi-site randomized clinical trial. *Journal of Positive Behavior Interventions, 15*(3), 133–143. doi:10.1177/1098300712458324
   Seligman, M.E.P. (1998). *Learned optimism: How to change your mind and your life.* New York, NY: Pocket Books.
2. Durand (2011).
3. Durand, V.M., & Hieneman, M. (2008). *Helping parents with challenging children: Positive family intervention facilitator's guide.* New York, NY: Oxford University Press.
   Durand, V.M., & Hieneman, M. (2008). *Helping parents with challenging children: Positive family intervention workbook.* New York, NY: Oxford University Press.
4. Seligman (1998).

CHAPTER 6

1. Adkins, K.W., Molloy, C., Weiss, S.K., Reynolds, A., Goldman, S.E., Burnette, C., . . . & Malow, B.A. (2012). Effects of a standardized pamphlet on insomnia in children with autism spectrum disorders. *Pediatrics, 130*(suppl. 2), S139–S144. doi:10.1542/peds.2012-0900K
   McCusker, R.R., Goldberger, B.A., & Cone, E.J. (2006). Caffeine content of energy drinks, carbonated sodas, and other beverages. *Journal of Analytical Toxicology, 30*(2), 112–114. doi:10.1093/jat/30.2.112
2. Durand (in press). Sleep problems.

CHAPTER 7

1. Vriend, J.L., Corkum, P.V., Moon, E.C., & Smith, I.M. (2011). Behavioral interventions for sleep problems in children with autism spectrum disorders: Current findings and future directions. *Journal of Pediatric Psychology, 36*(9), 1017–1029. doi:10.1093/jpepsy/jsr044
2. Piazza, C.C., & Fisher, W.W. (1991). Bedtime fading in the treatment of pediatric insomnia. *Journal of Behavior Therapy and Experimental Psychiatry, 22*(1), 53–56.
3. Mindell, J.A., & Durand, V.M. (1993). Treatment of childhood sleep disorders: Generalization across disorders and effects on family members. *Journal of Pediatric Psychology, 18,* 731–750.

CHAPTER 8

1. Durand (in press). Sleep problems.
2. Christodulu, K.V., & Durand, V.M. (2004). Reducing bedtime disturbance and night waking using positive bedtime routines and sleep restriction. *Focus on Autism and Other Developmental Disabilities, 19*(3), 130–139.

    Durand, V.M., & Christodulu, K.V. (2004). Description of a sleep-restriction program to reduce bedtime disturbances and night waking. *Journal of Positive Behavior Interventions, 6*(2), 83–91.

    Vincent, N., Lewycky, S., & Finnegan, H. (2008). Barriers to engagement in sleep restriction and stimulus control in chronic insomnia. *Journal of Consulting and Clinical Psychology, 76*(5), 820–828.
3. Durand, V.M. (2002). Treating sleep terrors in children with autism. *Journal of Positive Behavior Interventions, 4*(2), 66–72. doi:10.1177/109830070200400201

    Mindell, J.A., Kuhn, B., Lewin, D.S., Meltzer, L.J., Sadeh, A., & American Academy of Sleep, M. (2006). Behavioral treatment of bedtime problems and night wakings in infants and young children. *Sleep, 29*(10), 1263–1276. [Erratum appears in *Sleep, 29*(11), 1380].

CHAPTER 9

1. Kotagal, S., & Broomall, E. (2012). Sleep in children with autism spectrum disorder. *Pediatric Neurology, 47*(4), 242–251. doi:10.1016/j.pediatrneurol.2012.05.007
2. Piazza, C.C., Hagopian, L.P., Hughes, C.R., & Fisher, W.W. (1997). Using chronotherapy to treat severe sleep problems: A case study. *American Journal on Mental Retardation, 102*(4), 358–366.
3. Glickman (2010).
4. Guénolé, F., Godbout, R., Nicolas, A., Franco, P., Claustrat, B., & Baleyte, J.-M. (2011). Melatonin for disordered sleep in individuals with autism spectrum disorders: Systematic review and discussion. *Sleep Medicine Reviews, 15*(6), 379–387. doi:10.1016/j.smrv.2011.02.001

CHAPTER 10

1. Durand & Christodulu (2003).
2. Durand (2006).
3. Williams, P.G., Sears, L.L., & Allard, A. (2004). Sleep problems in children with autism. *Journal of Sleep Research, 13*(3), 265–268. doi:10.1111/j.1365--2869.2004.00405.x
4. Vinai, P., Ferri, R., Ferini-Strambi, L., Cardetti, S., Anelli, M., Vallauri, P., . . . & Manconi, M. (in press). Defining the borders between sleep-related eating disorder and night eating syndrome. *Sleep Medicine*.

CHAPTER 11

1. Ahmed & Thorpy (2012).
2. Badr (2012).
3. Parmet, S., Burke, A.E., & Golub, R.M. (2012). Sudden infant death syndrome. *JAMA: The Journal of the American Medical Association, 307*(16), 1766–1766.
4. Aurora et al. (2012).
5. Haywood & Hill (2012).

CHAPTER 12

1. Capdevila, O.S., & Delfraro, M.E.R. (2012). Enuresis and obstructive sleep apnea in children. In L. Kheirandish-Gozal & D. Gozal (Eds.), *Sleep-disordered breathing in children* (pp. 499–506). New York, NY: Springer.
   Harari, M.D. (in press). Nocturnal enuresis. *Journal of Paediatrics and Child Health.*
2. Chang, J.-W., Yang, L.-Y., Chin, T.-W., & Tsai, H.-L. (2012). Clinical character-istics, nocturnal antidiuretic hormone levels, and responsiveness to DDAVP of school children with primary nocturnal enuresis. *World Journal of Urology, 30*(4), 567–571.
3. Gim, C.S.Y., Lillystone, D., & Caldwell, P.H.Y. (2009). Efficacy of the bell and pad alarm therapy for nocturnal enuresis. *Journal of Paediatrics and Child Health, 45*(7–8), 405–408.
4. Brown, M.L., Pope, A.W., & Brown, E.J. (2011). Treatment of primary noctur-nal enuresis in children: A review. *Child: Care, Health and Development, 37*(2), 153–160.
5. Ibid.
6. Ibid.
7. Gregory, A.M., & Sadeh, A. (2012). Sleep, emotional and behavioral difficulties in children and adolescents. *Sleep Medicine Reviews, 16*(2), 129–136.
8. Adrien, J. (2002). Neurobiological bases for the relation between sleep and depres-sion. *Sleep Medicine Reviews, 6*(5), 341–351. doi:http://dx.doi.org/10.1053/smrv.2001.0200
9. Carra, Huynh, & Lavigne (2012).

CHAPTER 13

Information about the Motivation Assessment Scale (MAS) can be obtained from Monaco & Associates, Inc., 4125 Gage Center Drive, Suite 204, Topeka, KS 66604. Phone: 913-272-5501 or 1-800-798-1309.

1. Durand, V.M. (in press). Strategies for functional communication training. In J. Anderson, R.L. De Pry, & F. Brown (Eds.), *Individual positive behavior supports: A standards-based guide to practices in school and community-based settings.* Balti-more, MD: Paul H. Brookes Publishing Co.
2. Durand, V.M. (1990). *Severe behavior problems: A functional communication train-ing approach.* New York, NY: Guilford Press.
   Durand, V. M. (2011). *Optimistic parenting: Hope and help for you and your chal-lenging child.* Baltimore, MD: Paul H. Brookes Publishing Co.

CHAPTER 14

1. Mindell, J.A., Emslie, G., Blumer, J., Genel, M., Glaze, D.G., Ivanenko, A., . . . & Banas, B. (2006). Pharmacologic management of insomnia in children and adolescents: Consensus statement. *Pediatrics, 117*(6), e1223–1232. doi:10.1542/peds.2005-1693

2. Braam, W., Didden, R., Maas, A.P.H.M., Korzilius, H., Smits, M.G., & Curfs, L.M.G. (2010). Melatonin decreases daytime challenging behaviour in persons with intellectual disability and chronic insomnia. *Journal of Intellectual Disability Research, 54*(1), 52–59.

   Malow, B.A., Adkins, K.W., McGrew, S., Wang, L., Goldman, S.E., Fawkes, D., & Burnette, C. (in press). Melatonin for sleep in children with autism: A controlled trial examining dose, tolerability, and outcomes. *Journal of Autism and Developmental Disorders.* doi:10.1007/s10803-011-1418-3

CHAPTER 15

1. Cook, F., Bayer, J., Le, H.N.D., Mensah, F., Cann, W., & Hiscock, H. (2012). Baby business: A randomised controlled trial of a universal parenting program that aims to prevent early infant sleep and cry problems and associated parental depression. *BMC Pediatrics, 12*(1), 13–23.

   Kerr, S.M., Jowett, S.A., & Smith, L.N. (1996). Preventing sleep problems in infants: A randomised controlled trial. *Journal of Advanced Nursing, 24,* 928–942.

Appendix A

Support Groups and Associations

GENERAL SLEEP PROBLEMS

National Center on Sleep Disorders Research

National Heart, Lung, and Blood Institute

6701 Rockledge Drive
Bethesda, MD 20892
Phone: 301-435-0199
Fax: 301-480-3451
Web site: http://www.nhlbi.nih.gov/about/ncsdr/index.htm

National Sleep Foundation

1010 North Glebe Road, Suite 310
Arlington, VA 22201
Phone: 703-243-1697
E-mail: nsf@sleepfoundation.org
Web site: http://www.sleepfoundation.org

Sleep Research Society

2510 North Frontage Road
Darien, IL 60561
Phone: 630-737-9763

Fax: 630-737-9790
Web site: http://www.sleepresearchsociety.org

Society of Light Treatment and Biological Rhythms

Executive Office
10200 West 44th Avenue, Suite 304
Wheat Ridge, CO 80033
Phone: 303-424-3697
Fax: 303-422-8894
Web site: http://www.sltbr.org/Program%20book%20SLTBR%20
    Geneva%2013062012.pdf

NARCOLEPSY

Center for Narcolepsy Research

The University of Illinois at Chicago
845 S. Damen Avenue, (m/c 802)
Chicago, IL 60612-7350
Phone: 312-996-5176
Fax: 312-996-7008
E-mail: cnshr@listserv.uic.edu
Web site: http://www.uic.edu/orgs/cnshr

Narcolepsy Network

129 Waterwheel Lane
North Kingstown, RI 02852
Toll-Free: 1-888-292-6522
Phone: 401-667-2523
Fax: 401-633-6567
Web site: http://www.narcolepsynetwork.org/

SLEEP APNEA

American Sleep Apnea Association

6856 Eastern Avenue NW, Suite 203
Washington, D.C. 20012
Toll-Free: 1-888-293-3650
Web site: http://www.sleepapnea.org

LIMB MOVEMENT PROBLEMS

Restless Legs Syndrome Foundation

1530 Greenview Drive SW, Suite 210
Rochester, MN 55902
Phone: 507-287-6465
Fax: 507-287-6312
E-mail: rlsfoundation@rls.org
Web site: http://www.rls.org

BED-WETTING

Enuresis Associates, LLC

Chartwell Medical Center
8186 Lark Brown Road, Suite 301
Elkridge, MD 21075
Phone: 301-725-0963
Fax: 301-776-0716
Web site: http://www.dryatnight.com/bedwetting-association.htm

SPECIAL NEEDS-RELATED ORGANIZATIONS

American Association on Intellectual and Developmental Disabilities

501 3rd Street NW, Suite 200
Washington, D.C. 20001
Phone: 202-387-1968
Fax: 202-387-2193
Web site: http://aaidd.org/home

Attention Deficit Disorder Association

P.O. Box 7557
Wilmington, DE 19803-9997
Phone: 800-939-1019
E-mail: info@add.org
Web site: http://www.add.org

American Council of the Blind

220 Wilson Boulevard, Suite 650
Arlington, VA 22201-3354
Toll-Free: 1-800-424-8666
Phone: 202-467-5081
Fax: 202-467-5085
E-mail: info@acb.org
Web site: http://www.acb.org

The Arc of the United States

1825 K Street NW, Suite 1200
Washington, D.C. 20006
Toll-Free: 1-800-433-5255
Phone: 202-534-3700
Fax: 202-534-3731
E-mail: info@thearc.org
Web site: http://www.thearc.org/page.aspx?pid=2530

Autism Society of America

4340 East-West Highway, Suite 350
Bethesda, MD 20814
Toll-Free: 1-800-3AUTISM (1-800-328-8476)
Phone: 301-657-0881
Fax: 301-657-0869
Web site: http://www.autism-society.org

Autism Speaks

1 East 33rd Street, 4th Floor
New York, NY 70016
Phone: 212-252-8584
Fax: 212-252-8676
Web site: http://www.autismspeaks.org

National Consortium on Deaf-Blindness

345 Monmouth Avenue
Monmouth, OR 97361
Toll-Free: 800-438-9376
Toll-Free TTY: 800-854-7013

Fax: 503-838-8150
Email: info@nationaldb.org
Web site: http://www.nationaldb.org

Hydrocephalus Foundation, Inc.

910 Rear Broadway
Saugus, MA 01906
Phone: 781-942-1161
Fax: 781-231-5250
E-mail: HyFII@netscape.net
Web site: http://hydrocephalus.org

Hydrocephalus Support Group, Inc.

1933 Mistflower Glen Court
Chesterfield, MO 63005-4236
Phone: 636-532-8228
Fax: 314-251-5371
E-mail: hydrodb@earthlink.net
Web site: http://www.ninds.nih.gov/find_people/voluntary_orgs/
    volorg870.htm

National Center for PTSD

United States Department of Veteran Affairs
810 Vermont Avenue NW
Washington, D.C. 20420
Phone: 802-296-6300
E-mail: ncptsd@va.gov
Web site: http://www.ptsd.va.gov

The National Easter Seal Society

230 W. Monroe Street, Suite 1800
Chicago, IL 60606
Toll-Free: 1-800-221-6827
Fax: 312-726-1494
E-mail: info@easter-seals.org
Web site: http://www.php.com/national-easter-seal-society-inc

Spina Bifida Association of America

4590 MacArthur Boulevard NW, Suite 250
Washington, D.C. 20007-4226
Toll-Free: 1-800-621-3141
Phone: 202-944-3285
Fax: 202-944-3295
E-mail: sbaa@sbaa.org
Web site: http://www.spinabifidaassociation.org/site/c.evKRI7OXIo
    J8H/b.8028963/k.BE67/Home.htm

TASH

1001 Connecticut Avenue NW, Suite 235
Washington, D.C. 20036
Phone: 202-540-9020
Fax: 202-540-9019
E-mail: info@TASH.org
Web site: http://tash.org

Tourette Syndrome Association

4240 Bell Boulevard
Bayside, NY 11361 2820
Phone: 718-224-2999
Fax: 718-279-9596
Web site: http://tsa-usa.org

Appendix B

Internet Sleep Resources[1]

GENERAL SLEEP PAGES

Phantom Sleep Resources

http://www.newtechpub.com/phantom

The Phantom Sleep Page presents useful information about sleep and sleep disorders including snoring and sleep apnea for the public, patients, and professionals. It contains articles, bibliographies, connections to research and support groups, and newsletters from patient education and support groups worldwide.

Sleep Medicine Home Page

http://www.cloud9.net/~thorpy/sleep.html

This home page lists resources regarding all aspects of sleep, including the physiology of sleep, clinical sleep medicine, sleep research, federal and state information, patient information, and business-related groups.

---

[1] Because addresses to web sites change frequently, some of these addresses may no longer be valid. Usually, however, they will provide you with ways to track down the new address.

The Sleep Well
http://www.stanford.edu/~dement/index.html

The Sleep Well was created as a reservoir of information on sleep and sleep disorders. It is also a wish that everyone may *sleep well* and obtain the wisdom to do so from these pages. It provides a calendar of important sleep events and meetings, information on sleep disorders, and a way to search Mental Health Net for more information on sleep disorders.

SPECIFIC SLEEP-RELATED DISORDERS

American Sleep Apnea Association A.W.A.K.E. Network Map
http://www.sleepapnea.org/support/a.w.a.k.e.-network-map.html

This web site provides support group listings by state for the entire AWAKE Network.

Center for Narcolepsy Research
http://www.uic.edu/orgs/cnshr

In December 1986, the Center for Narcolepsy Research at the College of Nursing was established with private funds along with overhead support from the University of Illinois at Chicago to help increase knowledge about narcolepsy, a disorder of excessive sleepiness. This web site provides information about narcolepsy as well as links to other sites.

Children's Sleep Problems
http://www.aacap.org/AACAP/Families_and_Youth/Facts_for_Families/Facts_for_Families_Pages/Childrens_Sleep_Problems_34.aspxs

The American Academy of Child and Adolescent Psychiatry provides this "Facts for Families" sheet as a public service to assist parents and families in their most important roles. It provides a very brief overview of sleep problems in children.

Frequently Asked Questions About Coffee and Caffeine
https://cs.uwaterloo.ca/~alopez-o/Coffee/caffaq.html

The site provides information about all beverages and products that contain caffeine, including tea, coffee, chocolate, caffeinated soft drinks, caffeinated pills, coffee beans, and so forth.

Melatonin Information and References

http://www.mayoclinic.com/health/melatonin/NS_patient-melatonin/
DSECTION=evidence
http://www.nlm.nih.gov/medlineplus/druginfo/natural/940.html
http://www.sltbr.org

Due to the widespread press regarding melatonin and the popularity of melatonin reviews, http://www.nlm.nih.gov/medlineplus/drug
info/natural/940.html has organized a comprehensive set of references about melatonin. While not a complete list, it serves as a good
jumping-off point for people investigating melatonin.

Stanford University Center for Narcolepsy

http://med.stanford.edu/psychiatry/narcolepsy

This web site provides a great deal of information about narcolepsy
from the Stanford University Center for Narcolepsy, including information about the center and its research.

SIDS Network

http://sids-network.org

This site provides a great deal of information about sudden infant
death syndrome (SIDS): discussion groups, references, and downloadable brochures.

Sleep, Dreams, and Wakefulness

http://sommeil.univ-lyon1.fr/index_e.php

The Jouvet Sleep Lab in France (which is also an interchangeable
French/English language site) provides both clinical and basic sleep
researchers with a place to join in their community of interest. This
site provides comprehensive resources for those involved in sleep
research and the treatment of sleep-related disorders.

Appendix C

Accredited Sleep Disorders Centers

You can find the nearest sleep center to you by going to this web site and entering in your address: http://www.sleepeducation.com/find -a-center.

The first goal of these centers is to find out as much as possible about your child's sleep history. An interview will be conducted, and you will be asked to fill out forms such as the ones in this book to give the staff a good picture of your child's sleep and sleep-related behaviors. They then determine whether or not an overnight evaluation is needed. If they suspect, for example, that breathing problems may be a cause of sleep problems, they will likely recommend a more complete evaluation. A warning—in the past, some centers did not accept children for evaluation if they had severe disabilities, such as ones with intellectual disabilities or ASD, because the evaluation required keeping connections to monitoring equipment on throughout the night. This has changed in recent years, and you should bring this up when contacting them.

An overnight evaluation typically includes a *polysomnographic (PSG) evaluation*. This is a type of testing in which the person spends 1 or more nights sleeping in a "sleep laboratory" while being monitored on a number of measures, including respiration and oxygen desaturation (a measure of your airflow); leg movements; brain wave activity, measured by an *electroencephalograph* (*EEG*); eye movements, measured by an *electrooculograph* (*EOG*); muscle movements, measured by an *electromyograph* (*EMG*); and heart activity, measured by an *electrocardiogram* (*ECG/EKG*). The child will need to be able to sleep in this laboratory while attached to wires or electrodes to help monitor sleep activity. From these measures, the center can make recommendations for treatment based on the nature of your child's sleep problems.

Appendix D

Thoughts Quiz

Thoughts Quiz

Instructions: Reflect back on a recent problem situation surrounding your child's sleep problem and circle the responses that best matched what you were thinking at the time. For each of the following statements, estimate what was going through your mind at the time by indicating where in the range of "strongly disagree" to "strongly agree" you were thinking around the time of the difficult situation.

Thoughts	Strongly disagree				Strongly agree
1. I have little or no control over this situation.	1	2	3	4	5
2. I'm not sure how best to handle this situation.	1	2	3	4	5
3. In this situation, others are judging me negatively as a parent.	1	2	3	4	5
4. In this situation, others are judging my child negatively.	1	2	3	4	5
5. My child is not able to control this behavior.	1	2	3	4	5
6. My child's disability or condition is causing or contributing to this problem.	1	2	3	4	5
7. This type of situation is always a problem for my child.	1	2	3	4	5
8. This will never get better or may become worse.	1	2	3	4	5
9. I will never have time for just me.	1	2	3	4	5
10. My child is doing this on purpose.	1	2	3	4	5
11. This situation is (spouse's, partner's, family member's, or someone else's) fault for not handling this like I suggested.	1	2	3	4	5
12. It is my fault that this is a problem.	1	2	3	4	5
13. Why am I always responsible for my child's behavior?	1	2	3	4	5

Appendix E

Self-Talk Journal

Self-Talk Journal

Situation	Thoughts	Feelings	Disputation	Distraction	Substitution
What happened (success or difficulty)?	What did you think or say to yourself when this happened?	What emotions did you experience and how did you react physically when this happened?	Were your thoughts accurate and useful?	What did you do to shift your attention?	What is a more positive way to think about this?

Appendix F

Sleep Diary

Sleep Diary

Child: _____   Week of: _____

Day	Time put to bed	Time fell asleep	Nighttime awakening (time/how long)	Describe night-time awakening	Time awoke	Describe any naps
Sunday						
Monday						
Tuesday						
Wednesday						
Thursday						
Friday						
Saturday						

Appendix G

Behavior Log

Behavior Log

Date	Time	Behavior at bedtime	What did you do to handle the problem?	Behavior during awakenings	What did you do to handle the problem?

Fill out this log each time your child has difficulty going to sleep or wakes during the night.

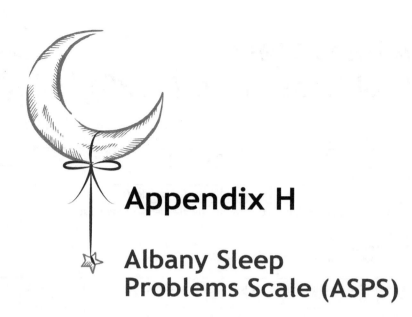

Appendix H

Albany Sleep Problems Scale (ASPS)

Albany Sleep Problems Scale (ASPS)

Name:	Date of birth:
Diagnoses:	Sex:
Date adm:	Name of respondent:

Instructions: Circle one number that best represents the frequency of the behavior.
0 = never
1 = less than once per week
2 = one to two times per week
3 = three to six times per week
4 = nightly

1. Does the person have a fairly regular bedtime and time that he or she awakens?	0	1	2	3	4
2. Does the person have a bedtime routine that is the same each evening?	0	1	2	3	4
3. Does this person work or play in bed often right up to the time he or she goes to bed?	0	1	2	3	4
4. Does this person sleep poorly in his or her own bed but better away from it?	Yes			No	
5. Does this person smoke, drink alcohol, or consume caffeine in any form?	0	1	2	3	4
6. Does this person engage in vigorous activity in the hours before bedtime?	0	1	2	3	4
7. Does the person resist going to bed?	0	1	2	3	4
8. Does the person take more than an hour to fall asleep but does not resist?	0	1	2	3	4
9. Does the person awaken during the night but remain quiet and in bed?	0	1	2	3	4
10. Does the person awaken during the night and is he/she disruptive (e.g., tantrums, oppositional)?	0	1	2	3	4
11. Does the person take naps during the day?	0	1	2	3	4
12. Does this person often feel exhausted during the day because of lack of sleep?	0	1	2	3	4
13. Has this person ever had an accident or near accident because of sleepiness from not being able to sleep the night before?	Yes			No	
14. Does this person ever use prescription drugs or over-the-counter medications to help him or her sleep?	0	1	2	3	4
15. Has this person found that sleep medication doesn't work as well as it did when he or she first started taking it?	Yes			No/NA	

16. If he or she takes sleep medication does this person find that he or she can't sleep on nights without it?	Yes		No/NA		
17. Does the person fall asleep early in the evening and awaken too early in the morning?	0	1	2	3	4
18. Does the person have difficulty falling asleep until a very late hour and difficulty awakening early in the morning?	0	1	2	3	4
19. Does this person wake up in the middle of the night upset?	0	1	2	3	4
20. Is the person relatively easy to comfort from these episodes?	Yes		No/NA		
21. Does the person have episodes during sleep where he/she screams loudly for several minutes but is not fully awake?	0	1	2	3	4
22. Is the person difficult to comfort during these episodes?	Yes		No/NA		
23. Does the person experience sleep attacks (falling asleep almost immediately and without warning) during the day?	0	1	2	3	4
24. Does the person experience excessive daytime sleepiness that is not accounted for by an inadequate amount of sleep?	0	1	2	3	4
25. Does this person snore when asleep?	0	1	2	3	4
26. Does this person sometimes stop breathing for a few seconds during sleep?	0	1	2	3	4
27. Does this person have trouble breathing?	0	1	2	3	4
28. Is this person overweight?	Yes		No		
29. Has this person often walked when asleep?	0	1	2	3	4
30. Does this person talk while asleep?	0	1	2	3	4
31. Are this person's sheets and blankets in extreme disarray in the morning when he or she wakes up?	0	1	2	3	4
32. Does this person wake up at night because of kicking legs?	0	1	2	3	4
33. While lying down, does this person ever experience unpleasant sensations in the legs?	Yes		No		
34. Does this person rock back and forth or bang a body part (e.g., head) to fall asleep?	0	1	2	3	4
35. Does this person wet the bed?	0	1	2	3	4
36. Does this person grind his or her teeth at night?	0	1	2	3	4
37. Does this person sleep well when it doesn't matter, such as on weekends, but sleeps poorly when he or she "must" sleep well, such as when a busy day at school is ahead?	Yes		No		

38. Does this person often have feelings of apprehension, anxiety, or dread when he or she is getting ready for bed?	0	1	2	3	4
39. Does this person worry in bed?	0	1	2	3	4
40. Does this person often have depressing thoughts, or do tomorrow's worries or plans buzz through their mind when they want to go to sleep?	0	1	2	3	4
41. Does this person have feelings of frustration when he or she can't sleep?	0	1	2	3	4
42. Has this person experienced a relatively recent change in eating habits?	Yes			No	
43. Does the person have behavior problems at times other than bedtime or upon awakening?	Yes			No	
44. When did this person's primary difficulty with sleep begin?					
45. What was happening in this person's life at that time, or a few months before?					
46. Is this person under a physician's care for any medical condition? (If yes, indicate condition below)	Yes			No	

OTHER COMMENTS:

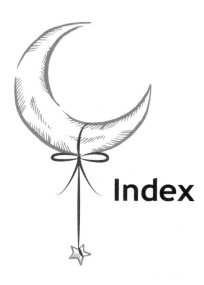

Index

Tables and figures are indicated by *t* and *f*, respectively.

Also by V. Mark Durand...

Mom's Choice Awards:
Parenting – Special & Exceptional Needs

USA "Best Books 2011" Award:
Parenting/Family: Reference

You've learned how to help your child *Sleep Better!*—now get the keys to **happier parents** and **better child behavior**! The secrets are in *Optimistic Parenting,* the book that helps moms and dads break the cycle of negative thinking, increase their confidence and parenting skills, and make lasting improvements to their family harmony. A highly regarded expert and a parent himself, V. Mark Durand delivers keen insights, gentle humor, and step-by-step strategies that help parents

- pinpoint the "why" behind challenging behavior
- tune in to negative thoughts, emotions, and self-talk
- interrupt and replace negative thoughts
- take care of their needs *and* the child's needs
- use emergency strategies for quick behavior intervention
- use long-term strategies for lasting behavior improvements
- address common problem areas such as sleep and transitions

WITH PRACTICAL TOOLS FOR PARENTS:

✓ Self-Talk Journal

✓ Behavioral Contract

✓ Sleep Diary

✓ and more

US$26.95 | Stock Number: BA-70526
2011 • 336 pages • 6 x 9 • paperback
ISBN 978-1-59857-052-6

Optimistic Parenting is a lifeline for overwhelmed parents—and a great source of insight for the professionals who work with them. Order it today and take the first step toward happier parenting!